Election 2008

4/08

Election

Franklin Foer
and the Editors of
The New Republic

2008

A VOTER'S GUIDE

ILLUSTRATIONS BY DAVID COWLES

A NEW REPUBLIC BOOK • YALE UNIVERSITY PRESS • NEW HAVEN & LONDON

Designed by Nancy Ovedovitz and set in Minion type by Keystone
Typesetting, Inc. Printed in the United States of America.

Library of Congress Cataloging-in-Publication Data
Election 2008 : a voter's guide / Franklin Foer and the Editors of The
New Republic.
p. cm.
ISBN 978-0-300-12652-5 (pbk.)
1. Presidents—United States—Election—2008. 2. United States—Politics
and government—2001–   . I. Foer, Franklin. II. New republic (New
York, N.Y.)
JK5262008 .E44 2007
324.973'0931—dc22   2007031394

A catalogue record for this book is available from the British Library.

The paper in this book meets the guidelines for permanence and
durability of the Committee on Production Guidelines for Book
Longevity of the Council on Library Resources.

10 9 8 7 6 5 4 3 2 1

Contents

Acknowledgments

Sacha Zimmerman deftly stewarded this project to completion, overseeing the editing and production of this anthology. Bradford Plumer produced the appendix and compiled the biographical data on the candidates. The profiles were edited by master craftsmen Richard Just, Katharine Marsh, Christopher Orr, and J. Peter Scoblic. And the profiles wouldn't have been possible were it not for the long nights put in by Kara Baskin, Adam B. Kushner, Britt Peterson, Henry Riggs, and Bruce Steinke. At Yale, this book benefited from the patient, thoughtful work of Keith Condon and Jenya Weinreb. Thanks also to Leonard Asper, Martin Peretz, and Elizabeth Sheldon for helping to provide such a hospitable home to this brand of journalism.

Many of the essays in this book appeared in earlier versions in *The New Republic:* Hillary Rodham Clinton (April 2, 2007); Barack Obama (March 19, 2007); John Edwards (January 22, 2007); Bill Richardson (June 18, 2007); Dennis Kucinich (July 2, 2007); John McCain (October 16, 2006); Mitt Romney (July 2, 2007); Rudy Giuliani (May 21, 2007); Fred Thompson (July 23, 2007); Sam Brownback (December 18, 2006); Newt Gingrich (July 24, 2006); Ron Paul (June 4, 2007); Chuck Hagel (June 4, 2007); and the Coda, "Warner and the Agony of Running for President" (October 30, 2006).

Introduction *Franklin Foer*

This book will appear in the fall of 2007, when the aborted campaign of former presidential flirt Mark Warner will already have been the subject of several retrospective tomes. At this late stage, it's a bit hard to understand why Warner justifies such treatment or to even conjure the former Virginia governor's fund-raising prowess or his grand plans for exploiting new technologies. But, at the peak of his prospective bid—that Paleozoic era of the presidential campaign known as last summer—he was regarded as a major contender for the Democratic nomination.

During the Warner boom, *The New Republic* assigned a substantial profile of the aspirant to our chief political correspondent, Ryan Lizza. And it wasn't long before my fellow editors and I began salivating over this piece. Lizza tagged along on Warner's campaign jet, while the candidate imbibed hard liquor with him and discoursed on his own foibles—that's what we in the business call some intense "color." As our deadline loomed, my desire for the piece reached an intensity that I remembered from waiting in line with my mother for Transformers, Cabbage Patch dolls, and other fad toys. Then, just as we were set to pry a draft from the writer, it was snatched away. For no clear reason, Warner announced that he wasn't going to bother with this whole campaign business.

It was not the last time during this longest-in-history campaign that the editors of *The New Republic* were stung in this fashion. Just as our profile of Indiana Senator Evan Bayh went to press, he, too, dropped from the race. And, within a week of publishing a lengthy number on Iowa Governor Tom Vilsack, he bit the dust. "Hotline," the political tip sheet, began to write about the "TNR Curse." They implied that our pieces—like those notorious *Sports Illustrated* covers—mystically doomed candidates, or perhaps re-shaped conventional wisdom to injure our subjects. But, the editors of these pieces, I can testify, were the prime victims of the curse.

There have been many other occasions when I have shouted obscenities about this never-ending election season: during the seventeenth mind-numbing South Carolina debate, for instance, or after listening to the two-hundred-seventeenth "Ask Mitt Anything" session. But, if we're honest about this ordeal, we would have to conclude that it is not all for the bad. By the time that voters select nominees, we will be intimate with them. We will be well-acquainted with their legislative histories, their hypocrisies, the sources of their financing, and their ideological proclivities—not to mention their adolescent pranks and their relationships with their mothers. It's not hard to recall recent nominees who we, unfortunately, hardly knew at the time of their ascension.

The New Republic began publishing lengthy pieces about the 2008 campaign in the spring of 2006. Our intention was to buck political journalism's rush to the Internet. While everyone invested greater resources in blogging and reconfigured their platforms to become ever more newsy, we sent our reporters to spend months delving into the biographies (and psyches) of the field, to produce profiles that would help define the coverage of their subjects. The pieces collected here, I hope, aren't just revelatory and infor-mative, but a tribute to the much-neglected genre of the deeply reported, stylishly written political profile—and a testament to the virtues of devoting time and space to journalism.

The press corps likes to wax enthusiastic about how this is the most interesting, least predictable race in memory. At times, during this slog, that hasn't seemed the case. But this race to replace George W. Bush has resulted in a strange inversion of recent campaigns. In recent campaigns, the Democrats have found themselves racked by internecine ideological warfare—with centrists battling the left. But, this year, the left really doesn't have a favorite son. John Edwards has done the most to carry the progressive banner, even though he supported the Iraq war and his last campaign was orchestrated, in part, by the president of the Democratic Leadership Council. Barack Obama has impeccable liberal credentials, yet he resists aligning himself with that wing of the party, preferring to champion the ideal of post-partisanship. And with President Bush essentially unifying the two wings of the party, Democratic debates have, thus far, launched few bolts of vituperation. As a lifelong Democrat, I find this absence of a center-versus-left battle to be a bit unnerving.

This year, most of the interesting ideological action is on the other side. For the first time in many years, the conservative monopoly on the nominating process seems imperiled. John McCain, Rudy Giuliani, Mitt Romney, and Fred Thompson may work desperately hard to portray themselves as rock-ribbed social conservatives, but they are evidently not that. (Which is not to say that these pols wouldn't follow in the path of Bush's economic radicalism or foreign policy.)

It's always tempting to extract grand lessons from a development like this. But, in this case, there's polling evidence to suggest an ideological metamorphosis. According to some of the data, all of the incendiary culture-war issues of the '90s—abortion, homosexuality, the general creep of modernity—have been subsumed by the war on terrorism. This development has thrown pundits for a loop. They all expected Giuliani, for instance, to quickly crumble thanks to his pro-choice stance and historic friendliness to the gay community. But, as of this writing, he has shockingly flourished.

That's what makes this election particularly consequential. The ideological foundations of the Republican Party have been shifting ever since the end of the cold war. But, over the later Bush era, we've seen signs that the party may be reconstituting itself. Libertarians, a small electoral fraction, to be sure, have despaired over the Bush administration's growth of the federal government and they have objected to the war on terrorism. More mainstream conservatives—from William F. Buckley to George F. Will—have despaired over the Iraq war, too. And a nominee like McCain or Giuliani sits just enough outside the traditional confines of conservatism to force a major intra-party reckoning. By dint of their heterodoxies, they will force Republican constituencies to reconsider their commitments to the coalition and to their ideological priorities.

It doesn't take too much imagination to foresee how changes within the Republican coalition could prompt third-party candidacies. Of course, there's New York Mayor Michael Bloomberg and rumors of his bid—a symbol of the center-right's alienation from Bush-ism. Then, there's the possibility that social conservatives could rally around their own independent standard-bearer should Giuliani (or even McCain) win the GOP crown. In other words, we're in for an extremely interesting next couple of months.

At *The New Republic*, we began assigning these profiles with this book in mind. Of course, there was a spirit of consumerism that always informed our efforts—an effort to help TNR readers sort through the scrum of candidates. And we've added an appendix that allows you to compare the stances struck by the campaigns. But we also hoped that the profiles anthologized here would add up to something more substantial—that they would explain something about ideological debates, the process of seeking the nomination, the type of person attracted to power in this age; we hoped that these pieces would serve as portraits not just of politicians, but of our politics.

1 • THE DEMOCRATS

Hillary Rodham Clinton

Full Name Hillary Diane Rodham Clinton

Current Residence Chappaqua, New York

Date and Place of Birth October 26, 1947; Chicago, Illinois

Education
B.A., Wellesley College, 1969
J.D., Yale Law School, 1973

Military Service
None

Nonpolitical Positions Held
Impeachment Inquiry Staff, 1974
Attorney, Rose Law Firm, 1976–1992
Chairwoman, Arkansas Educational Standards Committee, 1982–1992
First Lady of the United States, 1993–2001
Author, *It Takes A Village,* 1996
Author, *Living History,* 2003

Political Offices Held
U.S. Senator from New York, 2001–present

Family Married to former president Bill Clinton; children: daughter Chelsea

The Real Reason She Won't Apologize: Hillary's War
Michael Crowley

n October 2000, Hillary Clinton was entering the home stretch of one of the most unusual Senate campaigns in American history. Although her husband still occupied the Oval Office, she had decamped to a Dutch Colonial in Westchester County to run for the seat of retiring New York Democrat Daniel Patrick Moynihan. To compensate for the fact that she had never actually lived in the state she intended to represent, she immersed herself in Empire State minutiae. Off the top of her head, she would describe in detail the virtues of the Northeast dairy compact and the rate of upstate job growth. The aggressiveness of her New York provincialism tended to obscure the rare occasions on which Clinton would actually unfurl a broader worldview.

One such occasion took place on October 10, a few weeks before the election, when Clinton spoke before a group of investment bankers, magazine editors, and the sundry wonks who populate the Council on Foreign Relations. Although her address received little attention at the time, it outlined a clear vision of American power, one perhaps better-suited to a candidate for president than for the Senate. Many of the details were anodyne—she implored the United States to lead alliances against global problems like AIDS, poverty, and repression—but, when she came to the use of U.S. military force, her speech took a bracing turn:

> There is a refrain . . . that we should intervene with force only when we face splendid little wars that we surely can win, preferably by

overwhelming force in a relatively short period of time. To those who believe we should become involved only if it is easy to do, I think we have to say that America has never and should not ever shy away from the hard task if it is the right one.

These words, unthinkable for any Democrat to utter today, are revealing of the mindset that led her to support George W. Bush's confrontation with Iraq, a policy choice that has important implications for her presidential ambitions. And, even on that day nearly a year before September 11, her words struck one listener as alarming. During a question-and-answer session that followed, an audience member who identified himself as a banking executive rose to challenge her. "I seem to hear that we should pay any price, bear any burden, to spread our way of life abroad," he said. "I wonder if you think that every foreign country—the majority of countries—would actually welcome this new assertiveness, includ-ing the one billion Muslims that are out there? And whether or not there isn't some grave risk to the United States in this—what I would say, not new internationalism, but new imperialism."

This was perhaps an overreaction to Clinton's point, and she challenged it as "an extreme statement I do not subscribe to." Through the lens of recent American foreign policy, however, her inquisitor's words do have an eerily prescient ring. However acci-dentally, he had foreshadowed the events that would follow Clin-ton's infamous 2002 vote granting President Bush the authority to invade Iraq.

Hillary Clinton's entire political identity has become defined by that vote and her subsequent refusal to apologize for it. To most observers, her positioning on Iraq is simply the latest example in a long career of venal political calculation. In a zeitgeist-capturing "Saturday Night Live" sketch earlier this year, an actor playing Clinton appeared on a mock "Hardball" segment. "I think most

Democrats know me," the faux Hillary cloyingly explained. "They understand that my support for the war was always insincere."

But was it? The truth about how Clinton came to support Bush's war (albeit with reservations), and how she has thought about it since, has always been shrouded in mystery. People assume that Clinton is playing politics, that she voted for the war to look tough or because Bush was popular and that she won't apologize now for fear of looking like a flip-flopper. Political observers scour her daily statements—her head-nodding, even, in one recent *New York Times* article—for clues to her thinking. Or they speculate about what she might do in the future. But the key to understanding Hillary Clinton's foreign policy lies in the past. And, as one probes her inner circle and reconstructs her record, an alternative reading emerges: What if the hawkish Hillary of 2002 wasn't just motivated by political opportunism? What if she really believed in the war?

It's hard to get a handle on Clinton's foreign policy. That's partly because it's hard even to get a handle on the identity of her foreign policy advisers. "Look, I don't fucking know!" barks one former Clintonite when queried about whom Clinton relies on. "No one knows!" The topic breeds deep paranoia, as Hillary's campaign has been known to rebuke those who speak publicly without explicit license. The result is a confounding omertà code: Whereas other politicians eagerly expound on their worldviews and policy deliberations, asking Democrats about Hillary's foreign policy consultations sometimes feels like inquiring after Whitey Bulger in Irish South Boston. "Please don't take this conversation as confirming anything," pleaded one person I contacted, who would only identify himself as being in the "very distant, outer-most, orbital region" of the campaign. "I don't know how they want us to handle it." Such nervousness is a testament to the continued belief, despite the rise of Barack Obama, that Hillary will probably be the Democratic nominee—and that, if she wins, she'll have an administration full of jobs to fill. "This is one of those subjects where people are disinclined to say anything," explains Les Gelb of the Council on Foreign Relations. "People are very cautious when jobs are at stake."

As a result, it's not easy divining how Clinton thinks about national security in general, much less what factors led to her support for the Iraq war resolution. Her aides allowed me only a fleeting hallway encounter with Clinton herself. So I set out to unravel the mystery by calling dozens of former Clinton officials and Democratic aides. I also dug into her past, from her college career through eight years in the White House and six in the Senate. Sifting through Hillary's life, a portrait begins to emerge of a woman who has always been more comfortable with the military than many of her liberal boomer peers. I found that Clinton had aggressively pushed her husband to use force when he was president; that one of her most influential new advisers was a former senior aide to hawkish Senator Sam Nunn of Georgia; and that, although she opposed President Bush's Iraq "surge," she has consulted regularly with one of its prime architects. I even found that, in her late twenties, Hillary Rodham Clinton briefly attempted to enlist in the U.S. Marines.

That last fact—reported in 1994 but largely forgotten since—underlines the degree to which, unlike many of her peers, Clinton has never allowed Vietnam to define her vision of foreign policy. It's true that the war helped pull her from her roots as a Goldwater Girl and a president of Wellesley College's Young Republicans and drive her into the Democratic Party. During her junior year at Wellesley, she even knocked on doors for Eugene McCarthy's antiwar campaign. But Vietnam apparently didn't imbue Hillary with a loathing for the military. In 1975, just months after the last U.S. troops returned home, Hillary was living in Arkansas with Bill, who had mounted a failed bid for Congress the previous year. The young couple, who would marry later that year, were both teaching law at the University of Arkansas, when Hillary, for reasons never made entirely clear, decided to enlist in the Marines. When she walked into a recruiting office in Little Rock and inquired about joining, the recruiter on duty was unenthusiastic about the 27-year-old law professor in thick, goggle glasses. "You're too old, you can't see, and you're a woman," Clinton recalled him saying. "Maybe the dogs"—Marine slang for the Army—"would take you." Deflated, Clinton said she decided to "look for another way to serve my country."

From there, the trail seems to go cold. Hillary's geopolitical opportunities were limited in Arkansas, where she focused on her law career and advocacy on such domestic issues as children's rights. And, when she moved with Bill into the White House in 1993, in contrast to her public stewardship of health care, she had no formal foreign policy role. She was rarely, if ever, present at her husband's official national security meetings, and when she traveled abroad it was typically to promote relatively uncontroversial issues like women's rights and religious tolerance. "My staff used to tease me, suggesting that the State Department had a directive: If the place was too small, too dangerous or too poor—send Hillary," she writes in her memoir, *Living History*.

Behind the scenes, however, Hillary was an important figure in her husband's overseas agenda. "Much more than is usually the case with a first lady, she was interested in and knowledgeable about foreign policy," says Strobe Talbott, a former State Department official and longtime friend of the Clintons. In informal settings, "she was very much a part of the conversation."

That's no surprise, given how close Hillary was to Bill's top foreign policy mandarins. She had bonded with National Security Advisor Sandy Berger years before, while working for the presidential campaigns of George McGovern and Gary Hart, and remained close to Berger and his wife, Susan, ever since. As first lady, she talked regularly with Sandy, who she has said took an active interest in her overseas trips. More recently, in 2001, Susan, a Washington realtor, helped Hillary choose her $2.85 million brick Georgian house and even found her a posh interior decorator.

Hillary was tighter still with Madeleine Albright. Both had attended Wellesley (albeit a decade apart), and the pair famously hit it off on a 1996 trip to Eastern Europe when Albright was still ambassador to the United Nations. News reports painted a portrait of gal pals on a European holiday—window-shopping in Prague, sharing dumplings in a café, laughing hysterically as the wind turned their umbrellas inside-out. Their personal bond reportedly led Hillary to insist that Bill choose Albright for secretary of state in 1997. It also gave Hillary an informal line to America's top diplomat. The women met regularly, often with their top aides, for frank conversations about policy and politics in Albright's State Department dining room. In her memoir, *Madam Secretary*, Albright describes the relationship as an "unprecedented partnership." "I was once asked whether it was appropriate for the two of us to work together so closely," Albright writes. "I agreed that it was a departure from tradition," but she saw no problem with the first lady having a hand on the ship of state.

Perhaps most importantly, Hillary clearly helped to shape some of her husband's key foreign policy decisions. In March 1999, for instance, as Slobodan Milosevic's Serbian forces conducted a rising campaign of ethnic cleansing against Kosovar Albanians, her husband considered a series of airstrikes to stop the killing. His generals were nearly unanimous in opposition: Bombing wouldn't work, they said, and, in any case, military engagement wasn't worth the risk of American casualties. Russian opposition also guaranteed a lack of U.N. sanction for the mission; any military action would have to be a NATO operation of debatable international legitimacy. Hillary didn't care. As she later explained to *Talk* magazine, while on a trip in North Africa she phoned her husband in Washington and pleaded with him to unleash the military. "I urged him to bomb," she said. "You cannot let this go on at the end of a century that has seen the major holocaust of our time. What do we have NATO for if not to defend our way of life?"

Bill Clinton, of course, wound up agreeing with his wife. The subsequent 78-day bombing campaign was an astonishing success. The United States suffered zero casualties, and the Serbs capitulated, beginning the process of Milosevic's downfall. It was the third time Hillary had spoken up in favor of intervention. The first had been in 1994 in Haiti, according to one former Clintonite. The other had been the 1995 campaign of airstrikes to bring an end to the Bosnian conflict. Her memoir recounts hearing a speech by Elie Wiesel in April 1993 in which he invoked the Holocaust as he pleaded with the president to take action in the former Yugoslavia. "Sitting in the gray drizzle," Hillary writes, "I agreed with Elie's words, because I was convinced that the only way to stop the genocide in Bosnia was through selective air strikes against Serbian targets." This was more than two years before her husband finally brought himself to commence the bombing.

By the end of their reign, the Clintonites seemed to have demonstrated that the United States could flex its muscles with ease and precision—even without U.N. approval—and be loved for it. U.S. bombs had restored peace and stability to central Europe, and American values were on the march. Hillary's memoir recounts her 1996 meeting with an American peacekeeping soldier in Bosnia: "[W]herever we go, the kids wave at us and smile," he told her. "To me, that's reason enough to be here." Not only was it righteous, it held a certain glamour as well. As Hillary recounts in a typical passage, "Sheryl Crow, Sinbad and Chelsea and I flew in Black Hawk helicopters to visit soldiers in forward positions. . . . Chelsea had been a big hit with the soldiers and their families throughout the trip, shaking hands and signing autographs with her usual warmth and grace." All this filled her with a vivid optimism. On a flight back from the region, she recalls, "I remember thinking what a perfect day it was for flying and what a perfect moment to be alive."

Little wonder that, by 1999, Hillary was proclaiming in speeches, "I am very pleased that this president and administration have made democracy one of the centerpieces of our foreign policy." Or that, during her Senate campaign a year later, she would argue that America's military involvements should not be limited to "splendid little wars."

In the fall of 2002, Bush officials were having their own troubles divining what Hillary Clinton thought about Iraq. Although she was a regular attendee at Capitol Hill briefings conducted by senior administration officials like Colin Powell and Paul Wolfowitz, she listened far more than she spoke, recalls one former Bush official. (She was more open with then-deputy National Security Advisor Stephen Hadley, an old friend from Yale Law School, pulling him aside for private chats.) But in general, says the former Bush official, Clinton seemed more comfortable with confronting

Iraq than some other Democrats. "I was kind of pleasantly surprised by her attitude," he says. "Not that she was jumping up and down waving flags and saying, 'Hey, let's go after these guys.' But you take a John Kerry—he would sit back with his arms folded and a skeptical look."

At one point that fall, Clinton visited the White House, along with several other senators, to hear National Security Advisor Condoleezza Rice make her case for the Iraq resolution. Once again, Hillary kept her views largely to herself, leading Rice to call her personally afterward. Did the senator have any questions she might answer, Rice asked? Clinton asked Rice for assurance that Bush really intended to push diplomacy to the limit, that the resolution was not a de facto vote for war. On the contrary, Rice said, it was the best hope for peace: Only the clear threat of force could compel Saddam to accept the intrusive weapons inspections that might avert war.

Clinton says now that she took Rice at her word. She expected the administration to make a good-faith effort at diplomacy and to give arms inspectors ample time to do their work. According to her, it did neither. Her critics deride that as a naïve view, of course. A few weeks before, even her confidante Sandy Berger had noted that "the smell of gunpowder" was already in the Washington air. But a vote based on the notion that diplomacy required the threat of force behind it was entirely consistent with the worldview her husband's administration had developed. "I think there is a connection to her vote," says James P. Rubin, a former Clinton assistant secretary of state, "which is recognizing that the right combination of force and diplomacy can achieve America's objectives. Sometimes to get things done—like getting inspectors into Iraq—you do have to be prepared to threaten force. But you have to get the combination right. And, in Iraq, Bush got the combination wrong. To get it right means not dispensing with either force or diplomacy."

But, by 2002, some Clintonites seemed resigned to the inevitability of force as a solution. Iraq had been a persistent fly in the ointment during the latter years of the Clinton administration. Few things terrified the Clintonites more than the chemical and biological arsenal they were convinced Saddam possessed. Their phobia was illustrated in 1997, when Defense Secretary William Cohen appeared on television holding up a five-pound sack of sugar to illustrate how a small payload of Saddam's anthrax could kill half of Washington. Late in his presidency, Bill Clinton told one interviewer that the thought of a crop-duster spraying biological agents over the National Mall literally "keeps me awake at night." Thoughts like these led to an ever-more aggressive posture toward Saddam. In November 1998, the president signed the Iraq Liberation Act, making Saddam's ouster a stated goal of U.S. policy for the first time; a few months later, Albright toured the Middle East explaining to Arab governments that the United States was serious about "regime change." When Saddam kicked out U.N. weapons inspectors that year, Clinton ordered Operation Desert Fox, a four-day campaign of bombing and cruise-missile strikes. "So long as Saddam remains in power, he threatens the well-being of his people, the peace of his region, the security of the world," he explained at the time. "The credible threat to use force, and, when necessary, the actual use of force, is the surest way to contain Saddam's weapons of mass destruction program, curtail his aggression, and prevent another gulf war."

Whatever role Hillary played in her husband's Iraq policy remains a mystery. But it's clear that the Clintonites left office deeply frustrated at the unsolved problem of Iraq and perhaps believing that some final reckoning was inevitable. "President Clinton recognized, as did I," Albright writes in her memoir, "that the mixture of sanctions, containment, Iraqi defiance, and our own uncertainty about Saddam's weapons couldn't go on indefinitely."

Bush's approach was clearly blunter than what Clintonite foreign policy would have dictated. But, even as the "smell of gunpowder" turned into a stench, the foreign policy experts to whom Hillary was closest remained supportive of war with Iraq. "Most of the top [Clinton] national security team had sympathy for what Bush decided, in the broadest terms," says a Democratic foreign policy analyst.

The most hawkish among them was former U.N. Ambassador Richard Holbrooke, with whom Clinton conferred that fall. "If all else fails, collective action against Saddam is, in my view, justified by the situation and the record of the last decade," Holbrooke told the Senate Foreign Relations Committee in September 2002. Holbrooke's standard for "collective" seemed to include only the British and perhaps a handful of other allies. And Holbrooke made clear that a war to topple Saddam was unlikely to be easy and that U.S. forces might have to spend years in a postwar Iraq. Nor was Holbrooke alone. Varying degrees of support for the Bush resolution came from the likes of Rubin, former Defense Secretary William Perry, and former Deputy National Security Advisor Jim Steinberg. And, though she raised red flags about the war's risks, Hillary's close friend Albright ultimately concluded that Bush "should have this authority." This was hardly shocking: Albright's relatives had fled both Hitler and Stalin, instilling in her a belief that dictators must be challenged. "My mindset is Munich," she once said. "Most of my generation's is Vietnam." It may have been such thinking that once led Albright to query a stunned Colin Powell, "What's the point of having this superb military you're always talking about if we can't use it?" (In his memoir, Powell recalls, "I thought I would have an aneurysm.")

Hillary also conferred with Kenneth Pollack, the former Clinton national security aide whose book, *The Threatening Storm,* helped convince many Democrats that Saddam could not be peacefully contained indefinitely. (Although, in one encounter after the 2003 invasion, according to several sources, Clinton needled Pollack for his mistaken beliefs about Saddam. "Ken, where are those WMDs you were telling me about?" she said.)

To be sure, policy and politics have always been inexorably intertwined in Clintonland, and, while some close to Hillary made a principled case for supporting the war, others clearly billed it as a political winner. Among them was surely her pollster, Mark Penn, who has been a member of the Clinton inner circle since 1995. The disheveled, Harvard-educated Penn has long been obsessed with the political center. After September 11, he fixated on foreign policy, repeatedly warning Democrats that they needed to show voters that, as he put it in one essay, they are "capable of managing national security issues." For Penn, supporting the Iraq war was a fine opportunity to demonstrate this. In the 2004 Democratic primaries, he attached himself to a candidate who believed likewise, joining the ill-fated campaign of Joe Lieberman. According to one former Lieberman adviser, even as Iraq slid toward chaos Penn believed war supporters would be vindicated: "Penn was telling Lieberman he would be right about the war." It hardly seems a stretch to assume he told Hillary Clinton the same thing.

Of course, no Clintonite likely held more sway with Hillary than Bill himself, whose war position has never attracted the same scrutiny. Indeed, befitting the man who said of the 1991 Gulf War debate that he "agreed with the arguments of the minority," but "would have voted with the majority," Bill's views on the second Iraq war remain murky. When talk of a confrontation with Iraq first began brewing in 2002, he seemed wary about a possible distraction from the pursuit of Al Qaeda. "I don't have any use for Saddam Hussein," he said in a speech that June. "But I do think you have to ask yourself in what order do we have to do this." But, as the war drums grew louder, he grew increasingly supportive. While he stressed the importance of diplomacy and arms inspections, he seemed to value them more as a way to legitimate an invasion than to avoid one. On October 27, for instance, Clinton said in another speech that "I do think it would be better if we can go through the U.N. and try the inspections, even though if past is prologue, they'll fail." Though he regularly warned against acting without broad support, this, too, seemed less a critique of Bush administration aggressiveness than of U.N. timidity. In a mid-February speech, he told a Texas audience that Bush "deserves a lot of credit for saying we can't just ignore [Iraq] forever; it's time to deal with this again," before going on to argue that the credibility of the United Nations was at stake and urging recalcitrant European countries to show that they were serious about Iraq.

More strikingly, Clinton even seemed to embrace the neocon notion that, by toppling Saddam, the United States might reshape the Middle East. "[I]t's going to take years to rebuild Iraq," he said. "If we do this, we want it to be a secular democracy. We want it to be a shared model for other Middle Eastern countries. We want to do what a lot of people in the administration honestly want, which is to have it shake the foundations of autocracy in the Middle East and promote more freedom and decency. You've got to spend money and work hard and send people there to work over a long period of time." These could have been the words of Paul Wolfowitz. But, to Bill Clinton, this wasn't a blinkered fantasy—it was a legitimate and realistic U.S. foreign policy objective.

Still rotating in Hillary's orbit are many of the Clintonites who advised her prior to the war. "There's no way when you look at who's around her that you can't see it as a continuum" from her husband's administration, says representative and former Clinton White House aide Rahm Emanuel. But, when I pressed Hillary's advisers on the subject of whom she consults on foreign policy, they were eager to portray her—in convenient contrast to, say, Barack Obama and John Edwards—as an experienced foreign policy hand who doesn't need anyone telling her what to think. "This is not like Bush and the Vulcans," explains one, referring to the (supposed) policy titans who schooled the geopolitically clueless Texas governor. By contrast, Clinton advisers note, as first lady she visited 82 nations—each trip accompanied by a detailed briefing. "You'd be hard-pressed to say that there's anyone in this race with that experience," says one. The flattering image presented by Hillary's circle is of a policy mastermind who mainly calls in people with specific expertise when she needs to fill small gaps in her knowledge on particular regions or threats. (I learned the names of some of these experts—uncontroversial figures with high media profiles—but the paranoia in Clintonland runs so deep that I was not given permission to cite them.)

Hillary Clinton still talks regularly with her husband's senior foreign policy team, whose generally hawkish slant may help to explain why Hillary has been far slower than her Democratic rivals to shift left on the war. (It's telling that the three well-known former Clinton foreign policy officials who have signed up with Obama's campaign—former National Security Advisor Anthony Lake, State Department African affairs expert Susan Rice, and

Greg Craig, a lawyer and onetime adviser to Albright—are more dovish than many of their old colleagues.) Hillary's campaign still lacks a formally structured foreign policy team, perhaps in part because her lasting personal friendships provide much of the advice she needs. A month after Hillary's election to the Senate in 2000, for instance, Holbrooke hosted a gala dinner for her at his private residence in Manhattan's Waldorf Astoria Towers, featuring attendees like Robert De Niro and Harrison Ford. When Hillary traveled to Munich in 2005 for a speech about the United Nations, Holbrooke was there, taking notes in the front row. He's also inside enough to have recently solicited recommendations for a new full-time foreign policy aide to join Clinton's campaign. "He's obviously gunning for secretary of state," a Democratic foreign policy expert told me. "He's putting all his eggs in this basket."

Hillary is also still close to her former café-hopping buddy Albright, whom she recently named to a "rapid reaction" team of women who will defend her against attacks in the press. And she is said to confer constantly with Berger, her friend of more than 30 years, who, despite his opposition to the Iraq war, still defends the utility of force. In a 2004 *Foreign Affairs* essay calling for a return to internationalism, he nonetheless noted that "[a] Democratic administration will need to reaffirm the United States' willingness to use military power—alone if necessary—in defense of its vital interests." (That said, some Democrats suggest that Berger's involvement in the campaign will be limited—or at least concealed—thanks to his ham-fisted attempt to smuggle documents from the National Archives in 2003.)

Newer additions to Hillary's fold also suggest that her hawkish profile is about more than just polls. One is her Senate foreign policy staffer Andrew Shapiro. The 39-year-old Shapiro is affable but charged with nervous energy. (Sitting in the audience at a recent Clinton speech on the military, he rocked steadily back and forth like Rain Man at Wapner time.) A Gore-Lieberman campaign aide and Justice Department lawyer, Shapiro was also briefly a research assistant at the Washington Institute for Near East Policy, a center-right think tank. Shapiro is "a mainstream foreign Democratic policy establishment moderate," says a congressional foreign policy aide. "He's hawkish on defense issues and Israel." It is Shapiro, Hillaryites say, who is in the room for most of her important foreign policy decisions.

Hillary has also recruited a new and relatively unknown adviser: longtime defense establishment insider Jeffrey Smith. "When she went on Armed Services, she telephoned me and asked if I would come up and give her a sense of the issues she'd encounter," says Smith, who served as general counsel to the CIA in the mid-'90s and is now a partner at the Washington law firm Arnold & Porter. Though Smith has civil libertarian views on intelligence (he strongly opposes the Guantánamo Bay detainee program), he is a West Point graduate with roots in military culture who spent several years working for Nunn on the Senate Armed Services Committee. During the 2004 campaign, Smith said he had found John Kerry's 1971 charges of U.S. war crimes in Vietnam offensive. Smith has been a harsh critic of the Iraq war from the start, but, like Hillary, he has argued that the United States can't summarily withdraw. "[N]o one should question how difficult—or how important—it is to achieve our mission," he wrote in a 2003 op-ed.

Smith told me he's been surprised at the kinship Hillary finds with military and ex-military men. A case in point is her camaraderie with retired General Jack Keane, a gruff former vice army chief of staff and co-architect of Bush's Iraq "surge" plan. Keane, a New Yorker, contacted his new senator after her 2001 election and offered to keep her up to speed on the state's Fort Drum Army base and military issues generally. In 2003, Keane escorted Clinton on a visit to West Point to address students there. (A private chat about Iraq on the flight home prompted Clinton to take her first trip there two months later.) When Clinton joined the Senate Armed Services Committee in 2002, Shapiro says, Keane was among the first people she contacted. Although Clinton opposed Keane's surge plan, her aides say she still thinks enough of his opinion that she has debated it with him. It's hard to imagine that many other leading Democrats would have done the same.

Clinton's aides wouldn't grant me an extended interview with her, but I was afforded a brief, on-the-fly encounter. On a morning in March 2007, I merged into Clinton's bubble as she left a press conference on children's health care in the Russell Senate Office Building. Even on Capitol Hill, Clinton has massive star power, and it took her five minutes to work her way out of the room in her methodical style, head slowly turning this way and that like a giant radar dish as her pale blue eyes locked onto each new supplicant. Finally, Clinton greeted me warmly as we stepped onto an elevator closed to the rabble by her Secret Service detail.

I had time for two questions. First, I asked her about the influence her husband's foreign policy experience had on her Iraq vote: whether his successful use of force, even without U.N. approval, had shaped her decision. "It certainly did influence my thinking," she told me in her matter-of-fact tone. "What many of us thought was, the use of diplomacy backed up by the threat of force—that is a credible position for America to take in the world." But, she added, "there were those in the Congress who thought that the United States should never even threaten force—or certainly take force—in the absence of U.N. Security Council approval. Well, I had seen during the Clinton administration that sometimes, that's not even possible. Sometimes, it's not even possible for the president to get congressional approval to pursue vital national security interests." This does not sound like someone who, in her heart, had at the time thought George Bush's confrontation was a terrible mistake.

Then we were on the street. Clinton's black sedan was waiting with an open door. Though she was starting to look impatient, I wedged in my second question: What should people make of the fact that she had briefly tried to enlist in the military? At this her eyes narrowed and she threw me a glare of mistrust. "I have very deep and quite broad relationships with people in the military," she said. As for the meaning of the recruiting visit, "I can't tell you," she said with a dismissive wave. "You go look at that." And at that, the door shut, and she was gone, a faint silhouette behind tinted windows.

In her October 2002 speech explaining her vote for President Bush's war resolution, Hillary was clearly conflicted. She listed several reasons why war might be necessary, including the Iraqi chemical and biological arsenal—which she called "undisputed"— and her purported special perspective, as a New Yorker after September 11, on the "risks of action versus inaction." She also offered several counterarguments, including her fear that Bush might make a dangerous precedent of "preemption."

But, in concluding that she would support Bush, Clinton offered another rationale of a very different sort. She argued that she was inherently predisposed to grant the benefit of the doubt to a president asking Congress for support in matters of war. In the '90s, Clinton had watched congressional Republicans undermine her husband's foreign policy for political gain. They mocked his interventions in Haiti, Bosnia, and Kosovo—Tom DeLay called it "Clinton's war"—and they cried "wag the dog" when he launched a cruise-missile attack on Iraq in the midst of the Lewinsky scandal. "[P]erhaps," Hillary mused in her floor speech, "my decision is influenced by my eight years of experience on the other end of Pennsylvania Avenue in the White House, watching my husband deal with serious challenges to our nation. I want this president, or any future president, to be in the strongest possible position to lead our country in the United Nations or in war."

In short, Clinton was arguing that Congress should have an innate deference to presidential authority in matters of diplomacy and war. As she explained to ABC's George Stephanopoulos in December 2003, "I'm a strong believer in executive authority. I wish that, when my husband was president, people in Congress had been more willing to recognize presidential authority." To this day, when Clinton refuses to apologize for her war vote, she explains that she doesn't regret deferring to Bush's authority, but rather "the way he used that authority."

Thanks to the excesses of the Bush administration, the phrase "executive authority" has a dirty ring to it these days, and Hillary rarely talks much about it in public. But her advisers say it remains a guiding principle of her thinking. It also explains why Hillary, despite the vitriol of Cindy Sheehan and harassment by antiwar protesters, has been so much slower than Democratic primary rivals like John Edwards to call for a swift U.S. withdrawal.

Of course, there is another prominent Democrat, one beloved by the left, who has also shared Hillary's moderation on the question of exiting Iraq: Al Gore. Though he opposed the war full-throatedly, the former vice president has yet to endorse a quick withdrawal, saying that to do so would be to consign Iraq to complete anarchy. Clinton advisers note that the key thing Hillary and Gore have in common is eight years together at 1600 Pennsylvania Avenue. "On his press tour, Gore sounded like Hillary," says one

Clinton adviser. "And it's probably because those two understand the presidency better than anyone." Or, as Les Gelb puts it, "She thinks more like a president than a candidate."

Ultimately, perhaps the strangest thing about Hillary Clinton's war vote is that she actually seems to have related to George W. Bush's predicament. She remembered the feeling of being in the White House, looking at a dangerous and unstable world, and imagining that the United States had the power to make it safer and more humane. She knew the feeling of having a powerful military on call. She not only believed that Saddam had WMD, but also that, by deposing him, the United States could promote freedom and democracy.

Those beliefs made Clinton receptive to Bush's arguments for war, even if it was almost certainly not one she would have initiated. But the final straw for her decision may have had less to do with a vision of U.S. power than with a vision of herself. She had seen her husband in Bush's shoes, confronting a Congress that didn't trust his foreign policy leadership. And she knew that, someday, she might find herself in those same shoes as well. In that sense, for Hillary Clinton, supporting the Iraq war may have been as much about her future as it was about her past.

Barack Obama

Full Name Barack Hussein Obama, Jr.

Current Residence Chicago, Illinois

Date and Place of Birth August 4, 1961; Honolulu, Hawaii

Education
   B.A., Columbia University, 1983
   J.D., Harvard Law School, 1991

Military Service
   None

Nonpolitical Positions Held
   Financial Analyst, Business International Corporation,
      1984–1985
   Chicago Community Organizer, 1985–1988
   Associate Attorney, Miner, Barnhill & Galland, 1993–2004
   Author, *Dreams from My Father,* 2004
   Author, *The Audacity of Hope,* 2006

Political Offices Held
   Illinois State Senator, 1997–2004
   U.S. Senator from Illinois, 2005–present

Family
   Married to Michelle Obama; children: daughters Malia and
      Natasha

Barack Obama's Unlikely Political Education: The Agitator   *Ryan Lizza*

n 1985, Barack Obama traveled halfway across the country to take a job that he didn't fully understand. But, while he knew little about his new vocation—community organizer—it still had a romantic ring, at least to his 24-year-old ears. With his old classmates from Columbia, he had talked frequently about political change. Now, he was moving to Chicago to put that talk into action. His 1995 memoir, *Dreams from My Father,* recounts his idealistic effusions: "Change won't come from the top, I would say. Change will come from a mobilized grass roots. That's what I'll do. I'll organize black folks. At the grass roots. For change."

His excitement wasn't rooted merely in youthful enthusiasm but also in the psychology of a vagabond. By 1985, Obama had already lived in Hawaii, where he was born and raised by his white mother and grandparents; Indonesia, where he lived briefly as a child; Los Angeles, where he started college; and New York, where he finished it. After these itinerant years, he would finally be able to insinuate himself into a community—and not just any community, but, as he later put it, "the capital of the African American community in the country." Every strain of black political thought seemed to converge in Chicago in the 1980s. It was the intellectual center of black nationalism, the base both for Jesse Jackson's presidential campaigns and for Louis Farrakhan's Nation of Islam. Moreover, on the eve of Obama's arrival, Harold Washington had overthrown Richard J. Daley's white ethnic machine to become the city's first black mayor. It was, in short, an ideal place for an identity-starved Kenyan Kansan to immerse himself in a more typical black American experience.

Not long after Obama arrived, he sat down for a cup of coffee in Hyde Park with a fellow organizer named Mike Kruglik. Obama's work focused on helping poor blacks on Chicago's South Side fight the city for things like job banks and asbestos removal. His teachers were schooled in a style of organizing devised by Saul Alinsky, the radical University of Chicago trained social scientist. At the heart of the Alinsky method is the concept of "agitation"— making someone angry enough about the rotten state of his life that he agrees to take action to change it; or, as Alinsky himself described the job, to "rub raw the sores of discontent."

On this particular evening, Kruglik was debriefing Obama about his work when a panhandler approached. Instead of ignoring the man, Obama confronted him. "Now, young man, is that really what you want to be about?" Obama demanded. "I mean, come on, don't you want to be better than that? Let's get yourself together."

Kruglik remembers this episode as an example of why, in ten years of training organizers, Obama was the best student he ever had. He was a natural, the undisputed master of agitation, who could engage a room full of recruiting targets in a rapid-fire Socratic dialogue, nudging them to admit that they were not living up to their own standards. As with the panhandler, he could be aggressive and confrontational. With probing, sometimes personal questions, he would pinpoint the source of pain in their lives, tearing down their egos just enough before dangling a carrot of hope that they could make things better.

More than 20 years later, Obama presents himself as a post-partisan consensus builder, not a rabble-rouser, and certainly not a disciple of Alinsky, who disdained electoral politics and titled his organizing manifesto *Rules for Radicals*. On the stump, Obama makes a pitch for "common-sense, practical, nonideological solutions." And, although he's anchored to a center-left worldview, he gives the impression of being above the ideological fray—a fresh face who is a generation removed from the polarizing turmoil of the 1960s. The mirror he holds up is invariably flattering—reflecting back a tolerant, forward-looking electorate ready to unite around his consensus-minded brand of politics. Indeed, if there has been a knock on Obama's campaign in these early days, it's that it may be a bit too idealistic for the realities of a presidential race. With his lofty rhetoric and careful positioning as above politics, Obama in some ways recalls Bill Bradley, another candidate of moral purity—and one whose unwillingness to engage in the rough-and-tumble of modern politics ultimately proved his undoing.

Yet Obama connects his past as a Chicago organizer to his presidential bid with surprising ease. In early 2007, during his first visit to South Carolina since his campaign announcement, we discussed his community-organizing days. He sat at the head of a long table inside a dimly lit hotel conference room in Columbia and ate a chocolate energy bar. When I began to suggest links between his organizing work then and his current campaign, he interrupted: "I think there is. I don't think you need to strain for it." He was at home talking Alinskian jargon about "agitation," which he defined as "challenging people to scrape away habit," and he fondly recalled organizing workshops where he learned the concept of "being predisposed to other people's power."

Publicly, as well, Obama has made his organizing days central to his political identity. When he announced his candidacy for president last month, he said the "best education" he ever had was not his undergraduate years at Occidental and Columbia or even his time at Harvard Law School, but rather the four years he spent in the mid-'80s learning the science of community organizing in Chicago. The night after Obama's announcement speech, he made a similar point on "60 Minutes" as he led Steve Kroft around the old neighborhood.

Obama's self-conception as an organizer isn't just a campaign gimmick. Organizing remained central to Obama long after his stint on the South Side. In the 13 years between Obama's return to Chicago from law school and his Senate campaign, he was deeply involved with the city's constellation of community-organizing groups. He wrote about the subject. He attended organizing seminars. He served on the boards of foundations that support community organizing. He taught Alinsky's concepts and methods in workshops. When he first ran for office in 1996, he pledged to bring the spirit of community organizing to his job in the state Senate. And, after he was elected to the U.S. Senate, his wife, Michelle, told a reporter, "Barack is not a politician first and foremost. He's a community activist exploring the viability of politics to make change." Recalling her remark in 2005, Obama wrote, "I take that observation as a compliment."

By defining himself as a "community organizer" above all else, Obama is linking himself to America's radical democratic tradition and presenting himself as an heir to a particular political style and methodology that, at least superficially, contrasts sharply with the candidate Obama has become. Community organizers see themselves as disciples of Thomas Paine and the colonists who dumped tea in Boston Harbor. Historically, they have revered the tactics of the labor militants of the 1930s, and they became famous in the '60s for the political theater championed by Alinsky, illustrated most memorably by his threat of a "fart-in" at a Rochester, New York, opera house to bring attention to the Kodak company's refusal to hire blacks.

Needless to say, this doesn't sound much like the placid politician who wrote *The Audacity of Hope*. And it raises questions about Obama's authentic political identity that require traveling back to the years when community organizing gave him the best education of his life.

A year after graduating from Columbia, Obama spotted an intriguing help-wanted ad in *The New York Times*. The Calumet Community Religious Conference (CCRC), a group that aimed to convert the black churches of Chicago's South Side into agents of social change, was looking for a community organizer to run the group's inner-city arm, the Developing Communities Project (DCP). Obama soon arranged to meet in New York with the organizer heading up the job search.

Obama had spent the previous year on a fruitless quest. He worked briefly for a Ralph Nader outfit in Harlem teaching college kids about recycling and then on a losing assemblyman's race in Brooklyn. But he longed for an experience that connected him to the civil rights era. "In the sit-ins, the marches, the jailhouse songs," he wrote in *Dreams*, "I saw the African-American community becoming more than just the place where you'd been born or the house where you'd been raised. Through organizing, through shared sacrifice, membership had been earned." Obama wanted to join the club.

"What really inspired me," Obama told me during one of several conversations about his work as an organizer, "was the civil rights movement. And if you asked me who my role model was at that time, it would probably be Bob Moses, the famous SNCC

[Student Nonviolent Coordinating Committee] organizer. . . .
Those were the folks I was really inspired by—the John Lewises,
the Bob Moseses, the Fannie Lou Harmers, the Ella Bakers."

Instead, he got Gerald Kellman, a Jewish organizer in a rum-
pled, tea-stained shirt. While Obama was in search of an authentic
African American experience, Kellman was simply in search of an
authentic African American. His organization worked in black
neighborhoods decimated by the shuttering of economic behe-
moths like U.S. Steel, agitating the unemployed to demand jobs
and safer streets. But, for all the anger and poverty in these places,
Kellman and his comrades couldn't break through. Because he
and his fellow organizers, Mike Kruglik and Gregory Galluzzo,
were white (and two of the three were Jewish), the black pastors
viewed them with suspicion and, in some cases, outright disdain.
Kellman, who had paid what he considered a small fortune for the
Times ad, desperately needed a young black man to give the group
credibility.

The job with the DCP allowed Obama entrée into the poor
black neighborhoods with which he was so eager to connect. But
serving as the black representative for a trio of white organizers
wasn't exactly the community-organizing fantasy he had in mind.
Rather, as Obama says today, "This was the closest I could find."
Kellman, Kruglik, and Galluzzo weren't schooled in civil rights era
organizing, but in the teachings of Alinsky, who distrusted movement politics and even Martin Luther King Jr. But, although
Obama didn't quite find himself reliving the civil rights era,
he soon found himself succumbing to the appeal of Alinsky's
organizing methodology.

In *Dreams,* Obama spent some 150 pages on his four years in
Chicago working as an organizer, but there's little discussion of

the theory that undergirded his work and informed that of his teachers. Alinsky is the missing layer of his account.

Born in 1909 to Russian-Jewish immigrants, Alinsky had prowled the same neighborhoods that Obama now worked and internalized many of the same lessons. As a University of Chicago criminology graduate student, he ingratiated himself with Al Capone's mobsters to learn all he could about the dynamics of the city's underworld, an experience that helped foster a lifelong appreciation for seeing the world as it actually exists, rather than through the academic's idealized prism. Charming and self-absorbed, Alinsky would entertain friends with stories—some true, many embellished—from his mob days for decades after-ward. He was profane, outspoken, and narcissistic, always the center of attention despite his tweedy, academic look and thick, horn-rimmed glasses.

Alinsky was deeply influenced by the great social science insight of his times, one developed by his professors at Chicago: that the pathologies of the urban poor were not hereditary but environ-mental. This idea, that people could change their lives by chang-ing their surroundings, led him to take an obscure social science phrase—"the community organization"—and turn it into, in the words of Alinsky biographer Sanford Horwitt, "something con-troversial, important, even romantic." His starting point was an early fascination with John L. Lewis, the great labor leader and founder of the CIO. What if, Alinsky wondered, the same hard-headed tactics used by unions could be applied to the relationship between citizens and public officials?

To test his theory, Alinsky left the world of academia in the 1930s and set up shop in Chicago's meatpacking neighborhood, the "Back of the Yards"—the same wretched, multiethnic enclave that Upton Sinclair had chronicled three decades earlier in *The Jungle*. He created the Back of the Yards Neighborhood Council, which won a succession of victories against businesses and decreased crime, while increasing cooperation between rival ethnic groups. The results were impressive enough that they were celebrated far beyond Chicago in newspaper stories with headlines like, "they called him a 'red,' but young sociologist did the job."

Alinsky had been dead for more than a decade when Obama arrived in Chicago, but his legacy was still very much alive. Kruglik, Kellman, and Galluzzo had all studied his teachings through the Industrial Areas Foundation (IAF), the organizing school Alinsky founded. By the '80s, not even the IAF strictly adhered to every principle that Alinsky taught. But at least one of Obama's teachers considered himself a true believer: "I regard myself as St. Paul who never met Jesus," Galluzzo told me of Alinsky, who died shortly after Galluzzo moved to Chicago on a pilgrimage to meet him in 1972. "I'm his best disciple." Alinsky has attracted other, more famous admirers, including Hillary Clinton, who wrote an undergraduate thesis about him, a favorite bit of trivia for right-wingers.

But, while Alinsky is often viewed as an ideological figure— toward the end of his life, New Left radicals tried to claim him as one of their own—to place Alinsky within a taxonomy of left-wing politics is to miss the point. His legacy is less ideological than methodological. Alinsky's contribution to community organizing was to create a set of rules, a clear-eyed and systematic approach that ordinary citizens can use to gain public power. The first and most fundamental lesson Obama learned was to reassess his understanding of power. Horwitt says that, when Alinsky would ask new students why they wanted to organize, they would invariably respond with selfless bromides about wanting to help others. Alinsky would then scream back at them that there was a one-word answer: "You want to organize for power!"

Galluzzo shared with me the manual he uses to train new organizers, which is little different from the version he used to train Obama in the '80s. It is filled with workshops and chapter headings on understanding power: "power analysis," "elements of a power organization," "the path to power." Galluzzo told me that many new trainees have an aversion to Alinsky's gritty approach because they come to organizing as idealists rather than realists. But Galluzzo's manual instructs them to get over these hang-ups. "We are not virtuous by not wanting power," it says. "We are really cowards for not wanting power," because "power is good" and "powerlessness is evil."

The other fundamental lesson Obama was taught is Alinsky's maxim that self-interest is the only principle around which to organize people. (Galluzzo's manual goes so far as to advise trainees in block letters: "get rid of do-gooders in your church and your organization.") Obama was a fan of Alinsky's realistic streak. "The key to creating successful organizations was making sure people's self-interest was met," he told me, "and not just basing it on pie-in-the-sky idealism. So there were some basic principles that remained powerful then, and in fact I still believe in."

Chicago pastors still remember Obama making the rounds of local churches and conducting interviews—in organizing lingo, "one-on-ones"—where he would probe for self-interest. The Reverend Alvin Love, the Baptist minister of a modest brick church amid the clapboard bungalows of the South Side, was one of Obama's first one-on-ones. During a recent visit to his church, Love told me, "I remember he said this to me: There ought to be some way for us to help you meet your self-interest while at the same time meeting the real interests and the needs of the community.'"

Obama so mastered the workshops on power that he later taught them himself. On his campaign website, one can find a photo of Obama in a classroom teaching students Alinskian methods. He stands in front of a blackboard on which he has written "Power Analysis" and "Relationships Built on Self Interest," an idea illustrated by a diagram of the flow of money from corporations to the mayor.

But, although he was a first-class student of Alinsky's method, Obama also saw its limits. It appealed to his head but not his heart. For instance, Alinsky relished baiting politicians or low-level bureaucrats into public meetings where they would be humiliated. Obama found these "accountability sessions" unsettling, even cruel. "Oftentimes, these elected officials didn't have that much more power than the people they represented," he told me.

At one meeting, where residents of an asbestos-laden housing project confronted their property manager about whether their homes had been tested, Obama suddenly had the urge to warn his target. "I wanted to somehow let Mr. Anderson know that I understood his dilemma," Obama wrote in *Dreams*, with the kind of empathy that is the hallmark of his autobiography. He was sometimes more interested in connecting with folks on the South Side than organizing them. He studied the characters he encountered so closely that Kruglik says Obama turned his field reports into short stories about the hopes and struggles of the local pastors and congregants with whom he was trying to commune.

Where some of Alinsky's disciples speak of his work with religious fervor, Obama maintained some detachment during these years. In his memoir, he gently mocked Marty Kauffman, the character based on Kellman (and a touch of Kruglik), who is a little too clinical in his approach and never puts down any roots in the community. "[I]t occurred to me that he'd made no particular attachments to people or place during his three years in the area, that whatever human warmth or connection he might require came from elsewhere," he wrote. Obama was determined not to end up like that. He needed something more than organizing theory to make the South Side his home.

As it was, he ran into the same roadblock as his trainers had. "Obama," Galluzzo told me, "was constantly being harassed by people saying, 'Oh, you work for that white person.'" On one occasion, he eagerly tried to make his pitch about joining DCP to a Reverend Smalls. Smalls wasn't interested. "I think I remember some white man coming around talking about some developing something or other," he told Obama. "Funny-looking guy. Jewish name." His hostility only grew when Obama explained that Catholic priests were also involved. "Listen . . . what's your name again? Obamba?" Smalls asked without waiting for an answer. "Listen, Obamba, you may mean well. I'm sure you do. But the last thing we need is to join up with a bunch of white money and Catholic churches and Jewish organizers to solve our problems." Obama left the meeting crestfallen.

On a Sunday morning two weeks before he launches his presidential campaign, Obama is at Trinity United Church of Christ on the South Side, gently swaying from side to side under a giant iron cross. From the outside, the church looks more like a fortress than a house of worship, with high whitewashed brick walls topped with security cameras. Inside, Trinity is the sort of African American community that the young Obama longed to connect with when he first came to Chicago. The church's motto is "unashamedly black and unapologetically Christian," and sunlight streams through stained glass windows depicting the life of a black Jesus. The Reverend Doctor Jeremiah A. Wright Jr., Trinity's pastor since 1972, flies a red, black, and green flag near his altar and often preaches in a dashiki. He has spent decades writing about the African roots of Christianity, partly as a way to convince young blacks tempted by Islam that Christianity is not "a white man's religion."

On this particular Sunday, the sea of black worshippers is dotted with a few white folks up in the balcony, clutching copies of *The Audacity of Hope* they've brought for Obama's book-signing later. Obama, sitting in the third row with his wife and two daughters, Malia and Natasha, stands, claps, prays, and sways along with the rest of the congregation. During the sermon, he watches the preacher carefully and writes notes. When asked by Wright to say a few words, Obama grabs the microphone and stands. "I love you all," he says. "It's good to be back home." The 150-person choir breaks into a chorus of "Barack, Hallelujah! Barack, Hallelujah!"

This adulation is a far cry from how Obama was received by Wright when they first met in the mid-'80s, during Obama's initial round of one-on-ones. Like Smalls, Wright was unimpressed. "They were going to bring all different denominations together to have this grassroots movement," explained Wright, a white-haired man with a goatee and a booming voice. "I looked at him and I said, 'Do you know what Joseph's brother said when they saw him coming across the field?'" Obama said he didn't. "I said, 'Behold the dreamer! You're dreaming if you think you are going to do that.'"

From Wright and others, Obama learned that part of his problem as an organizer was that he was trying to build a confederation of churches but wasn't showing up in the pews on Sunday.

When pastors asked him the inevitable questions about his own spiritual life, Obama would duck them uncomfortably. A Reverend Philips put the problem to him squarely when he learned that Obama didn't attend services. "It might help your mission if you had a church home," he told Obama. "It doesn't matter where, really. What you're asking from pastors requires us to set aside some of our more priestly concerns in favor of prophesy. That requires a good deal of faith on our part. It makes us want to know just where you're getting yours from."

After many lectures like this, Obama decided to take a second look at Wright's church. Older pastors warned him that Trinity was for "Buppies"—black urban professionals—and didn't have enough street cred. But Wright was a former Muslim and black nationalist who had studied at Howard and Chicago, and Trinity's guiding principles—what the church calls the "Black Value System"—included a "Disavowal of the Pursuit of Middleclassness."

The crosscurrents appealed to Obama. He came to believe that the church could not only compensate for the limitations of Alinsky-style organizing but could help answer the nagging identity problem he had come to Chicago to solve. "It was a powerful program, this cultural community," he wrote, "one more pliant than simple nationalism, more sustaining than my own brand of organizing."

As a result, over the years, Wright became not only Obama's pastor, but his mentor. The title of Obama's recent book, *The Audacity of Hope,* is based on a sermon by Wright. (It's worth noting, however, that, while Obama's book is a coolheaded appeal for common ground in an age of political polarization, Wright's sermon, "The Audacity to Hope," is a fiery jeremiad about persevering in a world of nuclear arms and racial inequality.) Wright is one of the first people Obama thanked after his Senate victory in 2004, and he name-checked Wright in a celebrated speech to civil rights leaders in Selma, Alabama.

The church also helped Obama develop politically. It provided him with new insights about getting people to act, or agitating, that his organizing pals didn't always understand. "It's true that the notion of self-interest was critical," Obama told me. "But Alinsky understated the degree to which people's hopes and dreams and their ideals and their values were just as important in organizing as people's self-interest." He continued, "Sometimes the tendency in community organizing of the sort done by Alinsky was to downplay the power of words and of ideas when in fact ideas and words are pretty powerful. 'We hold these truths to be self-evident, all men are created equal.' Those are just words. 'I have a dream.' Just words. But they help move things. And I think it was partly that understanding that probably led me to try to do something similar in different arenas."

In 1995, Obama shocked his old friend Jean Rudd by telling her he wanted to run for the state Senate. Back in 1985, Rudd, then working at the Woods Fund—a Chicago foundation that gives grants for community organizing—had provided Kellman with his original $25,000 to hire Obama. When Obama returned to Chicago to practice law, he joined the board of Rudd's foundation. Now he was going to the other side. "That's a switch!" she told him. Obama insisted that nothing would change. "Oh no," he said, according to Rudd. "I'm going to use the same skills as a community organizer."

In fact, Obama had already been applying Alinsky's core concepts—rigorous analysis of an opponent's strengths, a hard-headed understanding of self-interest as a fundamental organizing principle, a knack for agitating people to act, and a streetwise sense of when a raw show of power is necessary—to situations beyond the South Side. In 1988, Obama left Chicago for Harvard Law, where his greatest political victory was getting himself elected president of the law review. He did it by convincing a crucial swing bloc of conservatives that their self-interests would be protected by electing him. He built that trust during the same kind of long listening sessions he had made use of in the depressed neighborhoods of Chicago. "He didn't get to be president of *Harvard Law Review* because he was first in his class," said Richard Epstein, a colleague of Obama's at the University of Chicago Law School, where Obama later taught. "He got it because people on the other side believed he would give them a fair shake."

Even at Harvard, Obama kept a foot in the world of organizing. He spent eight days in Los Angeles taking a national training course taught by the IAF, a station of the cross for Alinsky acolytes. And, after he returned to Chicago in 1991, he served on the boards of both the Woods Fund and the Joyce Foundation, which also gives grants to Alinsky-style groups, and continued to teach organizing workshops.

In 1992, he got a taste of the relationship between organizing and electoral politics when he led a voter registration drive that helped Carol Moseley Braun become the first black woman ever elected to the Senate. By 1995, he laid out his vision of the agitator-politician in an interview with the *Chicago Reader:* "What if a politician were to see his job as that of an organizer, as part teacher and part advocate, one who does not sell voters short but who educates them about the real choices before them? As an elected public official, for instance, I could bring church and community leaders together easier than I could as a community organizer or lawyer."

This high-minded mission statement, however, obscures the

real-world organizing skills that proved relevant to Obama's political career. They surface in the story of his first campaign. Obama initially planned to inherit the seat of a much-admired incumbent named Alice Palmer, a fixture in South Side activist circles since the '60s. Palmer had opted to run for Congress, clearing the way for Obama to replace her, but, when she lost the primary, she decided she wanted to keep her old Senate seat, after all.

Obama was faced with a decision: step aside and wait his turn or do everything he could to take down a popular incumbent. In one meeting, an old guard of black political leaders tried to force Obama to abandon the race, but he wouldn't budge. Instead of deferring to Palmer's seniority, Obama challenged the very legitimacy of her petitions to get on the ballot, dispatching aides to the Chicago Board of Elections to scour Palmer's filing papers, and, while they were at it, every other candidate's, signature by signature. Many were fake. Obama won the challenge and cleared not just Palmer but all his potential rivals from the field.

It was a brash maneuver that caught the attention of the Illinois political establishment. "His introduction to the political community was that he knocked off Alice," said Ron Davis, a longtime Obama political hand who filed the challenge against Palmer and still cackles with glee over their victory. "The [current] president of the state Senate, Emil Jones, pushed very hard to save Alice, but we beat his staff. So they heard about Barack before he came down there to Springfield: Who was this guy who came in and knocked Alice off the ballot?' "

In the wake of Obama's contretemps with the Clinton campaign early in 2007—she asked him to return money raised by Hollywood mogul David Geffen after Geffen had some acid words for her in the press; Obama declined—this episode acquires added resonance. The core question being raised today about Obama the candidate is whether he can be both a post-partisan, inspirational figure—the dreamer whom Wright first identified—and also the type of uncompromising political realist who can actually win. After all, the presidential campaign trail is littered with candidates, from Adlai Stevenson to Bradley, who, like Obama, bemoaned the dirty business that politics has become and tried to run campaigns that rose above the muck. Such candidates may maintain the high ground, but they always lose. Obama's assertion that he is, at heart, a community organizer suggests he might not fall into the same trap. He was, after all, trained to pursue the ideal but practice the pragmatic. Obama internalized the Alinsky maxim to always live in "the world as it is and not as we would like it to be," and, starting with his race against Palmer, he put it to use. In the world as we would like it to be, every election should have more than one contestant. In the world as it is, especially in Chicago, you challenge your opponents' signatures and knock them off the ballot.

The Palmer race was one of the earliest clues that Obama's sincere critique about what's wrong with politics should not be mistaken for a declaration of unilateral disarmament when it comes to campaigning. He is not running a protest campaign like Jerry Brown's in 1992, or one under the delusion that it is above politics, like Bradley's. He is operating in the world as it is. When I asked Ron Davis if Obama is too idealistic, he laughed. "Barack knows how to play the game!" he told me. "I would hope we would not have a pie-in-the-sky type for president. These are not the times." Galluzzo concurred: "First of all, he's committed to his values. They are not bullshit to him. He personally believes the principles he's espousing. Now, do I also believe he's ambitious and will do whatever it takes to win? Yes."

Speaking of what he learned as an organizer, Obama himself

told me, "I think that oftentimes ordinary citizens are taught that decisions are made based on the public interest or grand principles, when, in fact, what really moves things is money and votes and power."

After beating Palmer, Obama brought some of his old organizing lessons to Springfield. His successful career there owed much to a relationship he built with Emil Jones, the South Side machine pol whom Obama later described as his "political godfather." Jones was an improbable mentor for Obama: In the mid-'80s, Obama's group had organized protests against Jones when it wanted more help with funding for its projects. In *Dreams,* Obama portrayed Jones as an "old ward heeler" jockeying for position on a stage with the mayor. And Obama and Jones tangled over Alice Palmer, whom Jones had tried to rescue. Yet despite that history, or perhaps because of it, Obama sought out Jones in the legislature and let him know he was eager to work with him. Jones's mentoring frayed Obama's relationships with some other black colleagues—"petty jealousies," Jones told me—but it paved the way for all of Obama's legislative achievements.

"Emil was then, and is now, a powerhouse," Rudd told me. "One of the things that community organizing teaches you is to do something called power analysis. You have to understand how to have a relationship with people in power, to be a peer with them, not to go on your knees begging but understand yourself as a co-equal and find a way that someone who has power will understand your power. That's the whole point of organizing: What is it that people in power need to accommodate your needs?"

In 2000, Obama challenged Representative Bobby Rush, a former Black Panther whose connection to black Chicago once seemed unshakable. But, after Rush tried and failed to dislodge

Richard M. Daley from the mayor's office in 1999, Obama saw an opening. The contest proved particularly painful for him when his opponents picked at old wounds about his identity. Donne Trotter, another candidate and state Senate rival who resented Obama's meteoric rise, told the *Chicago Reader*, "Barack is viewed in part to be the white man in blackface in our community." But those accusations probably had more impact on Obama emotionally than they did on his poll numbers. A few months before the election, Rush's son was shot and killed during a robbery, creating a wave of sympathy that carried him to victory.

After his defeat, Obama doubled down on his efforts to secure Jones's patronage. "When he ran for the U.S. House and lost that race, he learned from that," Jones told me. "He recognized that, even though you feel it in yourself that you are the best person, you need others around you that can influence others in support of you—or keep some people from being obstructionists. You need people to open doors for you. I guess that's what he saw in me."

There was another door Obama thought Jones could open. When the Democrats took over the Illinois Senate in 2003, Obama paid Jones a visit. "After I was elected president, he came in to see me one day," Jones told me. "He said, 'You were just elected president. You have a lot of power now.' 'What kind of power do I have?' He said, 'You have the power to make a United States senator.' 'That sounds good. Do you have anybody in mind?' He said, 'Yeah, me.'"

Despite this history, Obama is still cast by the press as the candidate unwilling to stoop low enough to win, while Hillary is the machine politician whose last name has become synonymous with ruthlessness. But that David-versus-Goliath framing of the race is overstated. Obama's political team is seasoned and conventional.

His media adviser and strategic guru, David Axelrod, has spent decades in Chicago politics working for both the reformers (Harold Washington) and the machine (Richard M. Daley). Obama has all of the political machinery—ad-makers, fund-raisers, opposition-researchers—in place to run a serious but traditional campaign.

Moreover, when Obama's ideals clash with reality, he has been able to find compromises that don't put him at a political disadvantage. For instance, no Democrat can win the general election while adhering to the public financing system if the Republican nominee doesn't do the same. Clinton and John Edwards have simply conceded that the public financing system is dead and are ignoring fund-raising restrictions that would be triggered if either ends up playing within the public financing scheme. Facing the same situation, Obama—a longtime champion of campaign finance reform in general and public financing in particular—asked the Federal Election Commission if he could raise the potentially restricted money now (the world as it is) but then give it back if he wins the nomination and convinces his Republican opponent to stick with public financing (the world as we would like it to be).

Back home in Chicago's recent mayoral election, Obama endorsed Richard M. Daley—the symbol of machine politics, corruption, and racism for Hyde Park progressives and Obama's old organizing friends. Asked if she was disappointed, Rudd said, "Yeah. We all want our politicians to be pure and ideological, but I think it was a strategic move on his part and a well-considered one." Another member of Obama's organizing fraternity told me, "That's part of his political savvy. . . . He recognizes that Daley is a powerful man and to have him as an ally is important. While he was a state senator here and moving around in Chicago, he made sure to minimize the direct confrontational approach to people of influence and policymakers and civic leaders. These are the same people now who are very aggressively supporting his campaign."

But when those supporters become a liability, Obama has not been afraid to take a direct, confrontational approach. Reverend Wright learned this on the evening before he was scheduled to deliver the invocation at Obama's presidential announcement speech in Springfield. According to *The New York Times,* after Trinity's Afrocentrism—which had originally drawn Obama to the church in the 1980s—had become a sticky campaign issue, Obama called his old friend and told him it was probably best if the pastor didn't speak, after all. The following day, Wright could be seen silently watching the proceedings from the sidelines along with other Obama supporters.

The way that Obama and his team have responded to the opening skirmishes of the presidential race has also been telling. Every time Obama has been challenged this year, his campaign has responded with ferocity. When Fox News falsely reported that Obama attended a madrassa in Indonesia, his aides not only went into war-room mode, beating back the story—not that difficult, considering it was obviously untrue—but Robert Gibbs, Obama's communications director, also told Fox political reporter Carl Cameron that he wouldn't be allowed to travel on Obama's plane. What is Fox going to do to us, Gibbs asked Cameron, report that Obama attended a radical Islamic school? Oh, wait, you already did that!

When Australian Prime Minister John Howard said Obama's Iraq plan would embolden Al Qaeda, Obama delivered a rehearsed line to a room full of reporters about how Howard should send more Aussies to Iraq if he cares so much about the situation there. And, most famously, when the Clinton campaign called on Obama to distance himself from Geffen, his campaign shot back by referencing the Clintons' Lincoln Bedroom fund-raising scandal.

In our last conversation, a few days after the Geffen episode, I asked Obama if his reputation for purity is a little overblown. He chuckled. "I wouldn't be a U.S. senator or out of Chicago or a presidential candidate from Illinois if I didn't have some sense of the world as it actually works," he said. "When I arrived in Chicago at the age of twenty-four, I didn't know a single person in Chicago, and I know an awful lot of folks now. And so, obviously, some of that has to do with me being pretty clear-eyed about power."

But being clear-eyed about power also means understanding its limits.

"What I am constantly trying to do," he added, "is balance a hard head with a big heart."

John Edwards

Full Name John Reid Edwards

Current Residence Chapel Hill, North Carolina

Date and Place of Birth June 10, 1953; Seneca, South Carolina

Education

   B.S., North Carolina State University, 1974
   J.D., University of North Carolina, 1977

Military Service

   None

Nonpolitical Positions Held

   Attorney, Partner, Edwards & Kirby, 1993–1999
   Director, Center on Poverty, Work and Opportunity at the
      University of North Carolina School of Law, 2005–2006
   Author, *Four Trials,* 2003

Political Offices Held

   U.S. Senator from North Carolina, 1999–2005

Family

   Married to Mary Elizabeth Anania; children: sons Lucius Wade
      (died 1996) and Jack and daughters Catharine and Emma

John Edwards, Poor Man's Candidate:
The Accidental Populist   *Jason Zengerle*

Last October, the United Steelworkers of America went on strike against Goodyear, leading some 13,000 of its members to walk off the job. Once they did, it was only a matter of time before John Edwards went to see them. Like a moth to a flame—or Al Sharpton to a police shooting—Edwards of late seems inexorably drawn to labor strife. As he has laid the groundwork for his 2008 presidential campaign, he has become a fixture at union rallies and on picket lines across the country. Striking janitors at the University of Miami; disgruntled Teamsters at a helicopter plant in Connecticut; beleaguered hotel workers campaigning for better wages and health insurance in Chicago, Los Angeles, even Honolulu—Edwards has visited them all, offering words of encouragement and solidarity at every turn. "When I hear of a group of courageous workers engaged in a historic struggle," he told the janitors in Miami last spring, "it is important to me to show that I am with them."

And so, in early November, about five weeks into the Goodyear strike, Edwards paid a visit to the United Steelworkers (USW) hall in Akron, Ohio. It was a cold Saturday morning just three days before the midterm elections, and USW Local 2 was hosting a rally to support both the strike and Ohio Democratic candidates. Nearly 500 Local 2 members were participating in the strike, and it seemed as if all of them had come to kick off their weekends at the squat, concrete building that sits in the shadow of the tiremaker's world headquarters. Some were taking a break from the picket lines to warm themselves with ten-cent coffee and glazed doughnuts; others were there to inquire about getting much-needed checks from the union's strike benefit fund. As they waited for the rally to start in the hall's central meeting room, large men in windbreakers and varsity-style letterman jackets emblazoned with the USW logo traded gossip about if and when they would be going back to work.

While they did, Edwards huddled with a dozen or so union officials in a small conference room. Although he is now 53, Edwards still has the same slim build, foppish brown hair, and preternaturally youthful face that made him such a bright young thing nearly a decade ago, when he was elected to the Senate from North Carolina. He's also managed to hold on to the same friendly, almost deferential manner—the one he inherited from his father, who said to his son that he could "tell if someone was talking down to me in 30 seconds"; the one he easily could have lost once he became important enough to have his own Secret Service detail. As he made small talk with his hosts, discussing college football and past labor events he had attended, he immediately put them at ease.

After a while, the conversation turned to the meeting's real purpose: preparing Edwards for his speech to the rally. In order to know precisely what words of solidarity to offer, he needed a background briefing—which the union officials eagerly provided, telling him about the perfidy of Goodyear and the terribleness of the strike as he nodded and murmured in agreement. But there was one piece of business even more pressing than what Edwards was going to say: what he was going to wear. He had arrived at the union hall dressed in the standard Saturday uniform for a stumping politician—V-neck sweater, Oxford shirt, and khakis. But that, of course, wouldn't cut it for a labor rally. And so, with the expectant look of a suitor offering his intended a diamond ring, an official handed Edwards a blue USW t-shirt.

There was just one problem. When Edwards put the shirt on, it was huge. Even though he was wearing it over two other pieces of clothing, it fit him like a muumuu, billowing out and away from his body. It clearly had been tailored for the sort of exceptionally large man who tends to belong to an industrial labor union, not for a politician who's a bit of a fitness freak. As Edwards stood awkwardly, the shirt's shoulder seams dangling around his elbows, one of the union officials, a giant with a tremendous gut, slapped him on the back hard enough to knock him forward. "It's OK!" he roared. "It makes you look skinny!"

Like the shirt, Edwards's persona for the 2008 campaign—that of a combative champion of the working class—seems a strange fit. Although Edwards ran for president in 2004 as a populist, he did so as a sunny one—a disposition that appeared a natural extension of his congenitally cheerful personality. He dubbed his political organization the "New American Optimists" and presented himself as the "son of a millworker" whose later success as a lawyer and a senator was a hopeful story about American possibility. His stump speech, which called attention to the "Two Americas," was less an airing of grievances than a buoyant pledge to bridge the divide between rich and poor. And his policy proposals—including incremental reform of health care and micro-initiatives to help the poor—were fiscally friendly as well, showing that his populist heart was governed by a New Democrat brain.

Even when it came to campaign tactics, Edwards played nice. In the Democratic primaries, he abstained from going negative on his opponents—so much so that many assumed he was angling for the number-two spot on the ticket. And, after John Kerry gave him that spot, he didn't adopt the typical running mate's role of attack dog. When he faced off in his vice presidential debate against Dick Cheney—whom Democrats were hoping he would beat like a Darth Vader piñata—Edwards turned in a largely toothless performance. As one Edwards adviser puts it, "He was the smiley, happy candidate."

But now, Edwards is trying to turn that smile into a snarl, or at least a frown of concern. Since losing the vice presidential race in 2004—and subsequently leaving the Senate and Washington—he has spent his time focusing on the forgotten and neglected corners of the United States and, to a lesser extent, the world. Acting as a sort of latter-day Tom Joad, he has visited not just picket lines but homeless shelters, disaster zones, and refugee camps. And, in his current quest for the presidency, he intends to make the plight of the people he has encountered in those places his central issue. Accordingly, he has ditched his past commitment to fiscally restrained Rubinomics and now favors universal health coverage and an expensive raft of other policy initiatives to lift Americans—and even people in other countries—out of poverty. When he officially announced he was running for president in late December, he did so not sitting next to his wife in the comfort of their family home in a Raleigh neighborhood called Country Club Hills—as he had in the 2004 campaign—but standing by himself in the debris-strewn backyard of a hurricane-damaged house in New Orleans's Ninth Ward. "This campaign," he declared, "will be a grassroots, ground-up campaign, where we ask people to take action."

It's a campaign that seems off to a promising start. Edwards's reinvention has moved him to the left of Hillary Clinton, which, in the Democratic primaries, should be a good location. And, while Barack Obama—presumably the other top-tier Democratic candidate—is also to Clinton's left, he will have to face the questions about experience, or lack thereof, that Edwards dealt with in 2004. The election calendar could also play to Edwards's favor, as for much of 2007 he sat near the top of public opinion polls of Democrats in Iowa, the site of the first caucus; was strong in South Carolina, which holds the second primary; and was tight with the all-powerful culinary workers union in Nevada, which hosts the second caucus.

Still, while Edwards's new incarnation may bring him certain advantages in the race, it's nonetheless a peculiar bit of political positioning. The Democratic primaries have not, after all, been terribly generous to pro-union populists (just ask Dick Gephardt), and it has been a generation or more since a national Democrat has gotten far by campaigning against poverty. Indeed, for all the political calculations that have presumably played into Edwards's shift, it seems as though something else has been at work, as well.

"I can tell you one thing that's changed for me, and it's very significant for me personally," Edwards told me in one of several conversations we had in the weeks before he officially launched his campaign. "When I was running for president before, in 2003, 2004, I spent most of my time thinking about what I could do to be a better candidate." He paused, as if to let this confession sink in. "That's just not what I think about anymore," he went on. "Now what I spend my time thinking about is what I want to do as president of the United States." Often derided as "plastic" and "a lightweight" during his last national campaign, Edwards has, in other words, been searching for his own political essence, both as a source of gravitas and as a rationale for his continued presidential ambitions. And, in his role as a crusader for the working class, he seems to think he has found it.

It's hard to imagine a political defeat more devastating than the one Edwards suffered in November 2004. First, there was the shock of it: On the afternoon of Election Day, when he boarded a plane for Boston to await the official results, the early exit polls had convinced him—and the rest of the Kerry-Edwards campaign —that the Democratic ticket was on its way to victory; it was only a few hours later, after his plane landed, that he learned things didn't look so good. Then there was the frustration: The morning after the election, he participated in a campaign conference call and found himself alone in arguing that Kerry should not concede until the anecdotal reports of voting irregularities in Ohio were cleared up. But the truly crushing blow came immediately after Kerry's concession speech at Faneuil Hall, when Edwards and his wife Elizabeth paid a surreptitious visit to a Boston hospital. A few weeks earlier, she'd discovered a lump on her breast; then, a day after he lost the election, they were told that she had cancer.

John and Elizabeth Edwards have experienced tragedy before: In 1996, their 16-year-old son, Wade, was killed in a car accident. Both of them say that experience helped give them the strength to deal with her illness. Some family friends also believe that her cancer may have helped him better cope with his election defeat. "I never saw him become this morose, bitter person muttering, 'But for Ohio, I'd be on top of the world,'" says Ed Turlington, a North Carolina lawyer who served as the chairman of Edwards's 2004 presidential campaign. "He just threw himself into getting Elizabeth well."

After a few weeks—once Elizabeth had chosen a course of treatment and been given a good prognosis by her doctors—Edwards turned to the question of what he would do next, since his Senate term was up and he was now looking for a job. He had a number of options. Outgoing Democratic National Committee Chairman Terry McAuliffe had pushed him to pursue that post. There were people encouraging him to write a campaign memoir or a book laying out a vision for the future of the Democratic Party; others wanted him to do a TV talk show. Some investment houses and law firms were interested in having him join them, as well. Around Thanksgiving, Edwards convened a meeting at his Washington house of his inner circle—Elizabeth, people who'd worked for him in the Senate and on his presidential campaign, longtime family friends—to discuss his future options. According to multiple participants, it didn't take him long to dismiss them all. What he wanted to do, he told those assembled, was focus his energies on fighting poverty.

Shortly thereafter, Edwards founded a poverty think tank at the University of North Carolina at Chapel Hill, which he has since used as both a base of operations and a vehicle to familiarize himself with academic research on the issue. Jacob Hacker, a Yale political scientist who attended a two-day seminar at the think tank last year, came away impressed. "It wasn't as if the presentations were by rabble-rousing Democratic activists calling for revolution," Hacker says. "There were some very technical social-science discussions, and he seemed very engaged by them." He also conducted his own version of fieldwork. Robert Gordon, a domestic policy adviser to Edwards, recalls a trip they took to a community development corporation in the small town of Washington, North Carolina. "It was a roundtable with regular people like you see in campaigns," Gordon says, "except there were no cameras, and the regular people were really down on their luck. There were a couple of people who'd had pretty serious drug problems, a few who had HIV. There was a woman who'd lived in a homeless shelter and who'd had her kids taken from her." When a minister at the meeting reminded the group that they were sitting next to a man who was almost vice president, Gordon says Edwards interrupted. "He said, 'I might have almost been vice president, but I am no better than anybody in this room.'"

Edwards explains his focus on poverty matter-of-factly. He ran for the Senate, and then the presidency, to "serve." (His successful career as a trial lawyer left him with no real need to make more money: In 2003, his net worth was estimated to be between $12.8 million and $60 million.) Even though he no longer held elected office—and was unsure as to whether he ever would again—he says his commitment to service remained, and poverty was the issue where he thought his service would be most valuable. "It felt to me like there was a huge void in national engagement on this issue," he told me, "and it was something I really cared about, so it was a natural fit." For public consumption, at least, it's as simple as that.

But Edwards's decision to focus on poverty almost certainly involved a political calculation as well. Although he is not someone for whom the presidency has been a lifelong ambition, his 2004 defeat clearly galled him. He may not have been muttering "but for Ohio" while Elizabeth was sick, but, since then, there has been some grumbling "but for Howard Dean's scream." Many in the Edwards camp believe to this day that Dean's televised outburst denied Edwards the momentum he'd earned by finishing a strong second in the Iowa caucuses. The clearest summation of this view can be found in Elizabeth's recent memoir, *Saving Graces:*

We had always heard that two stories come out of Iowa, and what we wanted was for John to be one of them. If The Scream hadn't happened, Kerry and John would have been the stories coming out of Iowa. . . . Since it did happen, Kerry and The Scream were the stories. And there was no New Hampshire bump.

No New Hampshire bump for Edwards (it went solely to Kerry instead) meant no nomination. Add to this Edwards's displeasure with Kerry's general election campaign—he privately complained that it wasn't aggressive enough in attacking President Bush or competing in some red states—and it appears he felt he was tantalizingly close to the White House or the vice president's office but for other people's mistakes.

And, while focusing on poverty might seem like an odd choice for someone once again eyeing the White House, it makes a certain sense if you view politics the way Edwards does. For a politician of such immense talent, one of the most remarkable things about Edwards is just how politically unformed he is. Prior to his own Senate campaign in 1998, he—unlike most people who make a fortune and then run for office—wasn't even a political junkie: He voted only about half of the time and gave relatively little money in campaign contributions. Since then, Edwards has become a ferocious political animal, preparing himself for campaigns the way he once prepped for trials; but his political knowledge and experience, in many respects, goes back only to the second half of the Clinton administration. And, during that time, of course, questions of authenticity and a candidate's character have dominated presidential campaigns.

This helps explain why Edwards seems to view the presidential campaign less as a contest between ideologies or even policy proposals than as a referendum on each candidate as a person. "Do I have the strength and character to lead this country? I mean, that's the question," he told me. "The judgment should be made on vision, and strength, and character, and who you really are." In 2004, the perception (fair or not) of Edwards was that he was a young politician in a hurry, one defined more by personal ambition than a set of core convictions or a guiding vision for the country. But that's a much harder case to make about someone who has spent the last two years holding poverty seminars and visiting food banks. "Presidential campaigns are primarily about character and sort of a broad sense of priorities and values," says Harrison Hickman, Edwards's pollster. "In that sense, his attention to poverty as an issue defines a lot about where he comes from, about what he thinks the failings of the country are and what he thinks the priorities of the country are."

Nor does Edwards's crusade end at the water's edge. Lack of foreign policy experience was one of his greatest shortcomings in 2004, and, since then, he has been busy trying to make it a strong suit. First, of course, there is Iraq: As a senator, Edwards voted for the resolution authorizing Bush to use force—and defended that vote throughout the last presidential campaign—but, in November 2005, he became one of the first prominent Democrats who supported the war to say his vote had been a mistake. Speaking at an August rally for Democratic Senate candidate (and antiwar champion) Ned Lamont, Edwards reiterated his mea culpa. "I voted for this war. I was wrong. I should not have voted for this war," he told a crowd of several hundred Lamont supporters who had gathered in a courtyard at Yale Medical School. He then added a call for immediate withdrawal of U.S. forces: "We need to make it clear that we're going to leave Iraq, and the best way to make that clear is to obviously start leaving."

More broadly, Edwards—who, as a senator, wasn't a prodigious foreign junketeer—has become something of a globetrotter over the last two years, taking trips to Israel, Russia, China, India, and Uganda, among other exotic locales. And the lesson he has learned from those travels parallels what he has learned in the soup kitchens and union halls he's visited in this country. "We have two responsibilities," he told the Lamontsters. "One of those is to look after the interests of the United States of America. The second responsibility is to look after the interests of humanity."

Undoubtedly aware of the poor track record of foreign policy idealism in Iraq, Edwards tries to couch his call for American global do-goodism in realist terms. "The most important responsibility of the next president," he frequently says, "is to restore America's leadership in the world, because if we don't lead, there is chaos." But, for all the geo-strategic framing, Edwards's desire for increased U.S. engagement with the world sometimes seems to reflect the thinking of someone who has just recently realized how big—and how troubled—the world really is.

"We talk about poverty in America; poverty in America is moderate compared to poverty around the world," Edwards declared at the Lamont rally. He then proceeded to tell a story about how, "just before this past Christmas," he had visited some slums outside of Delhi. Asking the crowd to "picture in your mind for just a minute and be there with me," he described "little narrow alleyways filled with sewage, flies, animals everywhere" and how, amid all this misery, he saw "a little area about twice the size of this stage. There were four blankets laid out on the pavement, and there were probably 15 or 20 children on each blanket." He paused, waiting for his audience to let the picture develop in their minds. "And then I realized," he went on, his voice now tinged with wonder and regret, "these children were in school. This was their school."

It was a powerful story, told in a powerful fashion, but the crowd, while moved, also seemed somewhat puzzled. What was Edwards's point? That, while Lamont battled Joe Lieberman, there were children starving in India? So Edwards spelled it out for them, adding a final line to his tale. "And I walked away from there," he concluded, his voice now practically a whisper, "and I said to myself, 'Where is America?'"

On the second anniversary of one of the worst days of his life—the day that his running mate conceded the election and his wife was diagnosed with cancer—Edwards returned to the place where it all happened. He was in Boston to speak that night at an awards dinner for local community activists, although the trip also served as a convenient excuse to see his oldest daughter, 24-year-old Cate, who's attending Harvard Law School. (Edwards and his wife have two other children, eight-year-old Emma Claire and six-year-old Jack.) Before the speech, he met me at a seafood restaurant in his hotel for our first interview.

He wasn't in a particularly good mood. He was battling a cold—which seemed to have been exacerbated by the chilly New England weather—and he'd recently tweaked his hamstring, which meant that he'd been unable to go for one of his five-mile runs. When a waiter came to take our order, Edwards curtly informed him, "We're not eating," and asked for an iced tea. But, eventually, as he settled into the interview, he seemed to relax. Still, to most questions I asked, he gave answers that were deeply rehearsed. His comment about the "enormous freedom to choose what I am most interested in doing and spending my time on" sounded a lot like the "enormous freedom [of] being able to do what I am now" that he'd boasted of to a crowd of Democrats in New Hampshire the previous year. The observation he made to me that "China is going to become the largest English-speaking nation on the face of the planet" was one he'd make to Charlie Rose a couple of weeks later. Even his seemingly candid admission that, in the last presidential campaign, he was focused on being a "better candidate" as opposed to a better president was, in fact, a line he's given to numerous reporters.

In all, Edwards seemed at pains to avoid saying anything too candid or potentially controversial. When I asked him for his response to Bill Clinton's contention, as quoted in *The New Yorker*, that he ran for president prematurely in 2004, he dodged: "I think it's the wrong way [for candidates] to think about running for president of the United States . . . to evaluate what's in their best interest." (Elizabeth, for her part, is bracingly candid. When I later asked her about Clinton's comment, she shot back, "During the campaign, Bill Clinton was enormously supportive of John, constantly giving him advice and encouraging him in every conceivable way. At no point in my recollection did John ever get off the phone after a conversation with him where he said, 'Bill thinks it's too early for me.' Never. Not once." Was this just Bill trying to talk down a potential rival to Hillary? "I can come to the same supposition anybody else can about why he said that.") Even my mention of the strange coincidence of his being in Boston on the second anniversary of the traumatic day he spent here failed to elicit much of a response. "Is it really?" he asked, before quickly changing the subject to a retelling of his efforts to convince Kerry not to concede—a retelling identical to the one Elizabeth has laid out for public consumption in her book.

Presidential candidates, of course, are given to pat answers—partly because they're so often asked the same questions, partly because being candid carries so many risks. But Edwards's exceptional guardedness seems strange for a candidate who now makes such a fetish of authenticity—for a candidate, in fact, who makes a pointed distinction between guarded, pabulum-spewing politicians and candid, truth-telling leaders. "What happens with politicians," he recently told a public radio interviewer, "is that you're conditioned not to be yourself. You're conditioned to say the same thing over and over and over, because that's the safe route. . . . We need a leader, or leaders, who are willing to be themselves, who'll tell the truth as they see it." Or, as he complained to me about the last presidential campaign, during which he seems to think he acted more like a politician than a leader: "It was just plastic, there was a lot of plasticity to it. You know—young, Southern, dynamic, charismatic, beautiful family, all that. People need to see who I am, what my character is." Which, come to think of it, sounds a lot like something Edwards says in a "behind the scenes" video his campaign recently posted on YouTube: "I actually want the country to see who I am, who I really am. . . . I'd rather be successful or unsuccessful based on who I really am, not based on some plastic Ken doll you put up in front of audiences."

About the only time Edwards seemed to switch off autopilot during the interview was when he talked about poverty. "You should cut me off on this," he warned, "because I spend a lot of time talking about this." And he did. He talked about his various ideas for fighting poverty—raising the minimum wage, strengthening unions, reforming public housing, creating one million federally funded "stepping stone" jobs at nonprofits or government agencies. He talked about just how much he still had to learn and how even he sometimes felt despair about the intractable nature of the problem. "The cultural component of poverty and what feeds the cycle of poverty—I don't think I ever really got it until, like, for the fifteenth time I'm sitting with a 33-year-old, 32-year-old mother who has a 14-year-old who's having the third child," he said. "And you hear that and it's just, 'How will they ever get out?' You know, it's 'What can you do?' " He seemed genuinely offended when I asked him whether he was surprised that Americans' post-Katrina concern about poverty had waned so rapidly. "I think it's very superficial to suggest that there was interest [and] it's gone," he said. "It's not gone. It's still there. It's just not on the surface. . . . It's deeper down."

A few hours later, Edwards went to one of those places where the interest in poverty was anything but buried: the dinner banquet honoring local community activists. It wasn't the hottest political ticket in Boston that night—that honor went to the final big campaign rally for Massachusetts Democratic gubernatorial candidate Deval Patrick, where Barack Obama was giving a speech. But the event seemed like an opportunity for Edwards, since it allowed him to speak to people who were fighting poverty —in other words, his people. He congratulated them for their commitment to "the great moral cause in America today," which, he noted, "is now the cause of my own life." But then Edwards launched into a speech that followed, almost to the letter, the same trajectory as our interview: the same policy proposals, the same observations, even the same revelatory anecdotes. "One of the things that I've been struck by in the work that we've been doing over the last several years is that you sit with a mother, a single mom . . . and her 14-year-old daughter is giving birth to the third child. And it just feeds this cycle of poverty." What had sounded so fresh and genuine to me only hours before already seemed stale and scripted.

Yet it was anything but to the people in the room. When Edwards finished his speech, the vast banquet hall rose as one and gave him a standing ovation. He left the banquet early to have dinner with his daughter, but, as he snuck out through the hotel's kitchen, he was mobbed by some of the waiters and waitresses who'd watched his speech from the wings. "I listened to what you said out there," one told Edwards, her voice breaking. "Thank you so much for saying it. It means a lot. Please keep saying it."

It's a sentiment Edwards hears frequently. Although his spiel may be pat, although his words may be overly rehearsed, he's still saying things that no other candidate in this presidential race seems prepared to say—things that probably need to be said. There's a difference, after all, between spontaneity and sincerity. In his previous profession as a litigating attorney, Edwards was famous for the emotional power of his closing arguments. Other lawyers would pack the courtroom to hear him offer the final brief on behalf of the family of the little girl who'd had her intestines sucked out by a pool drain or the little boy whose parents had been killed by a speeding tractor-trailer. That those closing arguments were rehearsed to the point where Edwards could deliver them in his sleep didn't make the sentiment behind them any less genuine—or, for that matter, less effective. Indeed, that sometimes seems to be Edwards's signal gift—the ability to find the thread of emotional truth even in a line he's recited 20 times before. It's what made him a successful lawyer and makes him a formidable presidential candidate.

This was never more apparent than at the USW hall in Akron, where Edwards stood in his illfitting t-shirt as he waited for his turn to address the striking Goodyear workers. The speakers preceding him had offered stiff, stilted words of support to the workers—words that seemed to ring hollow to the crowd, which had grown anxious and restless. When Edwards's turn came, it wasn't hard to sense their skepticism. Here was a millionaire politician with Hollywood good looks who couldn't possibly know the first thing about what these workers were going through. But then Edwards stepped up to the podium, yanked the microphone out of its holder, and launched into his speech.

He began by striking his standard note of solidarity. He said that he had come to Akron on a "personal mission to stand with my brothers and sisters and for those who are standing up for men and women who have worked their entire lives and have earned dignity, and respect, and health care." He said the union was showing "backbone and courage to do what's right." What the workers were fighting for, after all, was a dignity that they already possessed and that their employer was trying to take away from them. "We're talking about standing up to protect what they're entitled to," he said. "That's what this is about."

Edwards went on in this vein for a little longer, casting the strike as part of a larger fight to honor the legacies of those who "have worked to make America what it is today." But, eventually, Edwards brought his speech—and the strike—back to himself. Although he didn't work in a tire factory, although he had every material possession a person could possibly desire, he wanted the striking workers to know that he truly understood their struggle. "I take this very personally," he said, as the crowd grew silent. "My mother and father have health care today because of the union. My brother, my only brother, and his family have health care today because of the union. This is a just and righteous cause. You stood up and made huge concessions for this company in 2003. You did what was right, and it's time to make Goodyear"—he said the company's name with a slight hiss—"do what they're supposed to do."

Before Edwards had even finished his sentence, the crowd began to whoop and cheer. He acknowledged the applause with a grin and a wave. "So I'm proud to be with you," he said, his words now nearly drowned out. The Goodyear strike would drag on for two more months and the USW, in the end, would agree to a contract with some provisions it once considered anathema. But, at that moment, as Edwards stood on the stage and the union hall reverberated with cheers, there was suddenly hope that a better outcome, and maybe even a better life, was possible. The t-shirt may have looked a little ridiculous on Edwards at first, but it turned out to be a perfect fit.

Bill Richardson

Full Name William Blaine Richardson III

Current Residence Santa Fe, New Mexico

Date and Place of Birth November 15, 1947; Pasadena, California

Education

    B.A., Tufts University, 1970

    M.A., Tufts' Fletcher School of Law and Diplomacy, 1971

Military Service

    None

Nonpolitical Positions Held

    Staff, U.S. House of Representatives, 1971–1972

    Staff, U.S. Department of State, 1973–1975

    Staff, Senate Foreign Relations Subcommittee, 1975–1978

    Executive Director, New Mexico Democratic Party, 1978

    Executive Director, Bernalillo County Democratic Committee, 1978

    President, Richardson Trade Group, 1978–1982

    U.S. Ambassador to the United Nations, 1997–1998

    Secretary, U.S. Department of Energy, 1998–2000

    Senior Managing Director, Kissinger McLarty, 2001–2002

    Author, *Between Worlds*, 2005

Political Offices Held

U.S. Representative from New Mexico, 1983–1997

Governor of New Mexico, 2003–present

Family

Married to Barbara Richardson; children: none

Bill Richardson v. His Resumé: Paper Candidate

Ryan Lizza

re you ready for some hot dogs?" says the ballpark announcer. "Let 'em know!"

Bill Richardson is ready. It's been a grueling day on the campaign trail—five events spread across some 350 miles of Iowa interstate—and, as we find our seats behind home plate for a minor league game in Des Moines, Richardson looks beat. A New Mexico wag once compared the governor's appearance to an unmade bed, and, right now, he looks the part. His black hair is tousled and his tie is gone. His collar is smeared with pancake makeup and his lapel is dusted with white specks of unknown origin.

But Richardson still has plenty of energy left—not only for a hot dog, a bag of popcorn, and a Diet Coke, which he asks his state trooper to fetch—but also to discuss his recent trip to North Korea to retrieve the remains of six American soldiers killed in the Korean war. "Maybe about two months ago," he casually explains, as if describing some political horse-trading with his legislature, "the North Koreans said to me, 'We want to do a gesture to you because we like you. You've been interested in remains. We're ready to give you from five to ten—unconditional. But you have to come and get them.' " The call, Richardson clarifies, came through the United Nations. "Their U.N. guy calls. His name is Ambassador Kim. K-I-M. They're all named Kim."

Richardson then contacted Bush's national security advisor, Steven Hadley, and told him he wanted to make the mission a bipartisan affair. Truth is, he just needed a ride. "What I was mainly interested in was an airplane," Richardson says as his food arrives and he maneuvers the overstuffed hot dog into his mouth. "So Hadley said—" Richardson pauses and turns to his trooper. "Jakey, you got a napkin?" The trooper passes Richardson a napkin, and he dabs his chin. "So Hadley said 'OK.' "

The hot dog is soon gone, and Richardson is finishing the popcorn now, as well as his North Korea yarn. "The White House said, 'We want to have Victor Cha' "—the National Security Council's top Korea expert—" 'come too.' I said, 'Well, that'd be a signal. The North Koreans will like that.' I said, 'We need a plane.' Hadley said, 'Yeah, I know you do. I knew you were going to ask.' And I said, 'Well, how the fuck else are we going to get there?' And so we got a nice G5."

This is the essence of Richardson's appeal—that he can blend seamlessly into a crowd of AAA baseball fans (unlike, say, John Kerry) while chatting about his negotiations with a member of the axis of evil (unlike, say, George W. Bush). Although many Democrats are smitten with Clinton, Obama, and Edwards, Richardson is enjoying a moment of heightened voter interest, even passing the psychologically crucial barrier of double-digit support in one Iowa poll. He is both the hot-dog-and-ballgame everyman and the seasoned international statesman. The latter is particularly alluring to an electorate yearning for the anti-Bush: someone with the foreign policy chops and diplomatic skills to repair America's tattered reputation and alliances, someone who understands the granular nuance of nuclear proliferation and the Iraq conflict and who isn't afraid to talk to our enemies.

This hunger for a leader who will undo the foreign policy of the Bush years is particularly powerful in internationalist Iowa, a state with a long tradition of peace churches, almost no military industry, and farmers who have always preferred selling to America's foes rather than isolating them. As Richardson and I chat about North Korean nukes, a middle-aged man shyly approaches the governor. "I just wanted to say, there's a lot of us here in Iowa who realize we need somebody like you to run our country," he tells Richardson. "I think your message of how much experience you've got in dealing with all the foreign policy, I think that rings really true here."

Everything about Richardson's impressive resumé seems to support the confidence that voters like this one have in him. He's a graduate of the Fletcher School of Law and Diplomacy at Tufts University, and he served as a foreign policy aide in Congress and at the State Department. As a congressman in the 1980s and 1990s, he made a name for himself as an international troubleshooter, parachuting into rogue states for face-to-face negotiations with dictators. His recent North Korean adventure shows that, even as governor of New Mexico, he has continued his role as America's de facto "undersecretary for thugs," a nickname he gave himself in the Clinton years.

Then again, a good resumé is not all it takes to win the nomination, and there are some signs that Richardson may not be the perfect candidate. In fact, as we get up from our seats to visit the play-by-play announcer's booth, Richardson does something I've never seen any politician do. There are two women sitting in front of us. They are both young and attractive, probably in their twenties. The governor rotates his large frame sideways and shimmies out of his row. The two women smile up at him. As he passes, Richardson reaches down and places his fingertips on the head of one of the women, tickling her scalp as he opens and closes his hand. Then, as he reaches for the next scalp, his hand suddenly aborts its mission, as if the governor realizes this wasn't such a good idea after all.

Richardson's touching problem isn't exactly news. In 2005, his lieutenant governor, Diane Denish, told *The Albuquerque Journal* that she goes out of her way to avoid sitting or standing next to Richardson because he's a little too grabby. "He pinches my neck. He touches my hip, my thigh, sort of the side of my leg," she told the newspaper, which illustrated the story with a photo of Richardson smiling mischievously as his hand reached around toward Denish's backside while the two sat next to each other at a public event.

The truth is that Richardson touches everyone this way. He routinely twists staffers into headlocks and pokes or bear-hugs people he's just met. At one event, I saw him grab a beefy union guy by the lapels and shout into his face, "Stay loose! No commitments yet!" His "political trait," he writes in his recent memoir, is to get "up close and personal." It's part of his charm and makes him a natural politician (he is, after all, the *Guinness Book of World Records* champion for a politician shaking the most hands in eight hours—13,392 at the New Mexico State Fair in 2002). It's also what enables him to negotiate with dictators—to treat them with the same level of cordiality as more upstanding members of the international community. But Richardson's informal style is not without its drawbacks. On the most basic level, giving an unsolicited scalp tickle to a stranger is peculiar behavior for a presidential candidate, and Richardson's touching has fueled a nasty whisper campaign that he's unelectable. But, even if you put aside those rumors, Richardson's style betrays deeper problems with him as a candidate.

It's midday, and 50 elderly Iowans are gathered at the Witwer Center in Cedar Rapids to hear Richardson's stump speech. He stands on a small stage in the cafeteria as members of the audience nibble cookies and listen carefully. He's no Bill Clinton. Richardson's feet are stiffly glued to the floor, but he gestures dramatically with his hands and bends his torso in all directions at the waist. It sometimes looks as if he is doing the robot. On the issues, Richardson is to the left of, but ideologically close to, his opponents. He says he would get the troops out of Iraq, though faster than Clinton, Obama, or Edwards. He favors energy independence, universal health care, and better schools. His real argument is that he's the most experienced candidate.

He delivers his pitch in a somewhat meta style. Rather than detailing his experience, more often than not, he simply tells his audience, "I have the most experience." Rather than radiating optimism through the power of his words, he simply explains, "I want you to know that I'm optimistic."

But, for all his talk of experience, Richardson is not so much a foreign policy expert as he is a born negotiator. Richardson himself traces this style to a life spent navigating "between worlds," which is the title of his memoir. Even today, Richardson's ability to embrace duality is impressive: He gets accolades for being the first

Latino presidential candidate, but he is also arguably the waspiest of the contenders, the only major Democrat to attend a New England prep school and certainly the only one who has written movingly about a cherished Brooks Brothers blazer. With a stern and demanding Anglo dad and a much younger and more indulgent Mexican mom, he grew up in luxury south of the border. He was chauffeured to school and saw up-close his father's hobnobbing with the Mexican and American elite, including his dad's friend Dwight Eisenhower. And yet, by day, Richardson would get into scrapes and play baseball with kids from the Mexico City slums surrounding his family's mansion.

When he was sent off to Middlesex in Massachusetts—where, Richardson has noted, "the boys all seemed to be upper-middle-class or wealthy and white"—he was no longer the elite son of an American bank executive but "Pancho," the Latino kid who still thought in Spanish and had trouble with his English. "Here we go again," Richardson thought upon arrival. "How am I going to fit in? How am I going to be accepted?" He figured out he could win over his classmates by impressing them as an athlete, and he was the first eighth-grader to make the varsity baseball team.

Richardson was similarly calculating about finding a place for himself at Tufts. He quickly established himself as cruise director of his class, personally organizing a trip to Mexico for his friends and rising through the ranks of his fraternity, Delta Tau Delta, to become its president. Ever the diplomat, one of his first decisions was to invite a group of Black Panthers to speak to his fellow Delts. But he also learned to relish hardnosed politics. During one contentious fraternity meeting, some brothers attempted to overturn President Richardson's ban on smoking pot in the house. A colleague recommended he invoke Robert's Rules of Order to discipline the proceedings. "What the hell is that?" a perplexed Richardson asked. Instead, he quelled the rebellion by threatening to bring in the dean of students. After that victory, he worked quietly to place political allies in key positions throughout the Tufts student government, what he's proudly called his "Lyndon Johnson moment."

Although Richardson was a college student in the late '60s, unlike most of his generation he hardly knew whether he was a Democrat or a Republican. Later on, as a Hill aide, he treasured deal-making far more than ideology. New Mexico proved to be the ideal political landscape for Richardson, and he audaciously moved there in 1977 without knowing a single person in the state. As *The Economist* once explained, "New Mexican politics is still about jobs, contracts and personal loyalty, not ideology. And Mr. Richardson personifies this." By 1982, he had won a congressional seat. As a freshman representative, Richardson was one of the most effective members in a class of unusually ambitious pols, including Harry Reid, Barbara Boxer, Dick Durbin, and Tom Ridge. He eventually convinced the leadership to appoint him to the Intelligence committee so he could indulge his foreign policy interests. It was through that assignment that he began his freelance diplomacy.

In 1992, Clinton passed over Richardson for a Cabinet slot. Richardson was crushed—"I'm hurting," he told Clinton when the president broke the news to him over the phone—but the rejection gave him the opportunity to play world statesman. The White House began to use Richardson as an unofficial envoy and back channel to regimes it wouldn't talk to directly. In 1994, he tried to convince the North Koreans to hand over two American airmen. The following year, he persuaded Saddam Hussein to give up two Western engineers who wandered into Iraq from Kuwait. And, in 1996, he sprang some Red Cross contractors from the clutches of a Sudanese warlord. At other times, he has met with Slobodan Milosevic ("wily" and "charming"), Haiti's Raoul Cédras, the leadership of Burma, and Fidel Castro ("more dandruff than I'd ever seen on anyone"). In his second term, Clinton rewarded Richardson with stints as U.N. ambassador and energy secretary. In his memoir, Richardson explains his basic diplomatic philosophy: "A personal connection can transcend even the deepest ideological differences."

That's how he approaches not just international thugs but Iowans, too. But there are limits to an approach that turns every personal encounter into a kind of negotiating session. Richardson's remarks to the senior citizens are over, and the first question for him is about military spending. A woman wants to know if the governor would favor eliminating what she says is the 5 percent of the Pentagon budget that goes to "our strategic air command" and "Star Wars–era type of missile defense systems" and earmark the money for education instead.

Nothing in Richardson's public statements or on his website suggests he agrees with the woman, but his instinct is to find points of agreement. First he tries the I'm-with-you-in-principle-but-not-the-details approach. "Look, I agree with you. I would redirect priorities toward human needs." But he also strains to point out that there are areas where he would increase the Pentagon budget. He wants more men and women in the Army and for them to have better armor. She frowns, and it looks like he might be losing her. He circles back to her question and promises to cut wasteful Pentagon spending, especially in Iraq, even throwing in a gratuitous jab at Halliburton. "So I'm with you," he assures the woman. But this is a negotiation, and Richardson doesn't want her to think she's won everything. "I don't want you to say, 'Well, you know, he's with me a hundred percent.'"

Now the woman is confused. "So to clarify, then," she asks precisely, "are you saying, though, that five percent, or even the fifteen percent, you'd sustain within the Pentagon budget to continue to pay for things for a war machine?" Richardson begins to fold. "No, no," he says. "I think you can easily maybe even go higher than the five percent." Again, the woman wants a clarification: "And shift it into education and health care?" Richardson is faced with a choice between making a personal connection and maintaining his ideological differences. He goes with the former. "Sure. Yeah, I believe so."

On March 20, 2003, the day after U.S. bombs dropped on Baghdad, Bill Richardson signed an optimistic neocon statement on the war. "Together with successful democratic reform in Iraq," it read, "the Gulf has the potential of making a clean break with a past rooted in repression and entering into the growing global community of democratic states." The statement was released by Freedom House, the human rights organization beloved by hawks and the interventionist wings of both parties. Richardson was a trustee of Freedom House and had been the organization's chairman before he became governor. Other signatories included Kenneth Adelman, Jeane Kirkpatrick, Diana Negroponte, and James Woolsey.

But, early this year, Richardson's neocon moment ended—right about the time he started campaigning in Iowa. His new position is about as far as possible from his old one: He wants all the troops out of Iraq this calendar year—"The difference I have with the other candidates is I'm saying no residual troops at all," he told me. And his first big speech on foreign policy, in contrast to his idealistic Freedom House declaration, called for "a new realism." In April, a few months after he gave it, I joined him in New York for a candidate forum with Al Sharpton and his National Action Network. After the event, a reporter asked Richardson under what circumstances he would use U.S. troops to intervene militarily. Without hesitation, he made the sound realist case. "Only if America's national security interests are affected," he said. I asked him what he would have done in the case of Rwanda. He paused for a moment and thought. "I would have intervened," he said, quickly adding, "I would have pushed for a peacekeeping force." And if it failed? Would he have sent U.S. troops? "I think in the case of human rights and genocide, the answer is yes."

Maybe Richardson is truly a realist and was just experiencing a temporary bout of foreign policy idealism back in 2003. Or else he's always been an idealist but the reality of the Iraq war reordered his views. Or perhaps there's a simpler answer, especially once you know that, even as he served as chairman of the hyper-idealist Freedom House, he had another job: senior managing director at Kissinger McLarty Associates, the private sector redoubt of hyper-realism. The safe bet is that Richardson, despite his years on the world stage, has never developed any fixed foreign policy ideology. Or any fixed political identity, either. In 1996, Richardson, who was then nearing the end of his 14 years representing New Mexico in the House, told a reporter, "I was a conservative Democrat who became a progressive Democrat who's now a moderate." And, these days, Richardson is methodically staking out ground to the left of all his Democratic rivals.

An absence of ideology might seem like the perfect antidote to the Bush years. And Richardson is not the only politician to have done an ideological flip-flop on Iraq. But, in Richardson's case, being unmoored from a clear set of principles has led to a series of errors in judgment that extends to more issues than just the war. His reputation as a foreign policy expert rests on his negotiating missions rather than on meaty policy work, and that has allowed the legend of Richardson the statesman to persist despite a history of bad calls.

In 1985, he voted for aid to the Contras, a controversial position for a Democrat to take. Then the Iran-Contra scandal broke out. Richardson reversed his position and admitted he'd made a mistake.

In 1991, Richardson voted against giving George H. W. Bush the authority to go to war against Saddam. Once again, he later admitted he got it wrong. "In retrospect, that was a mistake," he writes in his memoir. "The right vote was the one cast by the majority of my House and Senate colleagues, who supported the first President Bush's request for the authority to remove Iraq from Kuwait by force if necessary."

In that same book, Richardson recounts how his proudest achievement in the House was the starring role he played in helping Bill Clinton pass NAFTA. As the Democrat in charge of gathering votes for the pro-NAFTA side, he was so devoted to its passage that he actually set up a joint whip operation with Newt Gingrich's team. "NAFTA, in my view, was critically important," he writes in his memoir, which was published just two years ago. When I asked Richardson about his role in NAFTA, he said he doesn't regret his vote, but he has changed his mind about some aspects of free trade. "I guess you'd call me more of a fair-trader now," he admits.

Even if he doesn't measure up on substance, Richardson's style has always been a political asset. He so dominates New Mexico politics that back home they call him "King Bill" or "Govzilla." After being reelected with almost 70 percent of the vote, he figured his New Mexico success could easily translate into Prezilla.

Richardson thinks his informal approach is precisely the kind of authenticity that voters want. But, in presidential politics, where every utterance is sifted for its ideological content and examined for clues about the candidate's readiness for the job, style takes you only so far. After the first Democratic debate, during which he inexplicably declared that his model Supreme Court Justice was Byron White, one of the two dissenters in *Roe v. Wade,* Richardson was asked how that answer squares with his pro-choice views. Richardson challenged the very idea that White had anything to do with the Roe decision and argued that it was decided in the '80s, when White was no longer on the Court. After watching the scene unfold, the popular Democratic blogger Mark Kleiman was devastating: "He just doesn't seem very smart, or very thoughtful."

Some candidates can overcome a track record of poor judgment and inconsistencies with a polished presentation on the stump. (Think Mitt Romney or John Edwards.) But, as with the Byron White head-smacker, Richardson has again and again created the impression that he doesn't know the basics. In March, Alicia Menendez, a reporter for the news channel RNN, asked Richardson how he would vote on the Iraq supplemental if he were in the Senate. "I'm just not familiar with the supplemental," he told her. "Which one is that?" At the first Democratic debate, in April, Richardson was asked if he "would vote to fund the troops." He immediately answered "no," even though that's not his position. During a recent appearance on "Meet the Press," Tim Russert confronted Richardson with a devastating catalogue of the governor's contradictions on Iraq, immigration, his tenure as energy secretary, gun policy, and—the final, cruel shot—how he could be both a Red Sox fan, as he often says he is, and a Yankees fan, as he claims in his book. Richardson seemed deeply offended by the barrage. "I've been in public life twenty-five years. You're going to find a lot of these," he sputtered. "It seems you've found them all here."

Richardson is often just not that precise when he speaks, treating conversations with voters and reporters more like casual chats rather than interviews where his words will be scrutinized. Sometimes his gaffes are small and meaningless. After Al Sharpton, who has never held an elected position, introduced him at the forum in New York, Richardson said, "All the good things the governor said about me are true." Other mistakes are more eyebrow-raising. When discussing his plan to negotiate peace in Iraq, he often refers to the country's "three religious groups," a small but odd blunder for a candidate hawking his foreign policy experience, especially his deep familiarity with the Muslim world.

In one Iowa forum, Richardson noted that "we also are moving North Korea toward eliminating nuclear weapons." Not exactly. The negotiations are about shutting down a nuclear facility, not getting rid of their current stockpile, though that is, of course, an eventual goal. Richardson repeated the statement in a phone interview with me, which took place after his Byron White episode, when he was trying to be particularly careful about his statements. After placing me on hold—"put him on silent or whatever, because I want to just talk to Barbara"—he clarified the remark. "Let me just amend one thing I said. My view is that they will keep some kind of nuclear presence," he said. "I don't believe they will dismantle everything."

During a question-and-answer session after a speech about Darfur at the University of Northern Iowa, a student from Sierra Leone asked the governor a question about the causes of conflict. "Usually, when you have power, you don't want to give it up,"

Richardson said. "I remember in your country, Charles Taylor, he was around when I was at the U.N. He's no longer around, right? He's in exile somewhere. Your country still has conflict." Taylor was actually the leader of Liberia. He is not in exile but in a prison in the Hague, where he is standing trial this month. (It's one of the most important war-crimes cases since Nuremberg.) And the long-running conflict in Sierra Leone is over.

After the speech, Richardson was all back slaps, winks, and nods. He gamely posed for a picture with a student who is collecting photographs of candidates holding his Mr. Potato Head doll. "Do I look like a fool or what?" he laughed. And he tried to find those points of commonality that are his trademark, even if he had to strain a little to do it. To two Sudanese students, he asked, "Do you know who Manute Bol is?" Then, turning to me, he asked the same question, explaining that Bol, an American basketball star, is a member of the Dinka tribe of Sudan. Richardson held his hand above his head. "Very tall."

As I watched Richardson, I realized that there is no artifice to the man, which is an endearing quality for a presidential candidate. Lurking behind Richardson's grabby, clumsy style is a guy who will do anything to be loved. And that's how many Democrats view the United States right now—a nation that desperately needs the world to love us again. Richardson may be a good Cabinet member for the next president, but, despite his charm and likeability, the next president needs to be more than a frat-boy-in-chief who believes that personal connections can overcome all the world's ideological fissures. We've already been down that road.

Back at the baseball game, where the Iowa Cubs are crushing Richardson's own Albuquerque Isotopes, the governor is a whirl of energy and one-liners. We ride an elevator to the broadcast booth. "You're the owner, huh?" Richardson says to a man escorting us. "Why are you kicking the shit out of us?"

The governor settles into a chair between the Cubs' two play-by-play announcers. There's a pop fly to shallow right center. The Cubs shortstop falls down trying to make the catch, and an Isotope makes a sprint for second. "He's out!" Richardson interjects. The announcer, Toby Hyde, concurs. "Bill Richardson is right," he says. "He's out." He adds, with just a trace of sarcasm, "I'll let you call a couple of plays."

Richardson's bet that the personal always trumps the ideological is soon tested. This is Iowa, after all, where even the ballpark announcers are budding David Yepsens. Hyde asks Richardson what the one thing is that people should know about him, and the governor makes his resumé pitch. "It's that I've got experience," he says. "I've been secretary of energy. I'm governor of a state. I'm doing well. I've got foreign policy experience. I just got back from North Korea. . . . "

If Hyde is impressed, he doesn't let on. Richardson tries to keep things casual. "I just had the biggest, best hot dog I've ever had," he says. "And I'm on this diet. It makes me miserable. What a hot dog. I may have another one." But it turns out Hyde is a bit of an energy policy wonk, and, in between plays, he draws Richardson into a detailed discussion about the merits of cellulosic- versus corn-based ethanol. "How about wind?" Hyde asks. "Wind's sort of the forgotten of the renewables." Dictators may be susceptible to Richardson's nonideological approach, but Iowans, it turns out, are not.

After exiting the booth, with the announcers safely out of earshot, Richardson cackles and scrunches his face. "The guy was talking to me about wind energy!" It's clear from his amused expression that he feels like the interview—and the long day of campaigning—was a success. But, as we ride the elevator down to the ground floor of the stadium, the car is quiet, and the governor suddenly gets a pensive look on his face. Has he realized his mistakes? He breaks the silence. "I'm gonna get another hot dog on the way out," he declares. "Screw it."

Dennis Kucinich

Full Name Dennis John Kucinich

Current Residence Cleveland, Ohio

Date and Place of Birth October 10, 1946; Cleveland, Ohio

Education

B.A., Case Western University, 1973

M.A., Case Western University, 1974

Military Service

None

Nonpolitical Positions Held

Talk show host, 1981–1983

Author, *A Prayer for America,* 2003

Political Offices Held

Cleveland City Council, 1969–1975

Cleveland Mayor (was youngest mayor ever of a major U.S. city), 1977–1979

U.S. Representative from Ohio, 1997–present

Family

Married to Elizabeth Harper; previously married twice before; children: daughter Jackie from second marriage to Sandra Lee McCarthy

---

On His Terms: Taking Dennis Kucinich Seriously

Jason Zengerle

On a sunny Saturday in New Hampshire not long ago, Dennis Kucinich laid out for me the path that would lead him to the presidency. "I think what will happen," he explained, "is that the tremendous demand for integrity and authenticity is going to cause my candidacy to emerge powerfully in the closing weeks of the primary campaign to change it all." The two of us were sitting in the backseat of an SUV driven by an aide, shuttling between campaign events. Small in stature but loud in voice, Kucinich held forth on any number of matters related to his presidential bid, from his opposition to the ongoing war in Iraq to his opposition to a future war in Iran. But the issue that got him most energized was the very fact of the bid itself. "As there's increased awareness that my candidacy represents a real departure from business as usual, that I'm the only authentic peace candidate, that I'm the only one who has real consistency and integrity—" Kucinich paused, seeming to have lost his train of thought. Then, as if he had suddenly retrieved it, he blurted out, "You know, I expect to be the next president of the United States!"

As the underest of underdogs, it's Kucinich's right—and perhaps even his duty—to project an unrealistically outsized aura of confidence. But it would be hard for this confidence to be more misplaced. For one thing, there's the fresh memory of the Ohio representative's 2004 run for the White House, when the twice-divorced, then-bachelor candidate seemed to spend more time looking for a mate—participating in a "Dating Game"–style competition for potential first ladies—than he did looking for convention delegates. And then there's the reality of Kucinich's current campaign, which is actually in worse shape than the last one.

After all, in 2004, Kucinich managed to raise a respectable $13 million and had the support of a coterie of lefty celebrities, including Joaquin Phoenix and Danny Glover. This time around, Kucinich has taken in less than $350,000, according to campaign finance reports from spring 2007; and his most notable supporter is his new wife, Elizabeth, who—being 31 years younger and about a half-foot taller than her husband—turns many heads when she accompanies him on the campaign trail. (Elizabeth was not, for the record, a contestant in Kucinich's 2004 first lady search.) Worst of all, Kucinich has watched Mike Gravel fill the gadfly role in the race, stealing his thunder on Iraq and other issues at the two Democratic debates. Indeed, about the only thing as fantastical as Kucinich's claim that he'll be elected president is his claim that he's running in the first place.

Kucinich's '08 gambit is less a presidential campaign than it is an elaborate fiction. That's because, aside from participating in the debates, he does virtually none of the things a presidential candidate does.

Yes, Kucinich goes out and campaigns, but only in the narrowest slice of America—generally confining his stumping to vegan restaurants, small colleges, and other places that one finds within the listening area of a community radio station that broadcasts "Democracy Now!" And, as he hopscotches across this Pacifica archipelago, Kucinich doesn't offer much in the way of traditional presidential campaign rhetoric. While he does talk about de-funding the war in Iraq and instituting single-payer health insurance, he spends much of his time dishing out gooey, New Age sentiments—telling people about how "we are interconnected and interdependent" and that "the call for human unity is the call to save the planet and save the world and the universe, and we imbue all of our citizens with the sense of love for each other."

Even the straightforward task of public relations—which, for a money-strapped candidate like Kucinich, is crucial, since his campaign's lifeblood is free media—seems to be an afterthought. A reporter trying to reach the Kucinich campaign gets routed to press secretary David Bright's cell phone—which Bright rarely answers, because, as he explains in his outgoing message, he lives in "rural Maine," where cell phone coverage is spotty.

The notional nature of Kucinich's campaign is strange because, in some ways, he's in a good position to run a serious one, at least relatively speaking. As the only Democratic candidate who voted against the congressional resolution authorizing the Iraq war—Barack Obama, who opposed the war, was not elected to the U.S. Senate until after the war had started—Kucinich can plausibly argue that history has proved him right. Indeed, it's an argument that he has used to good effect before. After he was elected mayor of Cleveland in 1977 at the age of 31, Kucinich's political career crashed and burned when he refused to sell a city-owned electric utility, which resulted in the city going into default. He lost his reelection bid and went into political exile—moving to California and New Mexico, where he befriended Shirley MacLaine and became a vegan. By the early '90s, however, the correctness of Kucinich's decision not to sell the municipal power company had become apparent—by one calculation, the move had saved its customers more than $200 million, compared with what they would have paid to a private utility company—and he made his political comeback, winning a seat in the Ohio state Senate in 1994 and then his congressional seat in 1996. His slogan in his 1994 state Senate race was "Because he was right" and, in 1996, his campaign logo was a light bulb with the words "Light up Congress."

But that sort of campaign doesn't appear to interest Kucinich much this time around. Rather, his candidacy seems mostly an ego trip and a much-needed diversion. As Brent Larkin, the editorial page editor of *The Cleveland Plain-Dealer* who has been covering Kucinich for 37 years, puts it: "It's got to be more fun for him than doing the serious work of being a congressman in a Rust Belt city that's got a lot of issues."

So Kucinich wages a Potemkin campaign. He declares that he expects to be president while he does nothing that would make that possibility, remote as it already is, closer to being a reality. Every politician, to be sure, lives in a bubble; but Kucinich's campaign exists in its own biosphere. On his recent swing through New Hampshire, he began his day at a high school in the university town of Durham, where a group called "Teaching Peace" was holding a conference. There, amid booths selling "Unscented Peace Vigil Votives" and Native American crafts, he mingled with about 100 people. Many of the adults already seemed to know him. One, a self-described "awakening coach" named Robert Foulkrod, first met Kucinich when he came to a retreat on Foulkrod's Maine farm 20 years ago. "I'm trying to inspire the city of Nashua to be organized for Dennis," he explained, before adding, "I'm not organizing it myself. I'm into awakening people. Do you know anyone in Nashua?" Meanwhile, Kucinich's attempts to win the support of those he didn't personally know—namely, the high school students in attendance—were largely for naught. "I'm not old enough to vote," one explained apologetically after Kucinich asked for her support. "But you're old enough to influence thousands!" he pleaded in response.

The rest of his day was spent on similar endeavors—preaching to the politically converted or the politically irrelevant or, in many instances, both. But, in the afternoon, Kucinich finally participated in an event that seemed to bear some relation to a real presidential campaign. A group of about 20 retired generals and admirals—with approximately 700 years of combined military experience between them—had gathered at the Franklin Pierce Law Center in Concord and were meeting with any presidential candidate who wanted to discuss U.S. detention and interrogation policies. Hillary Clinton and Joe Biden had taken them up on the offer, and, at the last minute, so did Kucinich. Arriving 30 minutes late for the meeting, the candidate hurried into a conference room, where, for the next hour, he laid out his foreign policy. The meeting had a decidedly Model United Nations feel, with the group of 60-something white men wearing service academy rings pretending they were interested in what Kucinich would do as president, and Kucinich pretending that he would one day be president. But, when it was over, it seemed that no harm had been done by the military men's small courtesy of indulging a man who'd never be commander-in-chief. No harm, that is, until a young aide noticed me and my tape recorder and asked if I was a reporter. When I said I was, all hell broke loose. The meeting was supposed to be off-the-record, no press allowed. Every candidate had been provided a long set of instructions that explicitly spelled out that stipulation. And every candidate had abided by them— except for Kucinich, whose campaign had breezily invited me into the session. After an hour of furious negotiation with the meeting's organizers, I agreed not to write about what was said in the meeting, since it wasn't the fault of the retired generals that I'd been let in. But the episode made one thing clear: Taking Dennis Kucinich's presidential campaign seriously will bring you nothing but grief.

II • THE REPUBLICANS

John McCain

Full Name John Sidney McCain III

Current Residence Phoenix, Arizona

Date and Place of Birth August 29, 1936; Coco Solo, Panama Canal
   Zone

Education
   B.S., United States Naval Academy, 1956

Military Service
   Pilot, U.S. Navy, 1958–1981, retired as captain
   Prisoner of War in Hanoi, 1967–1973
   Awarded a Silver Star, a Bronze Star, the Legion of Merit, the
      Purple Heart, and a Distinguished Flying Cross

Nonpolitical Positions Held
   Worked for father-in-law's beer distributorship, 1981
   Author, *Faith of My Fathers,* 1999
   Author, *Why Courage Matters,* 2004

Political Offices Held
   U.S. Representative from Arizona, 1983–1987
   U.S. Senator from Arizona, 1987–present

Family

Married to Cindy Hensley McCain; children: sons John IV and
James and daughters Meghan and Bridget (adopted from a
Bangladeshi orphanage); previously married to Carol Shepp;
children: adopted Shepp's sons, Douglas and Andrew, and
had daughter Sidney with Shepp

The Making of an Überhawk: Neo-McCain

John B. Judis

I have liked John McCain ever since I met him almost a decade
ago. At the time, I was writing a profile of then-Senator Fred
Thompson, who was rumored to be considering a run for the
presidency. I had been playing phone tag with the press sec-
retaries of senators friendly with Thompson and was getting nowhere. I decided that, instead of calling McCain's office, I would
drop by. I spoke to one of his aides, who asked me whether I had
time to see the senator then. To my amazement, I was ushered into
McCain's office, where, without staffers present, he answered my
questions about Thompson.

Talking to a senator in this manner, and on such short notice, is unheard of in Washington. Senators like to stand on ceremony, and they also like to surround themselves with solicitous

and protective aides. But McCain is different. It is a difference that he refined after being caught up in the Keating Five scandal in the early '90s, but it fits his personality and jibes with his public-minded advocacy of campaign finance reform.

McCain is also another rarity in Washington: a centrist by conviction rather than by design. His political philosophy places him closer to Theodore Roosevelt than to his other idols, Barry Goldwater and Ronald Reagan: more noblesse oblige than libertarian populism or business conservatism. He says he favors "a minimum of government regulation in our lives," but what really matters is whether a policy or business practice is in the national interest. If it isn't, he'll use the power of the government to change it. Goldwater would not have voted for a bill tightening controls over the tobacco industry, and Reagan would have balked at curbing pollution. McCain has backed both. Liberals have recently chided him for wooing his party's evangelical base, but these have been nominal efforts. McCain pronounced himself in favor of teaching creationism as a theory; but he also devotes a chapter of his latest book to the genius of Charles Darwin. He gave a commencement speech at Jerry Falwell's Liberty University; but, in a subtle rebuke to Christian conservatives, he spoke entirely about foreign policy. Earlier this year, he voted to block a constitutional amendment banning gay marriage.

McCain's idiosyncratic approach to party politics also makes him an outlier. His commitment to bipartisanship is real—he worked with Russ Feingold on campaign finance reform, Ted Kennedy on immigration reform, and Joe Lieberman on global warming—as is his relish for battling his own party's leaders. In September 2006, when Bush and his congressional allies were using a bill flouting the Geneva Conventions to paint Democrats as soft on terrorism, McCain, along with John Warner and Lindsey

Graham, blocked the measure and insisted on a compromise. True, the compromise was flawed. Still, it undermined the administration's efforts to exploit the war on terrorism for political purposes.

McCain has one other attribute that separates him from many of his peers in Washington: He is willing to change his mind. This may be his most admirable quality; yet it is also frequently overlooked, probably because it seems to contradict McCain's reputation for stubbornness, even nastiness—a reputation his right-wing opponents are all too happy to speculate about. "Everyone knows McCain has a temperament problem, but no one is going to say anything about it," one prominent Washington conservative complains. Yet the most distinctive aspect of McCain's temperament is not his anger; rather, it is his penchant for reconsidering both old enmities and old convictions. Witness his work with John Kerry on normalizing relations with Vietnam, as well as his collaboration on campaign finance reform with activist Fred Wertheimer, who had sharply criticized McCain during the Keating Five scandal.

Nowhere has McCain's willingness to question his own previous assumptions been more dramatic than on foreign policy. When he first arrived in Washington, he was essentially a realist, arguing that U.S. military power should only be used to protect vital national interests. Since the late '90s, however, he has joined forces with neoconservatives to support a crusade aimed at overthrowing hostile and undemocratic regimes—by force, if necessary —and installing in their place democratic, pro-American governments. Unlike many Republicans, he enthusiastically backed Bill Clinton's intervention in Kosovo. Moreover, he was pushing for Saddam Hussein's forcible overthrow years before September 11— at a time when George W. Bush was still warning against the arrogant use of American might.

And therein lies my McCain dilemma—and, perhaps, yours. If, like me, you believe that the war in Iraq has been an unmitigated disaster, then you are likely disturbed by McCain's early and continuing support for it—indeed, he advocates sending more troops to that strife-torn land—and by his advocacy of an approach to Iran that could lead to another fruitless war. At the same time, he has shown an admirable willingness to reevalute his views when events have proved them wrong. The question, then, comes down to this: Is John McCain capable of changing his mind about a subject very close to his heart—again?

To begin to answer that question, you have to understand McCain's philosophical evolution on foreign policy. Not surprisingly, that evolution has everything to do with Vietnam.

McCain comes from a long line of military men. His father and grandfather were both four-star admirals. Attempting to follow in their footsteps, McCain attended Annapolis and, after graduating in 1958, became a naval aviator. By his own admission, he was brash, sometimes insubordinate—a maverick within a profession grounded in hierarchy. He longed to prove himself by going to war. Having absorbed his father's and grandfather's stories about World War II, he had no doubt that the United States would triumph. "I believed that militarily we could prevail in whatever conflict we were involved in," he told me.

McCain also acquired from his father a particular view of American power. The elder McCain admired the British Empire and conceived of the United States playing an analogous role in world affairs. In 1965, he commanded the U.S. invasion of the Dominican Republic, which blocked a previously ousted government—one that the Johnson administration believed was too friendly with Fidel Castro—from regaining power. The invasion was unpopular in both the United States and the Dominican Republic; but, afterwards, McCain's father said, "People may not love you for being strong when you have to be, but they respect you for it and learn to behave themselves when you are."

McCain's faith in this approach would be tested in Vietnam. He began bombing runs over North Vietnam in mid-1967, at a time when the Johnson administration was restricting the targets American pilots could hit. McCain soon became disillusioned with this strategy. He and his fellow pilots regarded their civilian leaders as "complete idiots" who "didn't have the least notion of what it took to win the war." In October 1967, McCain was shot down over Hanoi. He was imprisoned and tortured for five and a half years, and he emerged thoroughly chastened in his views on war and American might.

Like his father, who commanded U.S. forces in the Pacific during the last years of the Vietnam war, McCain continued to defend the decision to intervene—most notably in an article he wrote for *U.S. News & World Report* after his release—but he took a fairly narrow view of when wars were worth fighting. During a year spent studying the origins of the Vietnam conflict at the National War College, McCain began to develop a version of what would later be called the Powell Doctrine. He insisted that any intervention had to be demonstrably in the national interest, and he defined national interest in a limited way. Resisting global communism qualified; overthrowing brutal tyrannies or rescuing their victims did not. "The American people and Congress now appreciate that we are neither omniscient nor omnipotent," McCain would later tell the *Los Angeles Times*, "and they are not prepared to commit U.S. troops to combat unless there is a clear U.S. national security interest involved. If we do become involved in combat, that involvement must be of relatively short duration and must be readily explained to the man in the street in one or two sentences."

The McCain who arrived in Washington in 1983, after winning a House seat from Arizona, was still a hawk, but a very cautious one. He had abandoned the gung-ho idealism of the early cold war for a more tempered realism. And the U.S. defeat in Vietnam was still very much on his mind.

McCain's first application of his newfound realism came in September 1983, when he had to vote on a bill to extend the U.S. military presence in Lebanon. A year earlier, in the wake of Israel's invasion of Lebanon, the Reagan administration had sent Marines to Beirut to help oversee the evacuation of the Palestine Liberation Organization. But the Marines had lingered in Lebanon to aid the new government, which was fighting local militias as well as Syrian forces. Republican and Democratic leaders lined up in favor of extending the U.S. stay there, but the freshman McCain, to their displeasure, declared his opposition.

McCain called for a gradual U.S. withdrawal from Lebanon. He argued that there were not enough U.S. forces to protect the government. The United States could introduce more troops, he said, but that wouldn't be justified because there was no "clear U.S. interest at stake." McCain's concerns, of course, proved prescient—a month later, suicide bombers blew up Marine barracks in Beirut, killing 241 Americans and forcing a U.S. withdrawal—but, at the time of the September vote, his stance brought him only grief as Republican leaders, infuriated by his dissent, snubbed him in the halls.

The second major challenge to McCain's post-Vietnam worldview came when Iraq invaded Kuwait in August 1990. McCain, who had been elected to the Senate in 1986, shared the Bush administration's determination to protect Saudi Arabia and oust Iraqi forces from Kuwait. But, in the beginning, McCain played the cautious realist. He was concerned primarily about Saddam Hussein monopolizing the region's oil, and he was initially skeptical of the need to use U.S. ground forces. "I think that we have got to make use of the advantages that we have, and that is through the air," he told Judy Woodruff in early August. Later that month, he warned in a *Los Angeles Times* interview, "If you get involved in a major ground war in the Saudi desert, I think support will erode significantly. Nor should it be supported. We cannot even contemplate, in my view, trading American blood for Iraqi blood."

During Clinton's first term, McCain remained wary of sending troops overseas. He called for bringing U.S. forces home from Somalia and opposed intervening in Haiti. He also backed the administration's initial refusal to commit forces to Bosnia, where Serbs were engaged in a campaign of ethnic cleansing against the Muslim and Croat populations. McCain argued that, because the conflict did not bear on America's "vital national interests," it did not justify the use of force. Moreover, McCain doubted whether American power could really do any good in Bosnia. U.S. efforts in the Balkans, he lamented in May 1995, were "doomed to failure from the beginning, when we believed that we could keep peace in a place where there was no peace."

Given McCain's stance on Bosnia, one might have expected him to caution Clinton to stay out of Kosovo as well. Instead, by October 1998—five months before NATO would begin bombing Serbia in response to atrocities committed in Kosovo—McCain was telling CNN that he was "not in opposition to taking military action" to deal with a "humanitarian problem here of tens of thousands of innocent people dying." What had changed?

McCain's evolution did not take place overnight. According to people close to him, the senator's outlook had begun to shift in the early '90s, when he started to take an interest in democracy promotion and human rights. In 1993, McCain became chairman of the International Republican Institute, a government-funded group that promotes democracy and capitalism overseas. "We were all intoxicated by the fall of the Soviet Union and the collapse of its empire," he says.

There was another factor, too. Haunted by the American defeat in Vietnam, McCain had been reluctant to see troops deployed abroad. But his brother Joe says that the American victory in the first Gulf War restored the senator's confidence in U.S. power, allowing him to again contemplate military interventions. "Once the chess pieces were back on the board, then he thought he would play chess," Joe McCain says.

And then there was the shock of Srebrenica, where Serb forces murdered thousands of Bosnians in July 1995. Its full impact on his worldview may not have been immediate, but, today, McCain recalls the massacre as a key moment in his evolution on foreign policy. "My reluctance was eradicated by Srebrenica," he says. "I was belatedly aware of the terrible things going on there and that the only way we were going to solve it was militarily."

Yet, for a time, McCain held back, possibly because he lacked confidence in the Clinton administration. Days after Srebrenica, he said, "We cannot make a plausible argument to the American people that our security is so gravely threatened in Bosnia that it requires the sacrifice, in great numbers, of our sons and daughters to defend." When the Clinton administration successfully negotiated the Dayton peace accords in November, McCain initially opposed sending American peacekeepers to help enforce it. After Clinton promised the troops without consulting Congress,

McCain relented and supported efforts to secure funding. Still, he joined other Republicans in insisting that U.S. forces in Bosnia have an "exit strategy" and not engage in "nation building."

But that was the last time McCain would express significant skepticism about U.S. intervention. By 1997, his friend William Cohen was secretary of defense, and McCain was, to paraphrase his brother, ready to play chess. The first visible sign of a change in McCain's worldview came on Iraq. During the first Gulf War, McCain had backed President Bush's decision not to advance on Baghdad. But, in November 1997, he announced on Fox News that it had been a mistake not to oust Saddam during the war, and he called upon the Clinton administration to set up an Iraqi government in exile. The following fall—in the face of opposition from both the Pentagon and the State Department—McCain cosponsored the Iraq Liberation Act, which committed the United States to overthrowing Saddam's regime and to funding opposition groups. McCain welcomed Ahmed Chalabi, leader of the Iraqi National Congress (INC), to Washington and pressured the administration to give him money. When General Anthony Zinni cast doubt upon the effectiveness of the Iraqi opposition, McCain rebuked him at a hearing of the Senate Armed Services Committee.

The second, and perhaps clearest, indication that McCain was changing his outlook came in his response to the crisis in Kosovo. As in Bosnia, Serb forces were committing ethnic cleansing and atrocities but did not pose a direct military or economic threat to the United States. Yet, this time, when McCain chided Clinton, it was for using American power too cautiously. "The president of the United States," he said in May 1999, "is prepared to lose a war rather than do the hard work, the politically risky work, of fighting it as the leader of the greatest nation on Earth should fight when our interests and our values are imperiled." Note the word "values" alongside the word "interests." Clearly, this was a new McCain.

To be sure, Vietnam still loomed large in his worldview. But the shadow of defeat in Vietnam had lifted, allowing McCain to regain the expansive view of America's power and responsibility that he had inherited from his father. McCain was still using the example of Vietnam, but to argue for bolder—rather than more cautious—application of U.S. power. "We're now seeing things that are echoes of the Vietnam war," he complained in April 1999. "Targets being selected by the president of the United States; restraints on where and when we hit those targets; and, perhaps most importantly of all, an outright commitment that we will not use ground troops as necessary."

He also dropped his opposition to open-ended commitment of U.S. troops and to nation-building, which, for most Republicans, had become synonymous with everything that was wrong with Clinton's foreign policy. "Despite the unacceptable circumstances of the weak and endangered peace in Kosovo," he said on the Senate floor in March 2000, "it is infinitely preferable to the widespread atrocities committed during the course of Serbian aggression, atrocities that would surely reoccur were NATO to fail in our current mission."

McCain's position made sense. If U.S. forces could prevent atrocities without becoming bogged down in a long war and occupation, why shouldn't they? And, if they could encourage more democratic forms of government, why not do that as well? But what succeeded in Kosovo—where the United States was intervening as part of NATO and had no intention of single-handedly occupying and running a country—would not work everywhere.

Iraq would soon expose the perils of an overly aggressive idealism. Which is where my qualms with the new McCain begin.

Until the late '90s, McCain's foreign policy consisted largely of lessons from the past that he applied on a piecemeal basis. In 1998, when *The Weekly Standard* asked what kind of foreign policy he would practice if elected president, he responded, "The first thing I'd do is convene the best minds I know of in the field of foreign policy, and that would include members of previous Democratic and Republican administrations. I'd have [Zbigniew] Brzezinski, Jim Baker, [Brent] Scowcroft, Tom Pickering, [Henry] Kissinger, Warren Christopher—and I'm sure others. I'd say, 'Look, let's figure out where we are, where we need to go, what our conceptual framework is. Let's work out a cohesive foreign policy.'" That wasn't much of an answer.

But, in the months and years that followed, McCain, seeking to differentiate his views from those of other Republican presidential aspirants and from the growing isolationism of House Republicans, would place his new interventionist instincts within a larger ideological framework. That ideological framework was neoconservatism. McCain began reading *The Weekly Standard* and conferring with its editors, particularly Bill Kristol. Kristol is predictably modest about his influence on the Arizona senator, although he acknowledges, "I talked to McCain on the phone and compared notes." But when McCain wanted to hire a new legislative aide, his chief of staff, Mark Salter—himself a former aide to neoconservative Jeane Kirkpatrick—consulted with Kristol, who recommended a young protégé named Daniel McKivergan. Marshall Wittmann, one of Kristol's closest friends, became a key adviser during McCain's presidential campaign. Randy Scheunemann, who had drafted the Iraq Liberation Act and was on the board of Kristol's Project for a New American Century, became McCain's foreign policy adviser. One person who has worked closely with Kristol says of Kristol and McCain, "They are exceptionally, exceptionally close."

The senator's embrace of neoconservatism was accompanied by a reevaluation of his childhood hero, Theodore Roosevelt. McCain had long admired Roosevelt's adventurous spirit, but Kristol—as well as other neoconservative writers like Robert Kagan and David Brooks—was busy building the former president into something more: a model for "national greatness conservatism," a philosophy that linked the development of American character to the exercise of power overseas. Wittmann, a Roosevelt devotee who currently runs a website called The Bull Moose, gave McCain pieces by Kristol, Kagan, and Brooks on Roosevelt, as well as writings by Roosevelt himself. McCain began referring to Roosevelt in interviews, and Wittmann and Salter began working Rooseveltian themes into his speeches. The result was a growing emphasis on America's responsibility to transform the world.

McCain unveiled his new approach in a March 1999 speech at Kansas State University. The speech—which Wittmann, Salter, and Scheunemann all contributed to—echoed neoconservative themes. Long gone was the McCain who had worried about U.S. overreach. "The United States is the indispensable nation because we have proven to be the greatest force for good in human history," McCain said, adding that "we have every intention of continuing to use our primacy in world affairs for humanity's benefit." In an earlier essay, Kristol and Kagan had described Republican isolationism as "pinched." McCain now described it as "cramped." The centerpiece of the speech was a strategy that McCain called "rogue-state rollback." Scheunemann says he invented the term, adapting it from the conservative critics of 1950s cold war containment. According to this strategy, the United States would back "indigenous and outside forces that desire to overthrow the odious regimes that rule" illiberal states. At the head of this list of regimes was Saddam Hussein's.

Three years later, as debate broke out over whether to invade Iraq, McCain put himself squarely on the side of Dick Cheney, Donald Rumsfeld, and the neoconservatives. Like them, McCain evinced a blithe optimism about America's ability to transform Iraq. Asked by Chris Matthews in March 2003 whether the Iraqis would treat Americans as liberators, McCain replied, "Absolutely, absolutely." Echoing *The Weekly Standard,* he also promoted the most alarmist versions of the threat posed by Saddam, insisting that "Saddam Hussein is on a crash course to construct a nuclear weapon" and that "the interaction we know to have occurred between members of Al Qaeda and Saddam's regime may increasingly take the form of active cooperation to target the United States." And he indulged wildly optimistic scenarios about how the war might liberalize the Middle East, arguing that "regime change in Iraq" could result in "demand for self-determination" throughout the region.

As the war unfolded, McCain remained a Chalabi booster. With the Iraqi military crumbling in early April 2003, McCain signed a letter with four other Republican senators complaining that Chalabi's INC was not being funded. Appearing on "Good Morning America," he argued for "bringing in Chalabi and the Iraqi National Congress as soon as possible." And, though he would later criticize the Bush administration for giving the public "too rosy a scenario" about postwar Iraq, McCain was, in fact, a major player in this deception. In May, he wrote, "Thanks to a war plan that represented a revolutionary advance in military science, to the magnificent performance of our armed forces, and to the firm resolve of the President, the war in Iraq succeeded beyond the most optimistic expectations."

For McCain, disillusionment would begin to set in after he traveled to Iraq in August 2003. He returned home convinced that more troops were needed, but, in a meeting with Rumsfeld, his advice was dismissed. *The Weekly Standard* and McCain began a campaign for more troops—and against Rumsfeld. The arguments echoed what McCain had said decades earlier: that the Vietnam war had been lost because of ineffective civilian leadership. Now he was making the same charge about Iraq.

Yet, even as the administration resisted his call for more troops, McCain continued to insist that the war was being won. After the January 2005 elections, which Sunnis boycotted, McCain said, "I feel wonderful. I feel that the Iraqi people, by going to the polls in the numbers that they did, authenticated what the president said in his inaugural speech: that all people seek freedom and democracy and want to govern themselves." As late as this July, McCain was assuring viewers of "The Early Show" on CBS that "most of Iraq is pretty well under control."

In short, McCain's record on Iraq does not inspire confidence. He was wrong about Chalabi, he was wrong about Iraq's ties to Al Qaeda and WMD, he was wrong about the reaction of Iraqis to the invasion, and he was wrong about the effects on the wider Muslim world. As McCain prepares to run for president, it's worth asking: Does he understand that he made mistakes? Does he draw any lessons from these mistakes? And is he once again willing—as he was during the '90s, when Srebrenica laid bare the steep price of realism—to adjust his worldview accordingly?

I visited McCain on a hot summer afternoon in Washington and was shown into his office. This time, both his press aides were in attendance and were taking notes. I hadn't seen McCain in three years and had heard that he had aged significantly, but I thought he appeared to be in good shape. Like white-haired Barbara Bush, McCain, at one point, seemed older than his peers. But now, at age 69, he seems younger. The scar down his face from an operation for melanoma in 2000 is less pronounced than it once was. And he continues to have the best political voice—husky and commanding, without being condescending—since Ronald Reagan.

I asked McCain whether he had taken lessons from the Iraq war similar to the kinds of lessons he drew from Vietnam. He quickly invoked the need for more troops. "The lesson is almost the Powell Doctrine," he said. "Almost. Every smart person I knew said . . . in order to control this country there is almost a formula of the number of troops that are required."

I told him a story I had heard about the eminent British military historian, Sir Michael Howard. Speaking ten years ago at the Library of Congress, Howard, who had supported the war in Vietnam, was asked whether he still believed that the United States should have intervened. Howard reportedly replied, "It's a good thing you lost that war. Because if you had won, you'd still be there." McCain laughed at the story, but brushed aside its point. Instead, he returned to another tactical analogy with Vietnam: "One of the things that bothers me about Vietnam, I mean Iraq, is these grand sweeps that we are doing in urban areas . . . instead of clear-and-hold, which [General Creighton] Abrams employed in Vietnam and enjoyed a degree of success." McCain was saying that, if the United States would employ Abrams's strategy in Iraq, we might yet achieve the success that has eluded us.

McCain wasn't willing to concede that there was any flaw in the basic strategy of taking over and attempting to transform an Arab country highly sensitive to Western domination. I told McCain I thought that he failed to appreciate the power of nationalism, either in Vietnam or Iraq. "I hope I have a strong appreciation," McCain replied. "I think it is fundamental. The Ukraine revolution—they had their revolution to divorce themselves from Russia. I think it was the same thing in Georgia. Nationalism was the first thing that caused the breakup of the Soviet Union. I hope I place sufficient emphasis on nationalism." But McCain did not address longstanding Arab resistance to Western occupation—whatever the occupier's expressed motives.

I asked whether he had second thoughts about the case for war that he and the administration had made. I asked about his support of Chalabi in 1998. Hadn't Zinni been right about Chalabi and the INC? "I never supported Chalabi, per se," he said. "I supported getting Iraqis to stand up and help in the liberation of their country. Was I too enamored with the INC? I would say yes. I would say yes." He also conceded that he "underestimated the difficulty of bringing democracy to a people who had been driven to the ground and oppressed in such a brutal fashion."

McCain has blamed the misinformation that the public received before the war on a "colossal intelligence failure." But hadn't Bush officials, I pointed out, exaggerated and distorted what they knew? I read McCain excerpts from Cheney's March 16, 2003, "Meet the Press" appearance in which he claimed that Saddam "has a longstanding relationship with various terrorist groups, including the Al Qaeda organization" and had "reconstituted nuclear weapons." Isn't it true, I asked McCain, that Cheney didn't know these things, but rather asserted them in the face of considerable evidence to the contrary—for instance, from the International Atomic Energy Agency and the CIA? In response, McCain got a little testy. "I would remind you," he said, "that every intelligence service in the West shared the same view. That is compelling. When the French believed that, then it has weight. The French, the Germans, and the Israelis believed the same thing." (In fact, they didn't share Cheney's view that Iraq had reconstituted its nuclear program.)

I asked McCain about U.S. policy toward Iran. He had said previously that the only thing "worse than the United States exercising a military option" would be "Iran having nuclear weapons." This suggested that he favored a preventive strike. Citing Mahmoud Ahmadinejad's statements about Israel, he told me, "We haven't taken the military option off the table, but we should make it clear that is the very last option, only if we become convinced that they are about to acquire those weapons to use against Israel." Did that mean, I asked, that Ahmadinejad's statements about Israel made it unacceptable for Iran to acquire the sheer capability to use nuclear weapons? At this point, McCain seemed to back off. "I think that if they are capable with their repeatedly stated intention, that doesn't mean I would go to war even then. That means we have to exhaust every possible option. Going to the United Nations, working with our European allies. If we were going to impose sanctions, I would wait and see whether those sanctions were effective or not. I did not mean it as a declaration of war the day they acquired weapons."

As our hour was drawing to a close, I told McCain that, from what I had learned, he had been very influenced by the neoconservatism of Kristol, Kagan, and *The Weekly Standard*. "I don't know whether I fit that label or not," McCain replied. He added that he also talks to Brent Scowcroft and Henry Kissinger. I asked him whether he had ever had any major disagreements with Kristol, Kagan, or the magazine itself. "I am sure there have been issues that we have disagreed on," he said, "but I think, generally speaking, I agree with and respect them enormously. I would be glad to go back and look at it."

I saw McCain once again in fall 2006. I wanted to find out whether he had modified any of his positions, but I could detect little change. I asked him about a statement he had made arguing that Bush couldn't increase troop strength in Iraq because it would be impossible to "sell that" to Americans. This made me wonder whether McCain had abandoned his own call for more troops. But, during our interview, he said he wanted to "retract" that statement. "If I were president, if I thought that was still necessary, I would risk the presidency, because I would make the case if I thought it was necessary to prevail," he said. McCain's insistence on this point suggests that he still hasn't learned any lessons from our misadventure in Iraq.

That's too bad, because, if McCain were to reevaluate his positions on the Middle East, he might make a very effective president. He has the ability to lead and a good sense, domestically, of where the country ought to go. Indeed, I talked to several liberals who know McCain and who opposed the Iraq war but who still wouldn't mind seeing him in the White House. Gary Hart laments McCain's embrace of the neocons, but still likes the idea of a McCain presidency and was worried that his enthusiasm might "sink his chances." A former top aide to a leading Democratic presidential contender admitted being ready to pull the lever for McCain in 2008: "I would rather have someone standing up for their point of view than trimming their sails like Hillary [Clinton] or John [Kerry] are. A lot of my friends think that, too."

Part of McCain's attraction for me and other opponents of the Iraq war is that his hawkishness would give him the credibility to sell a diplomatic alternative to the imbroglio that Bush has created in the Middle East. Indeed, he is probably the best equipped of all the potential presidential candidates to extricate the United States from the ditch into which it has fallen. But doing so would require him to break substantially with his own recent history.

During our interview, I asked McCain whether he had changed his opinion that the Vietnam war was winnable—a view he had reaffirmed most recently in his memoir, *Faith of My Fathers*. His response surprised me. "I would say [it was a] noble cause," he said. "I still believe that. But do I believe it was winnable? I am not sure." If McCain is willing to reconsider his most basic belief about Vietnam, he could still change his mind about Iraq. It's true that little he said to me suggests he will adjust his worldview in the near future, but McCain has surprised his critics before. Perhaps he will do so again.

Mitt Romney

Full Name Willard Mitt Romney

Current Residence Belmont, Massachusetts

Date and Place of Birth March 12, 1957; Detroit, Michigan

Education

B.A., Brigham Young University, 1971
J.D., Harvard University, 1975
M.B.A., Harvard University, 1975

Military Service

None

Nonpolitical Positions Held

Author, *Turnaround: Crisis, Leadership, and the Olympic Games,* 2004

President, Salt Lake Organizing Committee (2002 Winter Olympics), 1999–2002

CEO, venture capital/leveraged buyout firm Bain Capital, 1984–2001

Political Offices Held

Governor of Massachusetts, 2003–2007

Family

Married to Ann Davies Romney; children: sons Taggart, Matthew, Joshua, Benjamin, and Craig

How Mitt Romney Un-Became His Father:
Parent Trap *Jonathan Cohn*

n July 8, 1964, 17-year-old Mitt Romney slipped into a front-row seat at a San Francisco hotel ballroom. The start of the Republican National Convention was just days away, and tensions in the room were high—not over the choice of nominee (Barry Goldwater had already locked up enough delegates) but over the ideological future of the party. Inside the ballroom, the committee in charge of writing the party platform was under attack from a small band of dissenters determined to make one final stand against the radical conservatism of Goldwater and his supporters. And one of the most prominent dissenters was Mitt's father, George Romney.

By 1964, the first-term Michigan governor had distinguished himself as a straight-talker who disdained partisanship. He had made such an impression on his fellow moderates that days later, at the convention, Gerald Ford would make the symbolic gesture of nominating Romney from the floor, saying of his fellow Michigander that "he has never let the temporary glitter of expediency obscure the path which his integrity dictated he must follow." When Romney's turn to speak before the platform committee came, he seized it—challenging the group, which was packed with Goldwater delegates, to accept language endorsing federal civil rights initiatives and the importance of labor unions, and, more generally, to distance the party from some of the right-wing extremists who had backed Goldwater. As Mitt looked on attentively, his father warned the group that "there is no place in either of our parties for the purveyors of hate."

The moment was one of great futility: The committee, which greeted the speech with polite but tepid applause, rejected the amendments, just as the full convention would later turn away efforts by Romney and his supporters to introduce those amendments from the floor. But, against this backdrop, Romney's speech conveyed the noble defense of a principled stand. That is how, over 40 years later, his son remembers it. "I watched that with great interest," Romney told me earlier this spring. "He believed that the Republican Party was aligning itself as an opponent of civil rights and was connecting with the extreme elements of the John Birch Society and felt that Goldwater was wrong in taking the party in that direction. He was passionate about that."

We were sitting in the green room of CNN's Los Angeles studios, just after Mitt's appearance on "Larry King Live" during a March fund-raising trip to California. He had just turned 60, making him roughly the same age his father was during the 1964 convention—and the similarities between the two are even more striking up-close than they had been the previous times I had seen him, either on television or before large crowds. Mitt has the same chiseled features as his father: the squared-off jaw and the deeply set eyes, plus the nose with impossibly perfect angles. And, although Mitt's words come out more slowly and more deliberately than the ones I heard on recordings of his father, the voice itself has an unmistakably familiar ring to it—crisp, deep, and forceful. "I never saw myself being like my dad," Mitt joked during our conversation. "Now that I'm older, I see a tape of myself giving a speech, I say, 'Holy cow, I'm turning into my dad.' I look like him a lot. I talk like him a lot. The things I value are very much the things he valued."

The similarities between Mitt and his father go well beyond appearances. He shares his father's competitive streak, his strong sense of political ambition. Twelve years after George's death, Mitt still sees him as a role model, describing him as "the definition of a successful human." His admiration for his father's approach to politics surfaced several times during our interview. When I asked him to explain why he had abandoned business for politics, for example, he didn't talk about crusading to save the United States from the left. Instead, he told me, "It's a family gene. There's something in the Romney makeup that longs to be able to make a difference, to make a contribution. . . . There's almost an obligation to step forward."

Until recently, Mitt Romney did indeed seem to be his father's son—with a life that evinced noblesse oblige and a political tendency toward principled moderation. But, in the course of his presidential campaign, Romney has called the sincerity of those poses into doubt, flamboyantly altering seemingly bedrock positions on abortion and stem-cell research and positioning himself as a right-wing crusader. During our interview, Romney methodically went through these positions, endeavoring to explain the switches as a natural and genuine evolution of thought—all proof, he said, that "I'm conservative."

Mitt Romney's makeover suggests a far more piercing critique than mere flip-flopping: the charge of filial betrayal, of running a campaign that would earn paternal disapproval were George still alive. At first glance, it's a charge that rings true. Like all father-son relationships, of course, it's also far more complicated than that. And these complications aren't psycho-biographical digressions but essential to answering the question: Despite all his twists and turns, could Mitt Romney make a good president?

George Romney's Mormon upbringing was a big influence in shaping the worldview that he passed down to Mitt. George's great-grandfather was an original Mormon apostle named Parley Pratt, who followed Brigham Young to Utah and was killed in 1857 by the disgruntled ex-husband of one of his wives. When the federal government began to crack down on polygamy, George's grandparents fled to Mexico. In 1907, George was born in Chihuahua, and, five years later, during the Mexican revolution, the Romney family fled back to the U.S., eventually settling in Salt Lake City.

George grew up devout but poor—his father was a builder who declared bankruptcy several times. But he developed a sense of the world—not only through his peripatetic family history but through his church mission to England in 1927. It was an experience that helped him hone his political skills. "I've seen pictures of George standing, holding on to a statue in Hyde Park, speaking to a crowd," says Charles Harmon, one of George Romney's old political advisers. "It's tough—people shouting at you, ridiculing you, while you're trying to sell your beliefs. I always felt he was a super salesman. And he got some of that training from his missionary work."

After working his way through college, but never finishing his studies, George got his first taste of U.S. politics as an aide to Democratic Massachusetts Senator David Walsh. But he had mainly come to Washington, D.C., because his future wife Lenore's family was there, and, after following her back and forth to the West Coast, where she was trying to build a movie career, the couple settled in Detroit. There, Romney worked his way up through the company that eventually became the American

Motors Corporation—and Detroit's fourth-biggest automaker. He became best known for his role promoting the AMC Rambler, a compact vehicle that offered higher fuel efficiency and a lower sticker price than most U.S. cars. Romney sold Ramblers with the same vigor he had once used to sell Mormonism, attacking the Big Three as dinosaurs. He eventually climbed all the way to the position of president.

Mitt was George and Lenore Romney's fourth child—born in 1947, a few years before George took over at AMC and with a six-year separation to his next-closest sibling, Scott. Lenore's pregnancy had come as a surprise—the couple had given up on conceiving again—and the difficult childbirth left Lenore bedridden for a year. Partly as a result, Mitt, from a very young age, developed an especially close relationship with his father—a relationship that would get even closer later in life, once the older children left home for college and Mitt had his parents to himself.

George Romney was an outsider who had made it into the elite on his own terms (he remained an active member of the Mormon Church throughout his life). To help his children accomplish this same feat, he practiced two main principles of childrearing. One was to prepare them intellectually by engaging them in adult conversation—and Mitt, as the last arrival, was part of those conversations from a very young age. "I was the baby of the family, so I got all the years of experience of listening to people debate the issues, talk about the future," Mitt recalls. According to Scott, Mitt consistently lobbed the smartest, most pointed inquiries at their father. "Dad would gather us around, in the living room, the four kids and mom," Scott says. "My sisters and I would say, 'That sounds great.' And Mitt would say . . . 'Dad, if these American Motors cars are so great, why doesn't anybody buy one?' "

George's other principle was to give his children a healthy sense of humility, particularly when it came to financial circumstances. George credited his own success to his strong work ethic—and he wanted his children to have it, too. So, even though the Romneys lived on a four-acre plot in the posh Detroit suburb of Bloomfield Hills, George insisted the children do extensive chores and then, during the summers, take real jobs outside the house—which, in Mitt's case, meant working as a security guard at a Chrysler plant one summer. "On weekends, those guys had a set of chores, and there wasn't a whole lot of extra time," recalls Phillip Maxwell, who first got to know Mitt when they were in the fourth grade together. "Their father was a real taskmaster—very fair, but he instilled real discipline."

George prepared Mitt for leadership in one other key way: by sending him to Cranbrook, the elite private academy that sprawls across 319 lush acres not far from the Romneys' Bloomfield home. Established in the 1930s, Cranbrook has trained generations of students in classical preparatory style—with intensive Latin, accelerated mathematics, and weekly writing assignments from seventh grade on. Its seniors routinely win admission to the nation's top colleges, and among its alumni are former Senator Alan Simpson and intellectual-turned-dissident Daniel Ellsberg, of Pentagon Papers fame.

But, despite his intellectual curiosity at home, Mitt wasn't a standout for most of his years at Cranbrook, which he attended from seventh to twelfth grades. Classmates describe him as a B-plus student who was happy to cede academic achievement to others. He was active in the Blue Key Club, a service organization that shepherded visitors around campus, and the Homecoming Committee. But he wasn't the student class president or leader of the prestigious debate society. Nor was he cut out for the football or the hockey teams, which perennially won state championships.

He made do as a team manager for the hockey squad—and, since Cranbrook was an all-boys school, as a cheerleader. "He wasn't an athlete, which was tough on him, because other members of his family were," says Philip Maxwell. "He just wasn't coordinated in that way." Other classmates remember Mitt as young for his age emotionally, at least by Cranbrook standards. They say he was more popular than admired, a "happy-go-lucky guy" known less for his achievements than his pranks—like the time he and some friends borrowed a state trooper's uniform from his father's security detail and pulled over students from the neighboring girls' school.

It was shortly after Mitt started at Cranbrook that George got into politics: first as the head of a committee to rescue the Detroit public schools; then as the head of an organization trying to rewrite the antiquated state constitution. That work led to his successful run for the governor's office, which took place when Mitt was in ninth grade and landed George on the cover of *Time,* fueling widespread speculation about a future in national politics. Once in office, George Romney quickly compiled accomplishments, including passage of the new constitution, enactment of a new minimum-wage law (something the Democrats had wanted for more than 25 years but could never make happen), and turning an $80 million budget deficit into a $100 million surplus.

Some classmates speculate that George's looming presence may have been what made Mitt so quick to retreat to the safety of humor. Eric Muirhead—a classmate who now teaches writing at San Jacinto College in Texas—says that, when students wanted to make fun of Mitt, they would say things like, "He's no George Romney." "I had the impression that Mitt was struggling for respect when he was at Cranbrook," Muirhead adds. "Mitt suffered because of his father's importance."

Muirhead admits that he didn't think much of Mitt's mettle, either—until senior year, when Mitt suddenly seemed a lot more serious about himself and decided to go out for the cross-country team. Although Mitt had never run track before, Muirhead, who was the team's captain, and the rest of the team were quickly impressed with Mitt's work ethic—so impressed, in fact, that when Muirhead fell ill before one of the season's first meets, he told the coach Mitt should take the open slot.

The race began and, as expected, Mitt fell behind the pack. Muirhead figured it wouldn't affect the end result. Given the strength of Cranbrook's top runners, the team would still win, just as long as Mitt actually finished. But, as Mitt neared the end, he was gasping for breath. And, as he staggered through the final stretch, along a track circling the football field, he fell onto his hands and knees. The crowd, there for the homecoming football game, stood up as one—including Lenore Romney, who'd come to see her son's first race. Muirhead ran out to help, but Mitt refused. "He got up, staggered, and fell again," Muirhead says. "He kept getting up, kept falling, but kept shouting at us—kept telling us not to touch him. I don't know how many times he fell, but he finished, he made his way around that track, and he got an ovation like I never heard. He won a lot of people's respect that day. . . . In all my years, I never saw a guttier performance."

After one year at Stanford, in June 1966, Mitt left for Paris, where he was assigned to Le Havre, on the northern French coast, to begin his two-and-a-half-year Mormon mission. In France, Romney was out of his father's shadow for the first time, and friends say he came into his own. His middle-aged mission president tapped him early as a leader and made him responsible for more than 50 of his fellow missionaries. When the 1968 student strikes set in, Romney threw himself into crisis-management mode—distributing funds, food, and good cheer to his frequently discouraged charges. "You've got young men a couple of thousand miles away from home, not getting communication, and oftentimes one hundred fifty miles from the mission headquarters, too," says Dane McBride, who served alongside Romney in France. "It's not natural for young men to put other young men on a pedestal, but I really admired his perceptiveness and his ability to lead and to lift and to reassure in very uncertain times."

At the same time that Mitt began to shine as a leader, his father's political career began to crumble. After Goldwater's disastrous defeat, Romney emerged as the front-runner to be the next Republican nominee for president. By late 1966, one poll showed Romney beating Lyndon Johnson in a hypothetical match-up. But Romney began to stumble on Vietnam, criticizing the war and then declaring his full-throated opposition. When asked by a TV interviewer why he had supported it in the first place, Romney said he had gotten a "brainwashing" from the military. His poll numbers plummeted. By the spring of 1968, he was out of the race altogether.

Mitt has always said that his father had no regrets about the race—that he had given it his best shot and spoken his mind. But, soon after, Mitt's own ambition kicked into overdrive. After returning from France, he married his high-school sweetheart, Ann Davies, and transferred from Stanford to Brigham Young University, eventually graduating as valedictorian. Mitt wanted to attend business school next, but his father hoped he'd pursue a degree in law. So Mitt compromised by pursuing both at Harvard, completing a joint degree.

Romney overlapped with another future politician there—one George W. Bush. But the two did not know each other, and, really, their experiences could not have been more different. While Bush was lounging his way through, coasting on his family's reputation, Romney was hitting the books. Once again, he finished near the top of his class—and, upon graduation, he had his choice of jobs in industry. Until that time, Mitt always figured he would go into the auto industry, like his father. (As Romney told *The American Spectator*, "I did not think I was going to be in politics. . . . I hoped to be head of Ford or American Motors or General Motors.") But, by that time, a new opportunity was opening up for the nation's best and brightest: management consulting. These firms recruited from the top tier of the top graduate schools and sought to create an army of analysts who could bring their unique intelligence to bear on a wide variety of businesses, rather than just one. Romney liked the sound of that challenge and accepted an offer from Boston Consulting Group, a pioneer in the field. A few years later, he joined a group of BCG partners who had broken with the firm to establish a new one, called Bain.

Mitt's knack for management would soon make him legendary throughout the business community. Here, all the leadership skills he had honed over the years served him well: He developed a reputation for unusually diligent research and analysis—for maintaining an open mind and calling in conflicting points of view. Not only did this produce better decisions, it also disarmed would-be critics. "He's quite good at managing big egos," says James Bailey, another Cranbrook classmate who, years later, ended up collaborating with Mitt on business dealings in Boston. "He's really an extraordinary manager, deserving of all the praise he gets." Eventually, Romney spun off an operation from within Bain, called Bain Capital—which invested money in its projects, effectively becoming its own venture-capital firm. The result was a litany of now-famous business success stories: Brookstone, Domino's Pizza, and Staples.

George Romney had always said the ideal time to run for public office was after you had achieved financial independence and your children were old enough to put up with the loss of privacy. So, in 1994, when Republican officials from Massachusetts began putting out feelers for someone to run against Ted Kennedy, Mitt said he was interested. It would be an incredibly daunting race in which to make his political debut: While Bill Clinton's troubles had improved prospects for Republicans in the rest of the country, unseating Ted Kennedy in Massachusetts was said to be impossible. Still, Romney did have one secret weapon: his father, who knew a thing or two about long-shot bids.

George Romney had also started his political career by challenging a popular Democrat in an overwhelmingly Democratic state. And a key to his victory was his ability to run as a fiercely independent Republican. He complained about labor's influence over the Democratic Party, but he also complained about business's influence over the Republicans. When the organizers of Detroit's Labor Day parade refused to let him participate, George simply showed up and marched at the front of the line, coat slung over his shoulder. When Mitt decided to run for senator, George helped lead the charge. He began by serving as an emissary to Republican power-brokers and as Mitt's de facto communications director: "He's better than the chip off the old block because he's had better preparation than I," George would tell audiences. And, once Mitt got his party's nomination, George moved in with Mitt and his family for six months. When it was time to hit the road, George and Ann would go off campaigning in one direction, while Mitt went off in another. Then they would return to confer some more over strategy. "We didn't disagree," Mitt recalls. "We saw issues in a very similar way."

Substantively speaking, Mitt's campaign in 1994 closely resembled the runs George made in the '60s. While he had clearly identified himself as a Republican by this point, he did not position himself as an ideologue. He attacked Kennedy by making him a proxy for wasteful spending and various episodes of Democratic Party corruption. "I think it's important to have people who can and will be able to challenge the country on ethics and principles," Romney said in his announcement speech. But he did not propose an all-out assault on the welfare state. Although personally opposed to abortion, Romney said it should be legal, recalling how a close family friend had died from an illegal abortion. He even reached out to groups representing gay voters, touting his support for domestic partnership rights and echoing his father's words from 1964. When the local gay newspaper, *Bay Windows,* asked Romney about Jesse Helms and Pat Robertson, he replied, "I think that extremists who would force their views on the party and try to shape the party are making a mistake."

Romney ran a strong campaign, at one point passing Kennedy in the polls. And, while he tried to manage expectations, his father talked them up—hinting at aspirations for his son that went beyond Massachusetts. A Romney win "is bound to get national attention," George reminded people. But Kennedy eventually came back, seizing on Romney's personal beliefs about abortion and using them to make a still-devastating indictment: "He's not pro-choice, he's not anti-choice, he's multiple choice." George Romney tried to enlist other members of the Romney clan to help the campaign, thinking they could fan out across the state as Mitt's emissaries in the closing weeks. But, as Mitt's numbers cratered— Kennedy would be the lone vulnerable Senate Democrat to hold his seat that year—Mitt quietly asked them to stay home. The election, he knew, was lost.

Only a few weeks later did he admit to Scott, his brother, how much the experience had bothered him. "He said he never expected to win, but then, at the end, when he lost, he said he absolutely hated it," Scott says. "He told me, 'I'm not going to go into another campaign unless I think I can win.' He said, 'I'm not going to do it again.'"

George Romney would not live to see his son in political action again: He died a year later, while exercising in the same Bloomfield home where Mitt had grown up. And it would be seven more years before Mitt gave politics another try. But this time the prospects were much brighter: He wouldn't be trying to take a Senate seat away from a Kennedy. Instead, he would be running for governor, a post Republicans had held continuously since the early '90s.

Mitt positioned himself much as he had during his Senate run eight years before. He campaigned primarily on economics and management skills; he would balance the state's out-of-control budget and attract new businesses to revive the economy. Once again, he assured social liberals that he had no intention of upending abortion rights. And, while he made clear his rejection of same-sex marriage, he went out of his way to cultivate the support of gay Republicans once again, meeting one-on-one with members of the Log Cabin Republicans. At Boston's Gay Pride parade, Romney flyers touted "equal rights . . . regardless of sexual preference" (although both Romney's former campaign manager and his deputy told me they did not authorize the flyers).

This time, Romney won easily. And, at least in the early going, he showed signs of governing the way he had campaigned—reprising, again, his father's early history in Michigan. He got intimately involved with the details of an initiative to change the state's school funding scheme, so that poorer districts would get more money. Romney also brought in advisers based on management instinct rather than partisan affiliation. "He never asked me if I was a Democrat or a Republican, and never asked most of the Cabinet members who came with me," says Barbara Berke, a BCG partner who served as his chief of economic development from 2002 through 2005. Romney also appointed several well-known gay activists to high-ranking positions in his administration, tapping one for a Cabinet post.

The episode in which Romney's stewardship instincts—and his father's influence—were perhaps most evident was his passage of major health care reform. That saga began in 2005, when it became apparent that, because of a quirk in the structure of federal Medicaid funding, Massachusetts actually stood to lose some money from Washington if it didn't find a way to expand health insurance coverage. When Democrats proposed that the state seize the opportunity to pass universal health coverage, Romney surprised virtually everybody by announcing that he agreed.

Romney's subsequent work on the health care bill showcased his best qualities—reminiscent, in many ways, of his days at Bain. For advice, he tapped some of the state's top minds on health—even those, like MIT's Jonathan Gruber, who had traditionally advised Democrats. For political support, he reached out to traditional champions of expanded coverage, such as former House member John McDonough, turning these would-be adversaries into allies. And, above all, he went into negotiations with an open mind. The result was a bill that had enough support to get all the way through the legislative process. Romney ended up signing the bill in a grand public ceremony on the steps of Faneuil Hall. Standing at his side was his old nemesis, Ted Kennedy—who, it turns out, had worked closely with Romney on sealing the deal. "I'm a partisan Democrat, and, in a lot of ways, I think he was a terrible governor," says one high-ranking legislative staffer who worked on the measure. "But I do give him credit for participating in the health care debate and helping to advance that agenda."

But Romney had even loftier ambitions on his mind than bringing universal health care to the people of Massachusetts. He wanted to do what his father couldn't—become president. And, around that time, Romney began to evolve into a more conservative politician. Following a controversial state court decision legalizing gay marriage in early 2004, Romney initially backed a civil unions proposal as a reasonable compromise, only to pull his support at the last minute and instead back a more harshly worded amendment that might have made partnership benefits illegal as well.

That fall, Romney—citing a meeting in his office with a pair of Harvard scientists working on stem-cell research—told his advisers that he wanted to start labeling himself "pro-life." He claimed to have been taken aback by the scientists' cavalier attitude toward the disposing of embryos. That surprised some of his advisers, since Romney had been outspoken in his support of stem-cell research (his wife has multiple sclerosis, and stem-cell research may lead to a cure) and had frequently championed it in speeches to biotech companies and industry groups he was hoping to lure to Massachusetts. Abortion rights activists were even more flummoxed. Here was a candidate who had compiled a long, very public record of defending abortion rights. Yet now, because of a single meeting over stem-cell research, he had suddenly done an about-face. And here was the candidate who, years before, like his father, had promised to work within the Republican Party to pull it away from conservative extremism sounding more and more like an extremist himself.

Romney maintains the shift represents a true evolution of thinking—a genuine change of heart. Several friends and members of his family confirmed hearing him talk about the stem-cell meeting shortly after it took place. But critics note that, when Romney decided to announce his new position on stem cells, he didn't do it at a local event or in an interview with a local reporter. He decided to tell a reporter from *The New York Times*—which most people interpreted as a sign that Romney was no longer pitching himself to the voters of Massachusetts.

As a presidential candidate, Romney has tried to position himself as the only true conservative among the front-runners, running ads in which he portrays himself as a lone right-wing warrior fighting the good fight against out-of-control liberals in Massachusetts. The conservative posturing has gone well beyond cultural issues, too. In one debate, when asked about the controversial enemy combatant camp at Guantánamo Bay, he quipped that, instead of closing it down—as even some Republicans have urged—he would double its size. When queried about his past support for the Brady Bill and the assault weapons ban, he replied that he was a veteran hunter and lifetime member of the National Rifle Association. (Later, he would admit that he had signed up for that lifetime membership only a year before—and that he had limited hunting experience.)

But, if any one moment epitomized the new Mitt Romney, it was his speech before the Conservative Political Action Committee (CPAC) in February 2007. There, gathered in one place, were the intellectual and ideological heirs to the conservative movement that first captured control of the Republican Party in the 1960s. But Mitt Romney had not come to carry on his father's fight against the right wing. He had come, instead, to do what every other aspiring Republican presidential nominee was doing: beg for the group's approval. After being introduced by Grover Norquist, the conservative activist perhaps most responsible for the radical makeover of government economic policy in the last decade, Romney began his speech by suggesting it was a "good thing" the crowd would soon hear from Ann Coulter, who was next on the speaking agenda. From there, he fed the crowd red meat— attacking Ted Kennedy, Nancy Pelosi, and the press; promising to fight the liberal social agenda, to close U.S. borders, and to never, ever raise taxes. "This is not the time for us to shrink from conservative principles," Romney thundered. "It is time for us to stand in strength." The next day, CPAC delegates voted on their presidential preferences. Romney, with 22 percent, came in first.

When I interviewed Romney, I asked him about the speech— which had taken place just a month earlier—and what he imagined his father might have said if it were him, and not Mitt, addressing the crowd. "Hopefully, he'd have given a speech just like mine," Mitt said. "I'm conservative. My dad was conservative." And, while Romney noted that he didn't line up with CPAC on every issue, he said he simply hadn't chosen to emphasize those differences. "In a speech to CPAC, I'll emphasize those areas we have in common," he said. "I won't get up and say, 'Let me tell you the places where you and I might disagree.' " But that, of course, is precisely what his father had made a practice of doing.

Still, there was a moment in our interview when I caught a glimpse of the Romney more familiar to the voters who elected him in 2002. It happened when I asked him to talk about the presidents he most admired—the ones he would most like to emulate if he were ever elected. Reagan, the father of modern conservatism and the usual centerpiece of his speeches, never came up. Instead, after working through some of the usual clichés—George Washington, Abraham Lincoln—he settled on a Democrat, Harry

Truman, and a moderate Republican, Dwight Eisenhower, the latter for steering the country through the 1950s without starting a nuclear war.

Eisenhower was also George Romney's patron. And it wasn't the only time during this campaign that Mitt Romney has linked himself to his father's legacy. I'd seen him do so at least once before—in the speech where he formally announced his candidacy. It was in Dearborn, Michigan, at the Henry Ford Museum. For the occasion, museum officials brought out a display with one of the old AMC Ramblers, which stood behind Romney as he spoke. The speech Romney gave that day was a lot more like one his father might have given, focusing on how to improve economic innovation (thus the museum setting) and better manage the government.

Some of the people who have known him the longest think that this version of Romney is closer to the one who would actually govern. "I know Mitt is taking positions that are uncharacteristically conservative, probably more conservative than the man behind closed doors, but it is what you have to do to get the nomination of the Republican Party," says Cranbrook alum Sidney Barthwell Jr. Although a Democrat, Barthwell says he will probably vote for Romney anyway. "He is of the highest character, a straight-ahead guy. . . . He would make a great president, even though I disagree with all the positions he takes."

Maybe he's right. Maybe the Romney who campaigned in 1994 and 2002—the one known for his fast intellect and superior management skills—really would make a fine president. And maybe that former incarnation of Romney is still lurking in there, somewhere, behind all the rigidly conservative rhetoric. But does that even matter? The people Romney is courting now have a claim on him. If he becomes president, they will hold him to his promises, pushing him to enact their agenda—and punishing him should he stray. George Romney's presidential hopes ended prematurely, on the day he gave that ill-advised interview about Vietnam. Mitt's candidacy will surely endure longer—maybe all the way until January 2009. But, in going further than his father ever could, Mitt Romney is also sacrificing something his father didn't: the governing philosophy that made him a promising leader in the first place.

Rudy Giuliani

Full Name Rudolph William Giuliani

Current Residence New York, New York

Date and Place of Birth May 28, 1944; Brooklyn, New York

Education

    B.A., Manhattan College, 1965

    J.D., New York University School of Law, 1968

Military Service

    None

Nonpolitical Positions Held

    Author, *Leadership*, 2002

    CEO, Giuliani Partners, a consulting firm, 2002–present

    Partner, the law firm of Bracewell & Giuliani, 2005–present

    U.S. Attorney for the Southern District of New York, 1983–1989

Political Offices Held

    Mayor of New York City, 1994–2001

Family

    Married to Judith Nathan; previously married first to Regina
        Peruggi, then to Donna Hanover; children: son Andrew and
        daughter Caroline from second marriage to Hanover

Why the GOP's Future Belongs to Rudy: Party Boy

Thomas B. Edsall

William "Rusty" DePass named his dogs Goldwater, Reagan, and Bush. He is, needless to say, a conservative man, one who lives in a conservative state where the psychological scars of the Civil War still run deep. Six bronze stars on the west wall of the Capitol building here in Columbia mark the trajectory of Sherman's 1865 cannon fire from across the Congaree River. A state senator points me to the deep gouges on the building's banisters—gashes left, he says, by the sabers of Union officers charging the stairs on horseback. The Confederate flag still flies proudly in front of the statehouse. This is not, in short, hospitable political terrain for a drag-dressing, gay-friendly, abortion-loving, serially married, abrasive presidential candidate from New York.

Indeed, it is thanks to voters like DePass and states like South Carolina that Rudy Giuliani is widely thought to be doomed. "You need to suspend all your analytical faculties to believe the GOP will nominate for president a Republican who supports abortion rights and is pro–gun control and pro–gay rights," says Stu Rothenberg, author of *The Rothenberg Political Report*. "It just isn't going to happen, at least not in my lifetime." Political analyst Charlie Cook said in late 2006 that he would "win the Tour de France before Rudy Giuliani wins the Republican nomination." More recently, he told me he was "nervously" sticking to that prediction. "If Giuliani wins," he said, "it means that everything that

I have ever learned about Republican presidential nomination politics is wrong."

As of spring 2007, Giuliani held an eight- to twelve-point lead in national polls of GOP voters; and, perhaps more significantly, according to some surveys, he was running neck and neck with John McCain in states like South Carolina, where he was expected to fare poorly. DePass, whom I spoke to while traveling with Rudy in South Carolina, explains how he became an unlikely Giuliani backer. "I am more conservative than he is on the abortion question, and, probably on all the social issues, I would be to the right of him," he says. "But the overarching issue of our time is this war on terror. I have a son on his way right now to Afghanistan. I think Rudy Giuliani understands better than anyone the whole business about the war on terror, how it has to be waged."

Many observers believe Giuliani's early success is the result of his calculated move rightward—a savvy effort to trick conservative voters into believing he is really one of them. But there is another possibility, one that assumes a bit more intelligence on the part of conservative voters like DePass: What if we are witnessing not Rudy moving toward the rest of the Republican Party, but rather the Republican Party moving toward Rudy? What if the salience of a certain kind of social conservatism is now in decline among GOP voters and a new set of conservative principles is emerging to take its place? What if Giuilianism represents the future of the Republican Party? Giuliani is the beneficiary of an upheaval within the Republican electorate—an upheaval that was catalyzed by September 11 but is becoming apparent only now, as the GOP hosts its first primary battle since the terrorist attacks. In brief, among Republican voters, the litmus test issues of abortion and gay marriage have been losing traction, subordinated to the Iraq war and terrorism. According to the Pew Research Center, 31 percent of GOP voters name Iraq as their top priority, and 17 percent choose terrorism and security. Just 7 percent name abortion and 1 percent name gay marriage.

The roots of this transformation predate September 11 and are partly the result of demographics. The lions of the Christian right—Pat Robertson, Jerry Falwell, James Dobson—no longer dominate Republican politics as they once did. Their grip is slackening as their older followers are slowly replaced by a generation for which the social, cultural, and sexual mores that were overturned by the 1960s are history, not memory. In retrospect, these men reached the height of their power in the late '80s, when, by a 51-to-42 majority, voters agreed that "school boards ought to have the right to fire teachers who are known homosexuals." Now a decisive 66-to-28 majority disagrees, according to Pew. In 1987, the electorate was roughly split on the question of whether "AIDS might be God's punishment for immoral sexual behavior." Today, 72 percent disagree with that statement, while just 23 percent concur.

Giuliani is on the cutting edge of these trends, seeking to exploit new ideological lines between conservatism and liberalism. He rejects conservatism based on sexuality and reproductive issues; and his personal life amounts to a repudiation of conservatism focused on family structure, parental responsibility, fidelity, and lifelong monogamy. Ed Gillespie, former chairman of the Republican National Committee, notes that, even as voters learn about Giuliani's more centrist positions, "it does not seem to move his numbers." The former mayor, Gillespie says, is "challenging the notion that abortion and gay marriage are vote-determinative for everybody in the party."

It isn't just average voters who are driving this shift; many members of the GOP elite—whose overwhelming concern is cutting taxes, a Giuliani forte—would privately welcome the chance to downplay, if not discard, the party's rearguard war against the sexual and women's rights revolutions. Much of the Republican Party's consulting community and country club elite always viewed abortion and gay rights as distasteful but necessary tools to win elections, easily disposable once they no longer served their purpose. Now, with most of the leading GOP contenders demonstrating at best equivocal support for the sexual status quo ante, that time appears to be drawing near.

For the moment, at least, September 11 has replaced abortion, gay marriage, and other social-sexual matters as the issue that binds the GOP together as a party. And no one, of course, owns September 11 quite like Rudy Giuliani. "This is a different world from 2000, when we last had Republican primaries without an incumbent president. 9/11 scrambled the priorities, and it may very well be that the war on terror pushes social issues down," says Whit Ayres, a Georgia-based pollster currently unaffiliated with any presidential campaign. "Giuliani is an authentic American hero, and Southerners love American heroes." No wonder the Yankee centrist suddenly has a chance in South Carolina.

If Giuliani's liberal inclinations on certain sexual issues represent his party's future, so does his decided conservatism on non-sexual domestic matters. Take, for instance, the question of how much risk is desirable in our economic system and what, if anything, government should do to encourage or discourage it. Ever since Reagan, Republicans have seen themselves as the party that embraces risk as a worthy feature of American life; and Giuliani, with his criticism of the social safety net, is very much an heir to this tradition. One *Weekly Standard* article quoted Giuliani as saying that Democrats want "a no-risk society." Explaining his opposition to health care mandates, he said, "We've got to let people make choices. We've got to let them take the risk—do they want to be covered? Do they want health insurance? Because ultimately, if they don't, well, then, they may not be taken care of. I suppose that's difficult."

Moreover, the centrality of risk to Giuliani's political philosophy is reflected in the kinds of people who have helped him raise a highly credible $15 million in the first quarter of this year. The list of his top fund-raisers is dominated by venture capitalists, takeover and merger specialists, hedge-fund operators, energy company CEOs, and nouveau riche investment bankers—men (and a few women) who have thrived in the financial culture of risk: Texas oilman T. Boone Pickens; billionaire investment banker Thomas Hicks; hedge-fund founder Paul Singer; multimillionaire Bill Simon; investment banker Ken Langone; and private-equity investor Douglas Korn, among others.

It is telling that Giuliani's fund-raising operation has tapped so deeply into Texas, a state where risk is central to the political and philosophical ethos. Texans treat campaign contributions like political venture capital, and they have been a financial mainstay of aggressive conservative candidacies and causes for two generations. They provided early backing to Ronald Reagan and to the House and Senate candidates who brought conservatism to Washington in 1980 and 1994. Texas does not rank among the top five states in donations for either Mitt Romney or McCain, and no Texas metropolitan area is a major source of cash for their bids. By contrast, for Giuliani, Texas ranks third—behind New York and California—while Dallas and Houston place second and fourth on his list of top donor cities.

Another element of the Reagan tradition to which Giuliani can lay claim—and that bolsters his chance of winning the nomination—is his appeal to white, working-class voters: the Reagan

Democrats who became the angry white men of the 1990s. Their switch to the GOP fractured the class basis of the New Deal coalition, and they have been crucial to every Republican presidential victory since 1968. These are Giuliani's people. He is pro-cop, anti-Sharpton, the mayor whose meritocratic streak led him to end the open admissions policy at the City University of New York. He stood in a flat-bed truck in front of City Hall in 1992 and told 10,000 beer-drinking cops that a proposed civilian review board was "bullshit" designed "to protect David Dinkins's political ass." He famously lectured a mother whose son had been killed in a hail of police bullets, "Maybe you should ask yourself some questions about the way he was brought up and the things that happened to him"—rhetoric that harkened back to George Wallace's insistence that the government stop "coddling" criminals because they "didn't have enough asparagus as a child." Giuliani was the tough guy who restored order to a city verging on chaos by breaking the back of the liberal interest groups that had once dominated local politics; and many white, lower- and middle-income voters in the outer boroughs loved him for it. They, more than any other factor, are the reason he was twice elected mayor of one of the country's most Democratic cities. And their hero now uses the same tough rhetoric that he once used to talk about criminals to talk about terrorists.

Giuliani's brand of conservatism also speaks to the Republican longing for managerial competence—something that has been woefully lacking under Bush. The statistics from Giuliani's tenure in New York suggest that he knows how to get results: Under his leadership, the city's murder rate fell by 63 percent; overall crime declined by 52 percent; vehicle thefts dropped by 71 percent; the number of children in foster care fell by 34 percent; the welfare case load declined by 59 percent; unemployment dropped by 40 percent; construction permits rose by 51 percent; and personal income rose by 53 percent. Of course, Giuliani's role in improving life for New Yorkers has almost certainly been overstated—most of all by Giuliani himself. The city's drop in crime was part of a national trend that actually began under Dinkins, and the economic boom of the '90s didn't hurt, either. What's more, Giuliani's managerial diligence is inseparable from his authoritarian streak, perhaps the least appealing aspect of his persona. Still, deserved or not, Giuliani's reputation as a skilled manager has been a very real asset in his campaign so far, allowing him to criticize Bush credibly on Iraq—the issue that, more than any other, symbolizes this administration's managerial shortcomings. "Here's what I would change," Giuliani told Larry King when asked how he would have handled the assault on Iraq. "Do it with more troops, maybe 100,000, 150,000 more." Giuliani harkens back to a time when Republicans were perceived as more competent, sober administrators than Democrats—and he affirms the nagging suspicion of many rank-and-file conservatives that Iraq could have been a stunning success if only George W. Bush weren't such a buffoon.

But perhaps the most striking way in which Giuliani captures the mood of contemporary Republican politics has nothing to do with ideology and everything to do with strategy. Both Reagan and Bush were masters of polarization. They calculated that it would be better to win by one vote, with a clear policy mandate, than to try to bring along a less committed 60 percent of the electorate with an appeal to consensus and compromise. In 2004, this strategy became clearer than ever, as Republicans sought to capitalize on deepening chasms between left and right. Deliberate polarization may or may not prove an effective strategy in the 2008 general election, but it is deeply attractive to conservative GOP primary voters whose antipathy to liberalism is intense.

Giuliani's entire career has been built on a willingness to polarize. Consider the vote totals in different neighborhoods in 1993, when he ousted Dinkins, New York's first black mayor. The election was close—Giuliani won by fewer than 50,000 votes—but the overall tally masked bitter partisan and racial divides. In heavily minority Crown Heights and Bedford-Stuyvesant, Dinkins won by margins of 38 to one. Meanwhile, Giuliani carried predominantly white Staten Island's South Shore by twelve to one, Howard Beach and Ozone Park by five to one, and Bensonhurst by eight to one. And, once he took office, Giuliani only seemed to grow more eager to stoke divisions through repeated head-on collisions with icons of the left, welfare-rights organizations, and the ACLU. Indeed, if there is one hallmark of Giuliani's career as a prosecutor and mayor, it is his compulsion to fight without restraint—whether the enemy is the mafia, the education establishment, or his estranged second wife.

Giuliani is now pursuing the same strategy of sowing division, only this time on a national level. To hear him tell it, the election will pit weak-kneed Democrats against hard-line Republicans. "I listen a little to the Democrats, and, if one of them gets elected, we are going on defense," he recently told an audience in New Hampshire. "We will wave the white flag on Iraq. We will cut back on the Patriot Act, electronic surveillance, interrogation, and we will be back to our pre–September 11 attitude of defense."

There is good reason to believe this rhetoric will win over a portion of GOP voters. As Rick Perlstein has pointed out in *The New Republic,* at a moment when conservatism is philosophically adrift—among other problems, it is currently tethered to an unsuccessful war, one whose premises may not have been all that conservative in the first place—the single thing that truly unites and energizes conservatives is a raw animosity toward liberals. With so many Republican policies having failed over the past six years, contemporary conservatism is less interested in policy and more defined by style. Nothing characterizes that style quite as well as bashing liberals. And Giuliani knows how to bash liberals. Neither McCain nor Romney nor even Newt Gingrich can match Rudy's record in confronting the ideological enemies on conservatism's Most Wanted list. It is in this climate that the tendency to say and do impolitic things—a characteristic that might ordinarily be seen as a drawback for a candidate—has become perhaps Rudy's greatest strength.

When you call Sunny Mindel, longtime Giuliani press aide and confidante, a woman answers the phone and says, "Giuliani Partners." After you ask to speak to Mindel, the woman asks in a slightly suspicious and hostile tone, "Who is trying to reach her?" After you identify yourself, there is a moment of silence. Then, if you pass muster, the woman says, "This is Sunny Mindel."

Mindel is among the old guard of Giuliani's tightly closed group of advisers—loyalists who have stuck with the mayor for years. In addition to Mindel, the group includes inner-circle top dog Tony Carbonetti, who has been with Giuliani since his first, failed campaign against Dinkins in 1989. Carbonetti later became the mayor's chief of staff, and he now works for Giuliani Partners. Another confidante is boyhood friend Peter Powers, who was campaign manager, transition chair, and deputy mayor for Giuliani. Powers now runs Powers Global Strategies, LLC, a lobbying and strategic consulting firm. Among the others closest to

Giuliani are former chief mayoral counsel Dennison Young Jr., campaign treasurer John Gross, and former New York Corporation Counsel and co-founder of Giuliani Partners Michael Hess.

If these were Giuliani's only advisers, his campaign would be in trouble. Part of the conventional wisdom that sees Giuliani as an outlier in Republican politics stems from the belief that he is surrounded only by New Yorkers and old friends—people who are themselves outliers in GOP circles. And, before the Giuliani campaign got off the ground, many Republican operatives believed that a major liability for the candidate would be his dependence on this closed circle of parochial advisers, none of whom is experienced in national elections. So it is noteworthy that Giuliani appears not to have fallen into this trap. Early on, Giuliani Partners hired Chris Henick, a Yazoo City, Mississippi–born political operative who trained under Lee Atwater and served as Karl Rove's deputy in Austin during the 2000 campaign—making him a protégé of the two men who, more than anyone else, fathered the GOP's strategy of polarization. Henick has become a bridge between the old guard and the new hires, including campaign manager Michael DuHaime, former political director at the RNC; strategy director Brent Seaborn, a specialist in datamining and microtargeting; senior communications adviser Jim Dyke; and political director Mark Campbell. The presence of Henick—combined with the considerable sums of money flowing out of the Lone Star state and into Giuliani's coffers—suggests that the campaign is being infused with a heavy dose of Texas to balance out its roots in New York.

To be sure, Giuliani's candidacy faces significant pitfalls. To begin with, there is his voluble support for gun control—a dispositive issue for many conservative Republicans. Then, of course, there is the religious right. Though their power is on the wane,

Christian conservatives are not going to allow Giuliani to have the nomination without a bitter fight. "Giuliani is the front-runner, but it's kind of like, here in D.C., you drive over the Potomac at night and it looks beautiful, but, if you get down near it, you certainly wouldn't want to take anything out of it and eat it. It's polluted; it's got problems," said Tony Perkins of the Family Research Center. Richard Land, president of the Southern Baptist Convention's Ethics & Religious Liberty Commission, put it this way: "If he wins, he'll do so without social conservatives." Then he added that a Republican presidential candidate can "no more win without conservative voters than a Democrat can without overwhelming support from blacks."

It's not just Giuliani's political positions that offend; his personal life is almost a caricature of family dysfunction. While mayor, Giuliani handled his marital difficulties with public displays that were flamboyantly irresponsible and vindictive. "What kind of man humiliates his children by escalating a private family controversy this way, even leaking—in a bid to gain sympathy—such lurid details as the impotence caused by his prostate treatments? What kind of president would such a man be?" wrote David Freddoso in *National Review Online*. Two months ago, *The New York Times* ran a story titled, "Noticeably Absent from the Giuliani Campaign: His Children." The article described how, in the wake of his failed second marriage, Rudy's relationship with his son Andrew, now 21, has turned distant, with the two not speaking for over a year. Gawker put the matter succinctly: "Rudy Giuliani Even Creepier Than You Thought." For a candidate who loves to say that "no government program can replace fatherhood," the hypocrisy is obvious.

Moreover, Giuliani's greatest strength—his ebulliently aggressive persona—can at times become a weakness. Rudy's public behavior as mayor was so egomaniacal as to be incomprehensible outside New York City limits. His firing of William Bratton—probably the best police commissioner the city ever had—appeared to be driven solely by jealousy over Bratton's rising profile. "It was the single biggest mistake of the Giuliani administration," wrote Fred Siegel in his generally sympathetic biography, *The Prince of the City*. In the years since he left Gracie Mansion, Giuliani has continued to feed his appetite for self-aggrandizement. Take his contract for giving speeches at $100,000 or more a pop, which includes the following language: "[T]he private aircraft MUST BE a Gulfstream IV or bigger.... The client agrees to supply two large sedans or SUVs and 1 van for luggage.... Client agrees to provide Mr. Giuliani with a pre-registered, large, two-bedroom, non-smoking suite with a king-sized bed, on an upper floor, with a balcony and a view, if applicable." New Yorkers may love public figures with outsized egos, but, in the rest of the country, such anecdotes are sure to make voters skeptical, at the very least.

Then there is the assortment of embarrassing characters lurking in Giuliani's past. His childhood friend, Alan Placa, is a Catholic priest and accused child molester whom the former mayor has continued to defend. A 2003 grand jury report, in which Placa was referred to as "Priest F," described his alleged crimes: "Priest F was cautious, but relentless in his pursuit of victims. He fondled boys over their clothes, usually in his office. Always, his actions were hidden by a poster, newspaper or a book. He talked continuously as he fondled them. Everyone in the school knew to stay away from Priest F." There is also the notorious Bernard Kerik, New York City's former police commissioner. When Bush tapped Kerik to serve as secretary of homeland security, his nomination foundered thanks to accusations that he employed an illegal immigrant and accepted illegal gifts and loans during his stint as top cop. Kerik owed his entire rise through the ranks to his friendship with Giuliani. And, according to Kerik's former girlfriend, the book publisher Judith Regan, this friendship could come back to haunt Giuliani's campaign. She told one of my *TNR* colleagues that Kerik and Giuliani would frequently discuss "sketchy" activities in her presence "as if I weren't there." Regan told my colleague that she would reveal the contents of the conversations in the event that Giuliani's presidential campaign took off. (Of course, Regan has her own scandal-ridden past. But she also has enough p.r. acumen and notoriety to win an audience for her accusations.)

And, yet, despite all his liabilities, Rudy retains a plausible chance of winning the nomination. In some respects, he has simply gotten lucky. He has the good fortune to be running against opponents who cannot lay an undisputed claim to the morality mantle. Romney earned the suspicion of social conservatives when he came out for abortion and gay rights during his 1994 Senate bid and his 2002 Massachusetts gubernatorial campaign. McCain, admitting infidelity, left his first wife, Carol (who had been severely injured in an auto accident), to marry a much younger heiress to an Arizona liquor fortune. His new wife further complicated his values profile by admitting in 1999 that she had been addicted to Percocet and Vicodin and that she stole these drugs from her own nonprofit medical organization. Moreover, McCain's anti-abortion credentials were tarnished when he spoke out against overturning Roe v. Wade in 1999, telling CNN, "We all know, and it's obvious, that, if we repeal Roe v. Wade tomorrow, thousands of young American women would be performing illegal and dangerous operations." McCain has since disowned those comments, but Focus on the Family's James Dobson, for one, does not believe him. "I pray that we won't get stuck with him," Dobson has said.

Giuliani is more than just lucky, however. He is also smart. The former New York mayor has chosen the right moment to take his idiosyncratic brand of conservatism to the national stage. Hawkish on defense, bullish on unrestrained capitalism, socially tolerant on some questions, acidly intolerant on others, despised by his foes, beloved by his allies, eminently comfortable with combative politics, he is plausibly positioned to capitalize on—and perhaps drive—the reconfiguration of the Republican Party. This would have seemed improbable a decade ago, given the substantial differences that separated him from his party's base. But, today, he seems less a misfit in the GOP than a candidate with the potential —if he doesn't short-circuit—to become a transformational figure at a crucial moment in the party's history: someone, like Goldwater, Reagan, or Bush, who could redefine how Republicans win elections and what the label "conservative" means. Perhaps Rusty DePass will name his next dog Giuliani.

Fred Thompson

Full Name Fred Dalton Thompson

Current Residence MacLean, Virginia

Date and Place of Birth August 19, 1942; Sheffield, Alabama

Education

  B.S., Memphis State University (now University of Memphis),
    1964

  J.D., Vanderbilt University Law School, 1967

Military Service

  None

Nonpolitical Positions Held

  Minority counsel, Senate Select Committee on Presidential
    Campaign Activities ("Watergate Committee"), 1973–1974

  Author, *At That Point in Time: The Inside Story of the Senate
    Watergate Committee*, 1975

  Attorney/lobbyist, private practice, 1974–1994

  Attorney at the Washington firm of Arent, Fox, Kintner,
    Plotkin & Kahn, 1991–1994

  Actor, 1985–present

  Commentator, ABC Radio Network, 2006–present

Political Offices Held

  U.S. Senator from Tennessee, 1994–2003

Family

Married to Jeri Kehn Thompson; children: daughter Hayden
and sons Daniel and Samuel; previously married to Sarah
Lindsey; children: son Fred "Tony" Jr. and daughter Elizabeth "Betsy" (died 2002)

Who's Your Daddy? the Masculine Mystique of
Fred Thompson   *Michelle Cottle*

Thwack! An elaborately beaded elephant handbag lands
solidly on Fred Thompson's upper arm. "Law and Order
on the Border!" the bag's owner, a short, sassy, middle-
aged brunette, crows at the presumed presidential candidate. "There's your campaign slogan right there!" Vibrating with
pride at her cleverness in linking Thompson's get-tough immigration stance with the title of the NBC series on which he until
recently starred, the Republican dame grins broadly and repeats
the line with even greater gusto: "Law and Order on the Border!"
The former Tennessee senator, characteristically imposing in dark
blue pinstripes, responds with a smile of indulgence and weary
amusement as he ambles through the herd of fans trailing him
across the lower level of the Greater Richmond Convention Center, where he has just headlined the Virginia Republican Party's
2007 Commonwealth Gala.

Thanks to poor acoustics, some in the audience were unable to understand Thompson's address, but this in no way dampened their ardor. "Can you hear him?" one of a gaggle of older ladies at the table in front of me demanded of her girlfriends as he launched into his stump speech. "I can't hear him! I can't hear him—but I love him!"

Now, as the actor and erstwhile politician rambles toward the back exit, autograph-seekers thrust programs and pens into his large hands. Digital cameras flash and giggling soccer moms in too-tight cocktail frocks wrap their arms around Thompson's trunk-like waist as their husbands struggle to snap cell phone pictures. Through it all, the phlegmatic senator nods, presses the flesh, mumbles an occasional response to inquiries about his presidential plans—"we're exploring away"; "the waters feel pretty warm to me"—and scribbles his signature over and over again. With his Droopy Dog mug, his virtually bald pate, and his bulky, six-foot-five frame overshadowing the throng, the 64-year-old candidate resembles nothing so much as a mildly beleaguered father surrounded by a pack of attention-seeking children.

To watch Thompson work a crowd like this is to glimpse the primordial roots of the Fred Fever currently gripping the GOP. Part of the appeal is obvious: A well-known actor, Thompson carries with him an inherent star quality that cannot be overestimated in our celebrity-obsessed culture. Moreover, after years of portraying a particular type of folksy authority figure, Thompson gives voters the sense that they already know who he is and what sort of leader he would be. Conversely, as a still relatively unknown political commodity, the candidate has a touch of the blank-slate phenomenon working for him, allowing savior-hungry Republicans to project onto him whichever personal and ideological traits they most desire. Underlying all of this, however, is an even more primal allure: In any given situation, Fred Thompson fundamentally seems like more of a man than anyone else around him.

If there's one thing conservatives are obsessed with these days, it's manliness. Saddled with a president they once cheered as a kick-ass cowboy but have come to scorn as weak on everything from immigration to government spending, Republicans are desperate for a competent, confident champion to make them feel good about themselves again. As Rudy Giuliani recently told a crowd of Delaware supporters, "What we're lacking is strong, aggressive, bold leadership like we had with Ronald Reagan."

Enter Fred Thompson. More than anyone in the field—more than Giuliani, more than John McCain, and certainly more than the altogether-too-well-coiffed Mitt Romney—Thompson exudes old-school masculinity. Along with the burly build, he has the rumbling baritone, the low-key self-assurance, and the sense of gravitas honed by years as a character actor playing Important Men. In Thompson's presence (live or on-screen), one is viscerally, intimately reassured that he can handle any crisis that arises, be it a renegade Russian sub or a botched rape case.

But therein lies the irony. For, while the veteran actor certainly looks and sounds the part of the man's man in this race, there's precious little in either his personal or political history to suggest that he overflows with any of the attributes commonly associated with manliness, such as determination, perseverance, leadership ability, or garden-variety toughness. By his own account, Thompson is a not especially hard-charging guy who has largely meandered through life, stumbling from one bit of good fortune to the next with an occasional nudge from those close to him. It is, to some extent, part of his much-ballyhooed comfortable-in-his-own-skin charm. But it also raises questions about whether he has the gumption to gut out a presidential race when it inevitably becomes difficult, or mean, or plain old boring. In short, is Fred Thompson really enough of a man for this fight?

Young Freddie Thompson never postured himself the future leader of the free world. He wanted to be a high school basketball coach. It was an obvious aim for a big guy from a small town who had the brains for academics but not the enthusiasm. Raised modestly middle-class in the central Tennessee town of Lawrenceburg, the teenage Thompson was regarded as likeable, outgoing, lazy (he had a tendency to doze off during class), and an incorrigible cutup. (As the *Nashville Tennessean* charmingly reported, Thompson's high school principal had to create a separate study hall for the mischief-making athlete and one of his close pals, accessible only through the principal's office.) Most folks assumed Freddie's future held nothing more exceptional than following his dad into the used-car business. The summer after his junior year, Thompson got his girlfriend, Sarah Lindsey, "in trouble," as people used to delicately put it. The couple married in September of Thompson's senior year and moved in with Sarah's parents while the groom finished high school. Fred Dalton "Tony" Thompson Jr. was born in spring 1960. Three years later, daughter Betsy arrived during her parents' junior year at Memphis State University. In 1964, Thompson enrolled at Vanderbilt Law School in Nashville, and, for the next three years, Sarah taught (when not on maternity leave with their third child, Dan) while Fred worked as everything from a shoe salesman to a hotel night clerk to help support the family.

Over the years, Thompson has made repeated reference to the fact that he isn't the kind of guy driven to achieve. "I have never beaten down a lot of doors in my life," he told Fox News in March.

"Occasionally doors have opened to me, and I had sense enough to see they were opening and I would walk through them, and they've always turned out well for me." Ironically, getting his high school sweetheart pregnant was the first and arguably most important of these doors. Considerably more goal-oriented than her young beau, Sarah has long been credited with starting Thompson on the road to personal maturity and professional direction. Better still: Her family, active in the local GOP, helped steer Freddie toward a career in law and politics. Sarah's grandfather, an attorney, is said to have been the inspiration behind Thompson becoming a Republican, and Thompson's first job out of law school was in the Lawrenceburg practice of Sarah's uncle, also a big GOP booster. Soon, Thompson began stretching his own political wings: helping organize a Young Republicans group for Lawrence County, managing a (failed) U.S. congressional campaign in 1968, and winning a spot on the county's Republican Executive Committee. From that post, he could network with state party bigwigs, including the man who would become his political Yoda, Senator Howard Baker.

The godfather of the modern Tennessee GOP, Baker was known for recruiting hot young talent in his quest to revivify the state party. (Lamar Alexander was another fabulous Baker boy.) Thompson swiftly emerged as one of the senator's most promising prospects. In 1969, Baker helped Thompson land a position as assistant U.S. attorney for the Middle District of Tennessee, a post that provided the fledgling lawyer with some early media training. "The U.S. attorney whom he worked for didn't like to try cases. Fred did, and soon he became a hot item in the local media," recalls William Kirkland, Thompson's best buddy from law school. "He was interviewed quite a bit—and he didn't shy away from that publicity." After working on Baker's 1972 reelection campaign, Thompson really hit the big time in 1973, when Baker, to the consternation of his Senate colleagues, drafted the unknown Tennessean to serve as minority counsel on the Watergate hearings. While Thompson didn't distinguish himself as a great legal mind during the proceedings, he did make a national splash when he famously asked White House aide Alexander Butterfield whether he knew of any listening devices in the Oval Office. The moment was pure political theater, as both parties' legal teams already knew the answer. But being chosen to ask the question in front of the TV cameras (a coup engineered by Baker) gave Thompson a healthy dose of national celebrity. By the hearings' end, the small-town lawyer with the unforgettable voice had signed with a major-league speakers' bureau in New York. "I got paid large sums of money for giving speeches in schools that I could never have gotten into," he later joked to *The New York Times*.

Post-Watergate, Thompson returned to private practice in Tennessee, where another door swung wide. In 1977, he represented Marie Ragghianti, a former head of the state parole board suing Democratic governor Ray Blanton for wrongful termination. The case brought to light a cash-for-clemency scheme that ultimately took down the corrupt administration. More importantly, it launched Thompson's acting career when he was cast to play himself in a movie about the scandal, titled *Marie*. A string of supporting roles in better-known films and TV shows followed, and, for the bulk of a decade, Thompson performed an impressive two-step, simultaneously forging political ties as a Beltway lobbyist and perfecting his public persona as the face (and voice) of institutional authority in such films as *No Way Out* (in which he played the director of the CIA), *Fat Man and Little Boy* (a major general), *The Hunt for Red October* (a rear admiral), *Thunderheart* (an FBI honcho), and *In the Line of Fire* (the White House chief of staff).

In 1994, Baker cracked yet another door for his protégé, approaching Thompson, by then a minor celebrity, with a new proposition: running for the Senate seat left vacant thanks to Al Gore's ascension to the vice presidency. Thompson, who had previously rejected his party's urgings to pursue elected office, reluctantly agreed. But his campaign against Democratic Representative Jim Cooper stalled out of the gate, with Thompson trailing by more than 20 points nine months out. As the story goes, over a meal at a local Cracker Barrel, campaign manager Tom Ingram asked a dispirited Thompson how he would run the race if he had his druthers. ("He wasn't having a good time," recalls Ingram, now a Senate aide to Lamar Alexander.) Thompson said he'd like to throw on a pair of jeans and drive around the state just chatting folks up. Voilà! A populist phenom was born. In early August, Thompson ditched his suits, rented a red Chevy pickup, and commenced his good ole boy charm offensive. Playing to the broad anti-Washington sentiment of the time, Fred cheered the virtues of "citizen legislators" over career pols, decried Washington's misguided efforts to "tax ourselves into prosperity," and vowed to "go up there and grab that place by the scruff of the neck and give it a good shake." Three months later, despite Cooper's attempts to paint him (not inaccurately) as a "Gucci-wearing, Lincoln-driving, Perrier-drinking, Grey Poupon–spreading millionaire Washington special interest lobbyist," Thompson won the race by 20 points. Two years later, he was reelected by an even fatter margin. Though touted as a prospective presidential candidate for 2000, he opted not to run after his Senate investigation into foreign contributions to the Clinton-Gore campaign failed to uncover any actionable misdeeds.

In January 2002, Thompson suffered a devastating personal loss when his daughter Betsy died of an accidental prescription-drug overdose. A few weeks later, he announced that he would not seek reelection to the Senate. Heading back into the private sector, Thompson looked to resume both his lobbying and his acting careers. Conveniently, before his term was even up, Thompson was cold-called by "Law & Order" creator Dick Wolf, who wanted to know if he would be interested in joining the cast of the spectacularly popular franchise. Since then, literally millions of Americans have come to know Thompson as the dashing, curmudgeonly, and comfortably conservative District Attorney Arthur Branch.

Thompson also kept a toe in the world of public policy. In addition to his lobbying and acting, he serves as a member of the Council on Foreign Relations, a visiting fellow at the conservative American Enterprise Institute, and chairman of the State Department's International Security Advisory Board. He has also been pinch-hitting for the venerable radio commentator Paul Harvey on the ABC radio network. By all accounts, Thompson is successful beyond his wildest childhood dreams. But, late last year, after fellow Tennessean and former Senate Majority Leader Bill Frist announced that he would not run for president, those closest to Thompson once again began whispering in his ear about bigger, better things. Perhaps the most influential of these whisperers has been Thompson's second wife, Jeri Kehn Thompson.

If Thompson's first wife put him on the path to law school, it's widely acknowledged that his second wife is the one driving his presidential run. Blonde, bodacious, and 24 years younger than her husband, Jeri is often sniffily referred to as Thompson's "trophy wife," but she is clearly more than that. A one-time Senate staffer and spokesperson for the Republican National Committee, Jeri is regarded around Washington as politically shrewd and fiercely ambitious on behalf of her spouse. In the wake of Frist's announcement, Jeri promptly contacted Republican p.r. veteran Mark Corallo about serving as her husband's spokesman and raising his profile inside the Beltway. More recently, after lefty filmmaker Michael Moore took a public poke at Thompson, challenging him to a health care debate and criticizing his penchant for embargoed Cuban cigars, Jeri brought the issue to her hubby's attention and urged him to call up a friend with a video camera and record his now-famous 30-second Web response. (In it, a cigar-chomping Thompson says he's too busy to meet with Moore, but wryly warns him to watch his step lest his "buddy Castro" decide to toss him in a mental institution as he has other documentarians. "A mental institution, Michael. That'd be something you oughta think about," intones Thompson with a meaningful arch of his brow.) Last month, at a reception for party bigwigs and top donors that preceded the GOP gala in Richmond, Jeri diligently stood in line to meet and greet every person in attendance. "She's been one of the key players," confirms Tom Ingram.

But while Jeri is clearly providing some of the fire-in-the-belly that Thompson otherwise lacks, there is much chatter about whether the brassy former operative realizes just how tough it is to be the wife of a candidate, much less of a president. The most oft-cited question mark is Jeri's very public pursuit of Thompson. (In romance, as in politics, Thompson has as often been the hunted as the hunter.) Divorced from Sarah in 1985, Thompson was an infamous ladies' man during his Senate days. (Former girlfriends include country singer Lorrie Morgan and GOP fund-raiser Georgette Mosbacher.) Falling under Thompson's spell at a Fourth of July picnic in 1996, Jeri's subsequent campaign to elbow out her competitors for his affection repeatedly made the gossip columns in Washington and New York, most memorably in April 2000, when she groused to the *New York Post*'s Page Six about "all these women" trying to move in on her man. "They just won't leave him alone," she fussed. "I can't get up to get a cocktail at a party without coming back and finding some girl sitting in my chair." Veteran journalist Margaret Carlson caught the worst flak. "She just won't get the hint that he has a girlfriend," Jeri charged, adding, "She calls his apartment all the time. I mean, what is the deal with these women? Don't they have any pride? It's the joke all over Washington that Margaret has this huge crush on him. And Fred is clearly not interested." The situation got nasty enough that the senator himself was forced to step in, issuing a public denial of Jeri's swipes at Carlson. Seven years later, the episode still prompts much tittering around the Beltway. But Jeri may have the last laugh: She wed her reformed Lothario in June 2002 and is today the proud mommy of a four-year-old daughter and a nine-month-old son. And with a little luck (Fred's specialty) and a lot of hard work (her department), she just might wind up First Lady.

Looking back over the sweep of Thompson's life, you get the picture of a nice, decent guy fortunate enough to have had a string of helping hands propel him along the road to success. "Fred's charmed," says Ingram. "I mean, from Lawrence County, which was [back then] a Democratic stronghold, to his relationship with Howard Baker, to representing Marie, to finding himself playing himself in her movie, to asking the pivotal Watergate question about the tapes . . . " Here, Ingram pauses and backtracks a bit to assure me: "He's very serious. He's very thorough. But he's also been at the right place at the right time with charmed results." Far from undercutting his presidential prospects, this laid-back reputation fuels the seductive story line of Thompson as a Natural Born Leader—a man who excels because of his intrinsic worthiness, not any grinding ambition. "It's part of his appeal," says Tennessee Representative John Duncan, co-chair of the "Draft Fred" committee. "I don't think people like people totally obsessed with politics." "He gives the impression of a man who has things in perspective," agrees Richard Land, head of the Southern Baptist Convention's lobbying shop. "It's been my impression that worka-holics don't work out in the White House." In this way, the candi-date is a lot like the man he is auditioning to replace: George W. Bush, who, perhaps more than any president in recent history, tapped the U.S. electorate's distaste for politicians who look like they're trying too hard. "You worry about some guys—Mondale, Gore, Kerry, and in some ways Bush Senior—who spent their entire life wanting to be president," says conservative activist Grover Norquist, head of Americans for Tax Reform. By contrast, he notes, "With Thompson, there's a sense of self-assuredness that Nixon didn't have and that Reagan did."

Ole Fred certainly knows this. Over the years, he has shrewdly cultivated his easygoing image, recognizing the advantages of appearing cool and in control under pressure. As his Watergate co-counsel Sam Dash once told me, "Fred knows how to look laid back when he's not. He'll tell a joke or drawl his voice slowly to make everybody feel he's not under anxiety." In recent months, as his team has quietly scrambled to lay the groundwork for a late entry into the race, Thompson has taken care to project a que sera sera vibe about this whole presidential business. "One advantage you have in not, you know, having this as a lifelong ambition is that if it turns out that your calculation is wrong, it's not the end of the world," he shrugged to Fox News.

As appealing as this laid-back image may be, it should raise some red flags about whether Thompson is enough of a go-getter to go all the way. During his Senate days (and even his Watergate days), Thompson wasn't known for his vigorous work ethic. "You can tell when somebody is going to be here for the long haul" in part by the amount of scut work they put in, says a veteran Democratic Hill staffer. "And Thompson clearly was never going to be a workhorse." The senator himself has long admitted that he found legislative life tedious. "I don't like spending fourteen- and sixteen-hour days voting on 'sense of the Senate' resolutions on irrelevant matters," he once grumbled. "The rap on him always was that he was obviously bored up here," says the Hill staffer. It's not that Thompson is lazy, per se. Rather, he doesn't want to do what he doesn't want to do.

The big question now is to what extent that includes all the grunt work demanded of a presidential candidate. Thompson has never been much of a political animal, and, as his old friend Kirkland notes, raising money has always been particularly "distasteful" to him. Ingram predicted back in May that Thompson will only run "if he believes he can do it differently." And, sure enough, the early rumblings from Team Thompson have focused on his plans to spend less time trudging through the snows of Iowa and New Hampshire and more time blogging, podcasting, and making other creative use of hot new techno-campaign tools. The campaign is plugging the strategy as a more populist approach to politics, allowing Thompson to bypass the biased mainstream media and speak directly to voters—a virtual variation on the red pickup truck. Of course, all his competitors are making similar online efforts. They just consider it a supplement to vigorous on-the-ground campaigning, not a substitute.

As for what sort of strong leadership Thompson would supply once in office, his legislative career offers little insight. Despite his early reformist zeal, Thompson left few footprints during his time on the Hill. And his one significant leadership test, the 1997 campaign finance investigation, is generally regarded as a flop. His attempts to make the hearings less partisan by probing allegations leveled at Republicans as well as at the Clinton-Gore campaign were swiftly undermined by his party's leaders. In the end, Thompson was deemed a well-intentioned chairman shamefully "sandbagged" by both teams—a verdict that may reflect well on his even-handedness and general character, but is hardly a tribute to his leadership skills.

Happily for Thompson, his on-screen record of leadership is more successful—and vastly better known. Indeed, his four-year stint playing District Attorney Arthur Branch on "Law & Order" is arguably his number-one qualification for a presidential run. It's not merely that Thompson's character is a commanding yet avuncular figure; it's that he's an explicitly and appealingly conservative one, a type you don't often find on network television. Within the context of the show, Branch is a down-to-earth, common-sense conservative surrounded by twitchy liberal Manhattan types whom he can lecture about their squeamishness on capital punishment and their ludicrously broad interpretations of the Constitution.

Authoritative but not authoritarian, paternal but not tyrannical, strong but not scary, Branch is, in many ways, the portrait of an ideal conservative. And, in the minds of countless Americans—including many inside the Beltway—Fred Thompson is Arthur Branch. As Bob Novak put it in a column a few months ago, "Sophisticated social conservative activists tell me they . . . are coming to see [Fred] Thompson as the only conservative who can be nominated. Their appreciation of him stems not from his eight years as a U.S. senator from Tennessee but from his role as district attorney of Manhattan on Law & Order." One shudders to think how the unsophisticated activists decide whom to support.

• • •

Reductively speaking, Thompson stands as the Daddy Party's dream Daddy—although a Daddy of a very particular type. Forget the nurturing, "compassionate conservative" model of Bush's 2000 candidacy, which has been roundly discredited on the right. Forget, too, the blustery, "Bring it on!" swagger that W. adopted after September 11, a little-guy machismo one also sees in Rudy Giuliani and John McCain. Thompson's manliness is laconic rather than feisty, a style more John Wayne than Jimmy Cagney. "He's a big man," says Duncan. "He has a way of filling or dominating a room." And, as all of us recall from our schoolyard days, big guys like Thompson don't need to run around picking fights, talking smack, and constantly reminding us of how tough they are because, well, look at them.

Certainly, the Thompson talk in both cyberspace and the traditional media is a study in hero worship, with grown conservatives swooning like cheerleaders smitten over the manliness of the varsity quarterback. There is much rejoicing about the senator's growling voice, his studly cigar habit, and his physical size. My favorite bit of macho Fred-worship making its way around the Internet is a widely circulated joke about the title of the recent film *300*, in which a small troop of Spartans holds the line against the massive Persian army: "If Fred Thompson had been at Thermopylae, the movie would have been called *1*." (Reading posts like this, it's unsurprising that, according to *USA Today*, 64 percent of Thompson's supporters are male, the highest percentage for any presidential hopeful.)

Among more serious journalists, *The Weekly Standard*'s Stephen Hayes has developed a particularly intense man-crush on Thompson, penning a series of breathless valentines about the fledgling campaign, starting with a 6,000-word profile in April that gushed: "As we spoke, I was struck by the fact that Thompson didn't seem to be calibrating his answers for a presidential run. On issue after contentious issue, I got the sense from both his manner and the answer he gave me that he was just speaking extemporaneously." Nor is it only the conservative media getting high on the smell of testosterone. The creepiest musings about Thompson's "sex appeal" thus far have come from NBC's Chris Matthews, the machismo-obsessed id of the Washington media, who recently cooed: "Can you smell the English leather on this guy, the Aqua Velva, the sort of mature man's shaving cream, or whatever, you know, after he shaved? Do you smell that sort of—a little bit of cigar smoke?"

More adolescent members of the chattering class, meanwhile, have taken to drooling over Mrs. Thompson, whose penchant for low-cut, form-fitting ensembles already has buttoned-down political types buzzing. MSNBC's Joe Scarborough recently created a stir when he and guest analyst Craig Crawford of *Congressional Quarterly* indulged in some lascivious speculation about whether the curvaceous Jeri's fitness regime makes use of a stripper's pole. Tacky as the comments were, they were essentially envious. "That's what a Hollywood career will do for you!" enthused Crawford.

Inevitably, with his official entry into the race, Thompson will lose a little luster as he morphs from above-the-fray candidate-in-waiting to flesh-and-blood (not to mention bloodied) combatant. Still, the lure of his manly charms should not be underestimated. As Bob Davis, a former Thompson staffer now chairing the Tennessee Republican Party, puts it, "When you put your children to bed at night, and you're laying your head down on your pillow, this is a guy people would trust to protect their backside no matter what happened."

This is an especially potent lure with the Republican Party feeling so lost and fragile. Just last month, former Thompson sweetie Lorrie Morgan predicted to the *Sunday Times* of London that Thompson will prove irresistible to women voters: "He's majestic. He's a soft, safe place to be, and that could be Fred's ticket. Women love a soft place to lay and a strong pair of hands to hold us." Team Thompson is betting that, these days, the same may be said of the entire GOP.

Sam Brownback

Full Name Samuel Dale Brownback

Current Residence Topeka, Kansas

Date and Place of Birth September 12, 1956; Garnett, Kansas

Education

B.S., Kansas State University, 1979

J.D., University of Kansas, 1982

Military Service

None

Nonpolitical Positions Held

Practicing attorney, 1982–1986

Author, *Building a Healthy Culture: Strategies for an American Renaissance,* 2001

Political Offices Held

Kansas Secretary of Agriculture, 1986–1993

U.S. Representative from Kansas, 1995–1996

U.S. Senator from Kansas, 1996–present

Family

Married to Mary Brownback; children: daughters Elizabeth, Abby, and Jenna (adopted) and sons Andy and Mark

---

The Many Conversions of Sam Brownback:
The Apostle *Noam Scheiber*

I t's a Tuesday in mid-October 2005, and Kansas Senator Sam Brownback is chairing a meeting of a little-known but highly influential Senate group called the Values Action Team (VAT). Think of it as a PTA board for the vast right-wing conspiracy: The Concerned Women for America has a standing invitation, as do the Family Research Council, the U.S. Conference of Catholic Bishops, and the National Right to Life Committee. The activists sit around a conference table in the Capitol building and plot strategy on matters like broadcast decency, Internet gambling, and anti-abortion legislation.

Typically, the group's weekly meetings draw 50 to 75 conservative activists. Today, however, there are well over 100 people crowded into the stately room. It's been two weeks since George W. Bush named Harriet Miers to fill a Supreme Court vacancy, and the nomination has flagged. So much so that, in the days before this meeting, the White House has readied plans for a renewed push. Brownback has long stated his opposition to Miers, but, as a gesture of goodwill, he's invited former Senator Dan Coats, Miers's steward on the Hill, to appear before the group. The activists are, if anything, even less generous than Brownback. Many have turned up just to watch the poor man squirm.

Coats makes the case for Miers as best he can: She was a managing partner of a big Texas firm. She'll be a reliable vote for the things you believe in. Then someone pipes up with an ominously simple question: Why did the president nominate Miers in the first place? Coats pauses for a moment before allowing, "I think neither the White House nor the members of the Senate wanted to make a nomination that would start a culture war." Wrong answer! "Everyone in that room, they are the culture war," Manny Miranda, one of the conservatives at the meeting, recalls thinking. The activists are furious. Several fume that Coats doesn't understand how judicial fights have changed in the years since he left the Hill.

Minutes pass before Brownback invokes an implicit slaughter rule. "Well, Dan, you've got some good feedback you can take back to the White House for when they choose their next nominee," he says. Though he is painstakingly polite, it appears he has just pronounced the Miers nomination dead. The activists look at one another and scratch their heads. Can he really do that? Belatedly, Brownback picks up on the implication of his statement and offers a qualification: "Of course, I don't mean that's going to happen any time soon."

Of all the GOP presidential contenders who could claim to have benefited from the recent midterm elections, Brownback may be the one for whom it is most true. For years, the social conservatives who brought down Miers have been having a fierce intramural debate on the merits of pragmatism versus purity. In the run-up to 2000, they resolved that debate in favor of the former, and the movement threw its support behind George W. Bush over conservative long shots like John Ashcroft and Gary Bauer. But, now, conservatives appear to have the worst of both worlds: Six years of disappointments on issues like abortion and gay marriage have resulted in a midterm rout and a lame-duck presidency. Purity is looking more attractive by the day.

Brownback is closing in on a decade as the leading social conservative in the U.S. Senate. He has impeccable credentials on issues like judges, abortion, and gay marriage. (And, for that matter, any combination of the three: He has threatened to hold up the nomination of a Michigan judge because she once attended a lesbian commitment ceremony.) And Brownback's leadership of the VAT gives him extraordinary day-to-day influence over the Senate's social conservative agenda.

There are crasser considerations, too. Brownback was an evangelical Christian before he converted to Catholicism. Iowa has large populations of both. Brownback's home in Topeka is a four-hour drive from Des Moines, giving him as close to a natural foothold in the state as any GOP contender will have. And, as a long-serving state agriculture secretary and former Future Farmers of America official, Brownback is as fluent in the language of ethanol subsidies and biodiesel production as any politician reared outside Iowa. Put this together, and you have a guy who could theoretically take one of the top two spots in the state's first-in-the-nation caucuses. With the Internet's track record of making juggernauts out of grassroots icons, even a third-place finish could give Brownback an E-Z Pass lane straight through to the final stages of the race. If everything breaks right, and social conservatives are particularly aggrieved over their party's standard bearer, Brownback could end up on the national ticket.

Brownback, in other words, is on the brink. He is savvy. He is righteous. He is committed. He would appear to have been born for this moment in politics. But looks can be deceiving, because birth is not at all how Brownback came by his place in the conservative cosmos. As recently as 1994, the year of his first campaign for Congress, Brownback was a member in good standing of the moderate Republican establishment. But, by the time he arrived in Congress that fall, he was emitting so much anti-government zeal he gave Newt Gingrich the willies. Within two years, Brownback had another epiphany, from which he emerged as a crusader for Christian causes.

Which raises a question for conservatives mulling a Brownback candidacy: Has the Kansas senator been finding himself? Or has he been finding himself a way to run for president?

In mid-October, I trailed Brownback through the Republican precincts of northwestern Iowa. The first stop was an unexpectedly frou-frou bistro in a town called Spirit Lake, where some 50 locals showed up for partisan red meat. What they got was more like mixed greens. Brownback opened with a riff about growing up in the "suburbs" of tiny Parker, Kansas, where his parents still mind a 1,400-acre farm. It took him several minutes to even mention Nancy Pelosi. When he finally did, he felt compelled to stipulate that "she represents her district well."

All in all, it sounded a lot like the way I imagine the young Sam Brownback sounded: humble, warm, gracious—and moderate. My mind drifted to a story I'd heard from Tim Golba, a former president of Kansans for Life, who'd met with Brownback in 1994 to discuss a possible primary endorsement. According to Golba, it quickly became clear that there was little to discuss. Brownback was not only unfamiliar with the anti-abortion lexicon, he had a habit of dropping the hints used by politicians on the other side. "I think you'll find me more in line with the view of Nancy Kassebaum," he told Golba, who still grumbles at the mention of the famously moderate Kansas senator.

For the most part, though, it's not the continuity between the young Brownback and today's Brownback that is striking: It's the change. Because the longer Brownback goes on, the more you sense a distinct lack of passion for standard Iowa fare like agriculture policy or the budget. Compared with the previous speaker, local Congressman Steve King, he's not even worked up about Iraq. What Sam Brownback clearly wants to talk about—what he thinks people need to know about—are the issues you might store in a mental file called "Judgment Day." The Judgment Day file begins with standard culture-war causes like gay marriage and abortion. But it is a sprawling file, and, before long, it sprawls to such far-flung locales as Sudan and the Congo, where Brownback wants to stop genocide and human trafficking. "We're a great nation," Brownback says. His voice is still composed, but now there's a firmness that wasn't there before. "And I believe, in my heart, that for our greatness to continue, our goodness must continue."

It is a long journey, this trip from heartland moderate to Judgment Day conservative. The crowd at Spirit Lake isn't entirely sure what to make of it. The self-deprecating comments, they can laugh at. The partisan comments, they can cheer. But this culture-war stuff. This Africa stuff. . . . I am seated next to a group of local businessmen, including two with name tags that read BANK MIDWEST. A few minutes ago, they were sporting Chamber of Commerce grins and clapping Chamber of Commerce claps. Now they just stare ahead, blankly.

There is a final thing you notice about Sam Brownback these days. The early accounts all depict a young man in a hurry. When he began high school, Brownback had—not quite a speech impediment, but a tendency to garble his words. He spent his afternoons working with a teacher named Marvin Creager until the tic had surrendered to his will. During his senior year, Brownback won a standing ovation at the state Future Farmers of America convention, where the delegates made him their president. When he applied for an internship at the local radio station in college, the station's manager, Ralph Titus, asked whether Brownback planned to go into broadcasting. "He said, 'No, I'm going to be president of the United States,'" recalls Titus. "I laughed. He did not."

It was a pattern that continued throughout early adulthood. "You always got the impression he was studying, prepping," says Will Gunn, who met Brownback when they were White House Fellows in the early '90s. The day Bob Dole resigned his Senate seat in 1996, a seat Brownback would soon claim, the freshman congressman strode into the chamber and schmoozed his future colleagues so extravagantly that the chamber had to be gaveled to order.

But, when Brownback sidles up to me and introduces himself after his remarks, what strikes me most is his calm. Truth be told, it is a little unsettling. There are too many silences, and the silences are too long. They goad you into filling them with small eruptions of chatter. I am, in fact, halfway through a mini-autobiography when Brownback looks down. My Israeli first name has piqued his interest, and he is taking a minute to reflect. Brownback is wearing a tweedy blazer and gray-green khakis. There is no tie around his neck, and his shoes evoke a recent trip to the Timberland outlet store. From a distance, I had mostly noticed his dark hair and trim, athletic build. This makes it all the more jarring to survey the deep grooves in his face.

When Brownback looks up, his hazel eyes have narrowed. He appears to be staring simultaneously at me and 30 feet behind me, if such a thing is possible. "It's a shame that country has always got to defend itself like that," he finally says, so softly I can barely hear him. Judgment Day may be here sooner than you think.

I have come to Manhattan, Kansas, to figure out how Sam Brownback took the critical first step from moderate to conservative, and I feel myself getting close when Dixie Roberts walks into a café and extends her hand. Roberts is a petite grandmother with frizzy black hair, stiletto heels, and bright pink lipstick. For years, she has enjoyed unofficial status in this university town as a kind of campus Mama. She put two sons through Kansas State and has amassed enough of her own credits to qualify as a junior. "Political science," she tells me.

Roberts has known Brownback since his 1978 term as student body president, when he told the *Kansas State Collegian* that his goals included a local mass transit system and a legislative network to convey students' concerns directly to state lawmakers. After law school at the University of Kansas, Brownback moved back to Manhattan to work at a small but politically connected firm, a job that eventually led to his appointment as state agricultural secretary. Roberts still gets wistful for the Brownback of this vintage. He was a mainline Protestant in those days, and when Brownback's current worldview comes up in our conversation, she scoffs slightly, then worries she's committed a faux pas: "You don't believe in that stuff, do you?"

When Brownback ran for Congress in 1994, Roberts held a seat in his kitchen cabinet. But, shortly after his primary victory, Roberts walked away and promised herself she wouldn't be back. Now she's offered to drive me to the place where it first dawned on her that Brownback had changed.

Ten minutes later, we've parked in front of the Little Apple Brewery, a local dive with a wood façade and a green awning. Roberts marches me back to an enclosed room toward the rear of the establishment. With the exception of the Southwestern décor, the room is mostly as Roberts remembers it. The Brownback campaign had called a meeting to thank supporters and begin planning for the general election. Brownback himself wasn't in attendance, but his campaign chairman, a former K-State dean named C. Clyde Jones, was there, as were other advisers.

Roberts was already seated when she noticed about a dozen of them enter the room—a group of local anti-abortion activists she'd never seen around the campaign. "It was like an army had come in," she says. "They just took over the meeting." It took all the composure Roberts could muster not to head straight for the door. She sat through the entire event feeling like the wind had been knocked out of her. When she got home, she called C. Clyde to tell him she was out.

To understand what happened, you have to start with Brownback's challenger in the GOP primary, a Manhattan chemical salesman named Bob Bennie. Everything you knew about Bennie told you his campaign would be a joke. He'd never run for office in his life. No one in Manhattan—much less the rest of the district—had ever heard of him. And he had no money to speak of. Just about the only thing Bennie had going for him was the early tremors of a political earthquake.

Up until 1991, Kansans for Life (KFL) had mostly restricted its activism to "citizen lobbying": They would show up in Topeka and buttonhole their representatives. But, despite the group's growing strength, passing legislation proved futile. "The leadership would always make promises, and then nothing happened," recalls Golba, the organization's then-president. That's when Golba realized it would be easier to change the politicians than to change the policies. He hired a savvy former legislator named David Miller to organize his ground troops and placed moderate Republicans in his crosshairs. The plan succeeded beyond all expectations. In 1992, KFL stunned the local political establishment by electing ten conservative representatives. One of the new state reps, a carpet-layer named Jene Vickrey, upset the speaker of the Kansas House.

Brownback's opponent, Bennie, was about as pro-life as you could get without earning yourself a restraining order. He had no trouble winning the KFL endorsement. This, in turn, formed the backbone of his campaign strategy. In every tiny Kansas town Bennie rolled into, dozens of KFL activists would turn up: 25 people in Erie (population 1,200); 50 in Burlington (population 2,700)—all of them to see a no-name with no chance of winning. After Bennie charged through his stump speech, the activists would fan out along the local streets, distributing literature and planting yard signs. It was like having a political operation thousands of workers strong.

From Brownback's perspective, it was also a nightmare. Before the congressional race, Brownback had never really had to justify his abortion views. Now he was getting an earful practically every time he stumped for a vote. There were days when it looked like the whole thing might slip away.

Then, as primary day approached, Bennie noticed a change in his opponent's language. Brownback never used to mention abortion on the campaign trail. Now he was publicly pronouncing himself an abortion opponent. When primary day rolled around in early August, Bennie ran up an impressive 36 percent of the vote to Brownback's 48. But he was still furious, believing Brownback had swiped the nomination by aping his positions. "I knew how I stood," he told me. "I didn't know how he stood."

It was a fair question. Four days before the vote, the local *Manhattan Mercury* had endorsed Brownback as a "moderate" who "displays a solid grasp of complex issues such as health care and foreign trade." The paper's editor-in-chief had known Brownback for years.

The Gingrich Revolution swept 73 new Republicans into office in November 1994, and being a freshman felt like standing at the center of the universe. Foreign leaders inquired about addressing the new class. K Street eminences turned up to offer advice.

Ideologically, Brownback was typical of his new colleagues. He strongly opposed abortion and had an abiding faith in God. But, most of all, he felt that big government in Washington was out of control. The idea of reining it in made him too excited to sleep.

Like any revolutionary junta—or, for that matter, any high school class—the freshmen needed a president. Brownback threw himself into the race. Between December, when the freshmen showed up for orientation, and the day of the vote in February, the field narrowed to two candidates: Brownback and a mild-mannered Mississippian named Roger Wicker. Wicker eked out a narrow victory largely because he didn't appear to be angling for the job. This forced Brownback to fall back on plan B. He'd been part of an informal group called the New Federalists since arriving in Washington. Now he installed himself as their leader.

Under Brownback, the New Federalists became a vanguard of about 25 House members, the purest of the pure. They churned out bills abolishing four Cabinet departments. They demanded huge cuts in congressional staff. They clamored for term limits and tossed around constitutional amendments the way most people edit a grocery list. Whatever it took to strip power from Washington, the New Federalists were prepared to do it.

The Cabinet departments never did get shuttered. Nor did the other items on the New Federalist agenda gain much traction. Instead, Brownback and his colleagues became the House's self-appointed enforcers. When, for example, the Clinton administration balked at the GOP's proposed spending and tax cuts, the New Federalists agitated for a shutdown. After the shutdown proved a p.r. fiasco, and the House leadership caved, Brownback was disappointed but not disillusioned. Then-Florida Representative Joe Scarborough remembers Brownback consoling him on the House floor in early 1996: "Sam came up and put his hand on my shoulder. He said, 'Don't worry, Joe. Even Rome wasn't burnt in a day.' "

That summer, Brownback challenged Sheila Frahm for the Republican nomination for Senate. Frahm was the lieutenant governor of Kansas and the epitome of moderate Republicanism. The state's governor was about to install her in the seat Dole had vacated to run for president when Brownback announced his candidacy. On the airwaves, Brownback attacked Frahm as a shiftless tax-raiser. At the grassroots level, he deployed the boundless energy of the anti-abortion movement. The old divide in Kansas politics had been geographic: the rural hinterlands versus a relatively populous enclave in the northeast. Frahm hailed from a prominent farming family in western Kansas, and—thanks to her years as a legislator in Topeka—she seemed known enough in the northeast to limit Brownback's native-son advantage. "I remember we were in Topeka when the [local] results came in. He had won, but I thought he hadn't won by enough," recalls Trent Ledoux, a former Frahm adviser. But the old geographic model had been obliterated. Brownback ran up huge margins across most of the state and then sailed to victory in the general.

Despite the triumph, Brownback was privately reeling. In August 1995, he'd noticed a small lump on his torso. The tumor was treatable with surgery, but cancer is cancer, and it has a way of focusing the mind. Brownback was participating in a weekly evangelical prayer group in Washington. But his newfound religiosity didn't calm his nerves; it only agitated them. Brownback couldn't stop wondering what he would have had to show for his life if this hadn't been a false alarm.

When Brownback arrived in the Senate, he sought a meeting with Chuck Colson, the Watergate felon turned born-again Christian. Officially, Colson ran the Prison Fellowship Ministries, an evangelical group that ministered to prisoners. Unofficially, he was the dean of the growing compassionate conservative movement. Brownback told Colson he wanted to put the "positive side" of his Christian faith to work in the Senate. The two men talked at length about how that might happen. Eventually, Colson mentioned William Wilberforce, the devoutly Christian English parliamentarian who had spearheaded the country's anti-slavery movement during the late eighteenth century. Colson encouraged Brownback to adopt Wilberforce as his model of Christian praxis.

Brownback began to read. Religiously. He devoured biographies of Wilberforce. Aides noticed how the boss would carry a copy of C. S. Lewis's *Screwtape Letters* everywhere he traveled. He delved into Daniel Patrick Moynihan's writings on politics and culture. People who knew Brownback during this time talk of metaphysical change. "I've had a sense that his faith has gotten stronger every year he's been in Congress," says former Democratic Representative Tony Hall, who regularly prayed with Brownback. Colson describes it as a "spiritual maturing."

The coup de grâce came later that year. At the time, Brownback was serving as chairman of the subcommittee that oversees Washington, D.C. David Kensinger, Brownback's longtime campaign manager and political Svengali, remembers when he and the senator noticed that the number of abortions in the District consistently rivaled the number of live births and that the vast majority of these mothers were unmarried. A little algebra revealed that only one in every six pregnancies ended with a married woman bringing a child to term. It was a jaw-dropping statistic. "You can do the flat tax, you can do school choice," says Kensinger. "But until you fix that, you're not going to fix what's wrong with D.C."

Brownback was done being a Gingrich Revolutionary. He sat down with Paul Ryan, his then-chief of staff, and told him as much. "It's one thing to introduce legislation to cut taxes, like 50 other members of the Senate. It's another thing to make a material difference in this country, or in Africa," says Ryan. "No one else was doing this, fighting the culture war. . . . That's the calculation he made."

Topeka Bible Church (TBC) occupies a multi-level, gray stone building in a racially mixed neighborhood of urban Topeka. Around the corner is a pair of apartment complexes that screams service-economy transience. A couple blocks away, a sign advertises Discount Smokes and Convenience Store.

When I ask Jim Congdon, the church's pastor, why TBC never relocated to the exurbs, he seems wearied by the question. Congdon is a trim, bearded man in his fifties, with cheeks you could store acorns in. He tells me he has considered moving out to the western edge of town, where much of his congregation now lives. But, each time, the tug of the old neighborhood wins out. "I just feel like it's good for us to stay here. I think that helps our congregation be more diverse," he says. Tomorrow, Congdon and 50 TBC volunteers will spend the day painting and mulching a nearby elementary school.

Sitting in Congdon's cluttered office, listening to his reflections on race and urban blight, you want to tell your secular friends that this whole culture-war thing is a huge misunderstanding. We can all go home now. But there is a sharper edge to Congdon's evangelicalism, and it can creep up on you in an instant.

Congdon's Sunday sermon, for example, is a meditation on the proper mindset for a Christian when Christ descends from heaven. This turns out to be highly relevant, because the current turbulence in the Middle East signifies that the end times are near. "For the first time in 40 years, an Israeli prime minister is worried about being annihilated," Congdon observes. One of the bigger divides among evangelicals is between pre- and post-millennialists. The post-millennialists believe Christ will only return after peace reigns on Earth. The pre-millennialists believe the apocalypse will usher in the messiah's return. Congdon, it turns out, is a pre-millennialist with an itchy trigger finger.

Once the service ends, I spot Brownback chatting up a woman manning a voter registration booth in the lobby. He's wearing a blue knit sweater and looking better rested than he did in Iowa. He invites me to join him at a reception for the outgoing youth pastor, and we make friendly banter while his two adopted children crawl all over him. From time to time I lose sight of eight-year-old Mark, only to see a small pair of legs emerge from between Brownback's arm and waist, at which point the senator gets to work retying a pair of white "Shaq" high-tops. (There are five Brownback children in all.)

After about ten minutes, a tallish woman in a sherbet-green outfit buttonholes Brownback, husband in tow. The woman gushes about how she prays for him every day and how lucky Kansans are to have a senator like him. She is the kind of excitable busybody you expect to find in every congregation, a big vacuum cleaner of opinions who repackages them as her own. Now she's off on a rant about how the press opposes President Bush because he's a Republican and a Christian. Before long, she's talking about Iraq, then the first Gulf War, then on to a lament about the attention span of our "microwave society." Finally it's back to the liberal media. "Well," Brownback says consolingly, "they have the newspapers and TV, but we have radio." The woman is, if not exactly appeased, at least out of material. "That's all I listen to is radio," she says.

As she's leaving, Brownback turns to me and explains his theory of red-state/blue-state relations. People who live in Red America know plenty about Blue America. They often work in large cities, or they travel to them on vacation, or they hear about them through popular culture. But the opposite is almost never true. "If they"—the people in Blue America—"travel at all," Brownback says, "they go abroad, like to Europe or Tokyo." I can't say for sure, but I think he is paying me a compliment.

In 2001, Brownback led a Senate delegation to the Vatican to award the Pope a Congressional Gold Medal. The group was bipartisan—in addition to Brownback, Catholic Republicans like Rick Santorum and Bob Smith of New Hampshire came along, as did Barbara Mikulski, a Maryland Democrat. The highlight of the trip was the Pope's private receiving line. Brownback would introduce each senator to John Paul II, and the three would chat privately for a few minutes. When it was Smith's turn, Brownback turned to the Pope and said, "This is Senator Bob Smith of New Hampshire. He's the leading pro-life advocate in the U.S. Senate." Smith then returned the favor. "The man sitting next to you has done more than his fair share," he said. Brownback was beaming.

Brownback's conversion the following year made him both a Catholic and a member of the rarefied flock of John McCloskey, priest to Washington's conservative establishment. McCloskey had previously converted conservative journalists Bob Novak and Larry Kudlow, and Brownback's "sponsor" was his fellow senator, Santorum. As with most secret societies, the accounts of Brownback's admission to this circle are remarkably thin. No one describes it as much more than a "quiet ceremony" officiated by McCloskey in a K Street chapel.

Even those closest to Brownback remain in the dark on the matter. When I asked Kensinger the reason his longtime boss converted, he told me simply, "I don't know." Will Gunn, a retired Air Force colonel who had met Brownback in the early '90s, was even more mystified. On Memorial Day weekend in 2002, Gunn had traveled to Brownback's home in Topeka for a reunion of their White House Fellows class. It turned out to be an extremely intimate gathering. All of the fellows had gone on to jobs with unrelenting schedules, and so, of the twelve alumni, only three could make the trip. Gunn arrived to find the senator and his wife, Mary, disarmingly down to earth. For dinner, the guests caught fish out of a backyard pond, which Brownback dutifully cleaned. By day, the families played pickup basketball; by night, they went dancing at a local honky-tonk club. On Sunday morning, Gunn, who is also an evangelical Christian, attended church with the Brownbacks.

Gunn and Brownback have been close ever since. They get together every two or three months to have dinner and talk about their obligations as fathers and believers and the role of Jesus Christ in their lives. Brownback once told Gunn he's in Washington because he believes the Lord wants him to be there. And yet, amazingly, Gunn says he didn't know about Brownback's conversion until he read about it in the newspaper several years later.

What we do know is that Brownback had taken a passing interest in Catholicism as early as 1997, when he teamed up with Ted Kennedy to arrange a Congressional Gold Medal for Mother Teresa. In the process, he'd begun reading up on Catholic teaching, including the writings of John Paul II. Brownback is what you might call a God geek. He is endlessly fascinated by all things religious. "If it's a spiritual thing, he loves it," says Congdon,

Brownback's pastor at TBC, where he still attends service after Mass most Sundays. Not surprisingly, Brownback's crash course on Catholicism seemed to stick with him. "It started working in the background," Kensinger speculates. "If these people are who they are, and I want to have a soul more like theirs, what helped them to become more like they are?"

Things proceeded in this vein for years. Paul Ryan, now a representative from Wisconsin, served as Brownback's chief of staff through his early days in the Senate. Long after he left the job, Ryan, who is Catholic, would periodically get calls from his former boss. The two men would talk about Catholic doctrine and the intellectual foundations of Catholicism. Over time, these musings began to fill out the gaps in Brownback's religious worldview. "I just think he found an articulation of the Christian faith in the Catholic tradition that he felt was more fully developed," says Brownback's friend Deal Hudson, a fellow convert and former Catholic outreach adviser to the Bush White House.

There are less flattering explanations as well. Brownback had always had a weakness for elite societies. He applied twice to be a White House Fellow before being admitted. When he got to Congress, *Rolling Stone* has reported, he sought admission to a small "cell" overseen by "The Fellowship," an organization of evangelical elites. Catholicism in general, and McCloskey's flock in particular, may have been just another upscale fraternity to pledge.

Nor is it easy to ignore how Brownback's conversion has given him a beachhead in each of the two most powerful communities on the religious right. Even Congdon concedes there was some skepticism in the pews of TBC when news of the conversion made the rounds. "I fielded a lot of questions from suspicious people who thought that was just a political conversion," he says.

A generation ago, being Catholic would have been a clear liability in certain evangelical quarters. But, over the last 20 years, conservative Catholic and evangelical groups have forged a semi-official alliance, evocatively dubbed "co-belligerency," to help advance their shared political agenda. Kensinger says Team Brownback has no idea how the senator's conversion will play among evangelicals, but there's clearly a hope that it will net him the best of both worlds—a candidate who can address each group in its own language.

Political or not, Brownback's path to Catholicism appears to have motivated his broadening interest in human rights. In the years since September 11, Brownback has taken on more or less the entire Republican Party in a fight to protect the rights of political refugees, not exactly a popular crusade in the middle of the war on terrorism. In recent years, Brownback has even begun a very public reconsideration of his support for the death penalty. At a hearing earlier this year, Brownback solicited testimony from families of victims on both sides of the issue. Afterward, a *Kansas City Star* reporter asked which stance he found more compelling. Brownback wouldn't say, but he noted how the death penalty supporters looked angry and "hard." "In Christian theology, the burden is on the person who has not forgiven," he said.

Then there is the immigration issue, which is either a colossal political miscalculation or the policy equivalent of Catholic self-flagellation. In 2005, Brownback signed on as a co-sponsor to the relatively moderate Kennedy-McCain bill. The reaction from rank-and-file Republicans has not been kind. Steve Scheffler, the head of a conservative evangelical group in Iowa, told me, "The biggest thing [Brownback would] have to address is why did he vote for that horrendous bill?" Kensinger says Brownback's answer is simple: "The Bible says you will be judged by how you treat the

widow, the orphan, the foreign among you. That's the end of it."
He believes the key is how Brownback manages his position—not
the position itself. But Chuck Hurley, a Brownback law school
classmate who runs the influential Iowa Family Policy Center, has
hinted a shift could be in the works. "I understand he's been doing
some consulting about that issue," Hurley told me conspiratori-
ally, citing an upcoming meeting with a local anti-immigration
politician.

So just who, exactly, is Sam Brownback? Answering that question is difficult, but it helps to go back to the beginning of his
political career and to a woman named Kim Smith. A longtime
conservative activist, Smith is the kind of person whose name
inspires shifty eyes and labored euphemisms in a small town like
Manhattan, Kansas. When I mentioned her to Dixie Roberts, she
hemmed and hawed, then told me that Smith's sons "had always
been in trouble" and that she found Smith's constant preaching a
little tough to take. "Here you are, espousing all these religious
views, and someone has a troubled personal life," she sighed,
before hastening to add, "we've always been friends."

Smith had been one of Bob Bennie's most loyal supporters during the 1994 GOP primary. She shared his "out there" views on
abortion and had derided Brownback as an operator. "Sam, like so
many others, was just a 'good ole guy' and abortion was a nasty
subject you didn't talk about," Smith recently wrote me. Smith
seemed to derive a sadistic pleasure from making Brownback
sweat. One of her sons worked at a Christian radio station and
would receive updates on his public appearances. Smith made a
point of dispatching activists to these events to hector him about
abortion.

But, by the end of the primary, Brownback had started to gener-
ate favorable chatter in Smith's circles. She decided to meet him in

person. Smith watched the way Brownback treated his family. She grilled his longtime scheduler about what he was like to work for. And, most important of all, she opened a long, anguished dialogue with him on abortion. Smith told Brownback how, back in the mid-'70s, she had terminated a six-week-old pregnancy. She was 19 and didn't have a high school diploma or marketable skills. She showed up at a Planned Parenthood clinic with dozens of questions, only to be given what she says was a "high-pressure sales job," to which she acceded. "It was the most devastating decision I have ever made," she wrote me.

Brownback was shocked to hear that abortion was so prevalent, that a 14-year-old girl could have an abortion without her parents knowing, and that the procedure was legal up to the minute of birth (which is not, in fact, true). He had never even heard of a technique called partial-birth abortion. After a few weeks of this, Smith got in touch with Golba and the other leaders of the local pro-life movement. She told them that Brownback had become an ally in their cause. She felt so strongly about this, she said, that she was ready to vouch for him personally.

By the time Brownback and Golba met again, it was obvious that he had changed. Brownback had been a mild-mannered Methodist at the outset of the campaign. Now, as a result of his conversations with Smith and Robert Tyson (Brownback's former Sunday school teacher), he had begun to opine on the abortion issue with a religious sense of purpose. "His talk was completely different," says Golba. "We felt an honesty. . . . I could tell he knew the issue; he had studied it. We felt that's where his heart was."

A few years later, Brownback's old primary opponent, Bob Bennie, received an invitation to a breakfast in Omaha, Nebraska, featuring a local gubernatorial candidate. A Christian men's organization had sponsored the event, and Bennie—who had since relocated to nearby Lincoln—was just "filling a seat at a table." Then he realized he knew the keynote speaker: Sam Brownback. Brownback's remarks were unusually personal—really more of a testimonial than a speech. He talked largely about the spiritual change he'd undergone during his first congressional campaign. Bennie had been livid over what he'd seen as Brownback's insincere positioning on abortion. But at the breakfast, he told me, it was obvious that "he'd had a change of heart in the way he thought about things." When Brownback finished, Bennie stood off to the side as the other men filed by. Finally the senator turned and recognized him. "Bob," he said, holding out his hand. But Bennie wasn't in a handshaking mood. He walked up to Brownback and the two men embraced.

Newt Gingrich

Full Name Newton Leroy Gingrich

Current Residence McLean, Virginia

Date and Place of Birth June 17, 1943; Harrisburg, Pennsylvania

Education

    B.A., Emory University, 1965

    M.A., Ph.D., Tulane University, 1968 and 1971

Military Service

    None

Nonpolitical Positions Held

Teacher of History and Environmental Studies, West Georgia
    College, 1970–1978

News and political analyst, Fox News Channel, 1999–present

Founder, Gingrich Group, 1999–present

Distinguished Visiting Fellow, Hoover Institution at Stanford
    University, 1999–present

Honorary Chairman, NanoBusiness Alliance, 2000–present

Founder, Center for Health Transformation, 2003–present

Senior Fellow at American Enterprise Institute, present

Author of nine books, both fiction and non-fiction

Political Offices Held

    U.S. Representative from Georgia, 1978–1999

    Speaker of the House of Representatives, 1995–1999

Family

    Married to Callista Bilek; previously married to Marianne Ginther and Jackie Battley; children: daughters Kathy and Jackie with Battley

---

Cogito Ergo Sum Newt: The Thinker

Jason Zengerle

Who's that gray-haired guy in there with the monkeys and the Kennedy?"

It's a hot, humid summer afternoon at Providence's Roger Williams Park Zoo, and a young woman is asking about the enthusiastic gentleman who, along with Rhode Island Representative Patrick Kennedy, is behind the glass wall feeding mealworms to the white-faced saki monkeys. Kennedy, who is only a couple of weeks removed from an embarrassing stint in drug rehab, has the sheepish look of a man who would rather be somewhere—anywhere—else. But his silver-haired companion is having the time of his life. Wearing a squinty-eyed smile, his ample belly protruding over his belt and the white mop atop his head charmingly mussed, he holds out a palm filled with mealworms and watches the monkeys go to town. When his hand is emptied of the slimy treats, he turns to a zookeeper and asks for more. It's just another day in the life of former House Speaker Newt Gingrich—once the second-most powerful politician in the United States, but now just some guy feeding monkeys at the zoo.

The zoo trip, needless to say, was Gingrich's idea—his treat for appearing with Kennedy earlier in the day to give a bipartisan talk about health care at a business conference. It's not that Gingrich minds talking about health care; he just loves going to zoos. The Providence zoo, Gingrich eagerly tells its director, is the seventy-fifth or seventy-sixth zoo he's visited. In fact, before he decided to become an academic and then a politician, Gingrich confesses, he wanted to be a zookeeper.

As the zoo director leads Gingrich and Kennedy on a tour of the facilities, it's difficult not to wonder whether Gingrich made the wrong career choice. While Kennedy—who is dressed appropriately for the oppressive weather in a polo shirt and khaki shorts but still looks miserable—occasionally chimes in with an unconvincing "Isn't that the coolest?," Gingrich, who is sweating in suit pants and an Oxford shirt, asks questions that betray a startling degree of zoological expertise. How big does a flamingo herd have to be before the birds begin breeding? Are larger kangaroos as aggressive among themselves as wallabies? Does the zoo have "roar & snore" nights, when it allows visitors to sleep over? For more than an hour, Gingrich peppers the zoo director with such queries, stopping only to offer his own insights. "That's the darkest Masai I've ever seen," he marvels as he stands outside the giraffe enclosure.

Finally, it's time for Gingrich to leave, and, as he steps into a silver Lincoln Town Car, the zoo director shakes his hand, looking happy but also a bit dazed. (Most VIP visitors, he will later explain, aren't that interested in the zoo.) And then Gingrich is off to do the things he does when he's not conducting fact-finding zoological missions: writing books, giving $50,000-a-pop speeches, running his health care consulting business, offering the Bush administration advice on the war on terrorism, and, oh yes, laying the groundwork for his 2008 presidential campaign.

That's right, Newt Gingrich is running for president. Granted, he's not yet an official candidate, and, if you ask him whether he's running, he—like virtually everyone eyeing the White House this early in the process—will deny it. But, as soon as that denial leaves his lips, Gingrich, unlike other presidential candidates, will not-so-subtly undercut it—inviting you, for instance, to ask him again in August, when he'll be in Iowa glad-handing at the state fair. Because, as Gingrich himself seems to realize, the notion that he is running for president is, at least at first glance, unbelievable.

After all, it has been almost eight years since Gingrich last held elected office, and he didn't exactly leave on his own terms, resigning as speaker and from Congress after overseeing the Republicans' disastrous performance in the 1998 midterm elections. His time out of office has been similarly inglorious. Shortly after slinking off the political stage, Gingrich, who had mercilessly hounded Bill Clinton about the Monica Lewinsky scandal, went through marital difficulties of his own—ditching his second wife for the woman who would eventually become his third, a congressional aide 23 years his junior. More significantly, Gingrich has spent the last few years impotently watching from the sidelines as his crowning achievement, the 1994 Republican Revolution, succumbed to decadence and corruption, and many of the men whom Gingrich played a key role in bringing to prominence and power—men like Tom DeLay and Jack Abramoff—became poster children for political corruption. Suffice it to say, these are not the items of which presidential resumés are made.

And yet, were it not for these misfortunes, it's doubtful that the 63-year-old Gingrich would be contemplating the White House at all. First, there is the not insignificant matter of personal redemption: A presidential campaign, even an unsuccessful one, would go a long way toward erasing the bad memories of Gingrich's rushed and gloomy exit from the House. It would afford Gingrich the opportunity to defend the legacy of the 1994 Republican Revolution and rescue it from the grubby paws of people like DeLay and Abramoff, who, to some extent, have replaced Gingrich as the faces of that revolution.

More importantly, running for president would allow Gingrich to assume the role that comes most naturally to him: savior. Gingrich has always had an outsized image of himself—likening the political strategizing he did as speaker to Ulysses S. Grant's command of the Union Army or dubbing the course he taught at Kennesaw State University "Renewing American Civilization." And, despite the remarkable distance he has traveled from those heady days, that titanic self-regard remains. Gingrich's current political positioning, he explains, is about something much bigger than a mere presidential campaign. It's about "defining the idea context and solution context of the next generation of American politics." It's about "winning the future" (the title, incidentally, of one of his recent books). It's about nothing less than saving the United States from ruin.

One recent morning in Washington, Gingrich gives me a laundry list of the momentous challenges he believes the country currently faces—from the war with what he calls "the irreconcilable wing of Islam" to the rise of China and India to the epidemic of diabetes. But these aren't the only challenges, he explains. "I think the deeper problem," he says, a tinge of weariness creeping into his voice, "is the whole nature of the modern world." He grimaces. "I think that we are almost nowhere in explaining to ourselves how hard this is going to be." No one, Gingrich seems to believe, is capable of offering that explanation, much less acting on it. Not John McCain. Not Rudy Giuliani. Not even George W. Bush. No one, that is, except Newt Gingrich.

Talk about Gingrich these days with any of his friends and admirers, let alone with the man himself, and you'll undoubtedly hear the same word: ideas. "If there was ever anyone in politics who's an ideas man," says New Hampshire Representative Charlie Bass, "it's Newt Gingrich." "Newt obviously has ideas," says Gingrich's former spokesman and *Washington Times* editorial page editor Tony Blankley, "so he gains cachet from the contrast with people just wandering around repeating slogans." Joe Klein, writing in *Time* in April 2006, went so far as to jokingly propose a new federal position for Gingrich akin to party ideologist in the old Soviet Union—"party ideaologist."

Indeed, Gingrich is so full of ideas that he has actually created a physical repository for them—a twelve-by-eight windowless office at the American Enterprise Institute (where Gingrich is a senior fellow) in which, he says, "we're trying to literally organize layer after layer of ideas." There, two twentysomething Newtoids pore over copies of *Winning the Future*, boiling the book's essence down to short maxims that they then type on small sheets of white paper and thumbtack to the wall under headings like Defeating America's Enemies, Defending God in the Public Square, and Promoting Active, Healthy Aging. "It's a work in progress," one of them says when I visit, apologetically pointing to a bare spot on the wall.

The notion that Gingrich is brimming with ideas—on everything from animal husbandry to the health care system—is, of course, nothing new. An old joke in Republican circles, dating back to the early '80s, when Gingrich was just a backbencher, was that his office had file cabinets stuffed to the point of overflow with Newt's Ideas and one uncluttered desk drawer labeled Newt's Good Ideas. But the degree to which Gingrich and his allies go out of their way these days to portray him as a "man of ideas" almost certainly has something to do with their desire to distinguish him from DeLay—and to try to separate the House leadership under Gingrich from the House leadership that followed. As one Gingrich booster puts it rather explicitly, "DeLay was about power. Newt was about ideas."

When Gingrich talks about his speakership, he does so in the way Democrats of a certain age talk about the Kennedy administration. "It's a little bit like Camelot," he says. "There was this golden moment when Republicans cared about ideas and kept their word." He adds, "There's a certain virtue to my having left, because there's a clear break point, and then, after I left, gradually the spirit of DeLay and Abramoff became symbolic."

It's a nice story, if not an entirely accurate one. After all, while Gingrich was never personally fond of DeLay, he did bring him onto his leadership team, making the man known as "the Hammer" his whip. He also supported DeLay's efforts to turn K Street into a solidly Republican enclave. "I remember Newt talking about how the K Street Project was important," says DeLay's former spokesman John Feehery, "because, ultimately, the real place where the fund-raising happens starts with K Street." Abramoff, meanwhile, didn't make the career transition from Hollywood producer to Washington lobbyist until after the 1994 midterms, when his old pals from his College Republican days became ascendant. "Yesterday I had the opportunity to meet privately with

Speaker Newt Gingrich," the new lobbyist wrote in a February 1995 letter pitching his services to the governor of the Commonwealth of the Northern Mariana Islands, "and was able to raise the issue of the desire of the CNMI for more latitude in dealing with its own affairs."

And then there were Gingrich's own scandals—including a run-in with the House Ethics Committee over the use of tax-exempt funds to pay for his political activities that resulted in a formal reprimand and a $300,000 penalty. Gingrich blamed these troubles on Democratic efforts to demonize him—a somewhat ironic charge from a man who had disseminated to GOP colleagues a list of recommended terms to describe their Democratic opponents, including "sick," "corrupt," and "traitors." In other words, most of the problems that crippled the House Republicans during the days of DeLay and Abramoff—the raw exercise of power, the rampant corruption, the hyper-partisanship—were also there, at least in embryonic form, during Gingrich's reign. "Newt wasn't just a piano player while all this stuff was going on upstairs," says Marshall Wittmann, who served as the Christian Coalition's director of legislative affairs during the beginning of Gingrich's speakership. "The seeds were being sown for what eventually took place back in those early years."

Gingrich prefers to ignore these inconvenient facts. In his retelling, the House under his leadership was a laboratory of problem-solving that not only cut taxes, reduced the debt, and balanced the budget, but even took crucial steps that benefited the war on terrorism. "The 9/11 Commission described the Gingrich plus-up and said it was the only increase in intelligence spending in the '90s," the man responsible for said plus-up boasts, "and [George] Tenet has said that, without that plus-up, the system would have broken down." The sum total of his and the Republican revolutionaries' actions, Gingrich argues, was nothing short of monumental. "What we did was create a solution-oriented, idea-based, grassroots movement that led Washington by changing the country."

Gingrich says all this, he hastens to add, not to brag but to impart a lesson—a lesson not everyone has learned. "I think neither Bush and Rove in Texas nor the DeLay faction ever understood what we did," he tells me. "They didn't study it, they didn't think about it." On another occasion, addressing a group of scholars and reporters at the Brookings Institution, Gingrich is still more specific. "I think the Gingrich model of an idea-led, contentious Republican Party that fought and argued and debated is a lot better as a model than 'the Hammer,' " he says. "If you just think about it, if you think you're in an age where you need new ideas, a hammer is a relatively dumb symbol."

A prolific author, Gingrich has written four alternative historical fictions—spinning tales of what would have happened had the Confederates won at Gettysburg or had the United States not confronted Nazi Germany—and is currently at work on a fifth about the Pacific theater in World War II. But there is no alternative history that seems to interest him so much as the one about what would have happened had he not politically imploded in the late '90s. Had he remained speaker, Gingrich tells me, DeLay, for one, would have been held in check. "He never would have had the level of power that he had," Gingrich says. "It wouldn't have happened, and I would have been consciously organizing and helping younger members create countervailing centers of ideas."

But his political downfall, Gingrich believes, had ramifications that stretch far beyond what transpired in the House after his departure. "I think, when I was speaker, you could argue that it was the second-most powerful office in the country," Gingrich says. And there was a time—prior to the government shutdown, prior to the impeachment debacle—when Gingrich seemed to be on a glide-path to the most powerful office in the country. He was viewed by Republicans as both Moses and Joshua, having led his people out of bondage and into the promised land, and many assumed he would be their presidential nominee in 2000. It's an agonizing game of "what if" for Gingrich, because, as he never tires of pointing out, he was right about so many things that others were wrong about—leaving implicit the suggestion that, had he been in charge, certain catastrophes could have been avoided.

Like September 11. Gingrich guides the skeptical to his 1984 book *Window of Opportunity*, in which he urged the United States to confront terrorism.

Or Katrina. Gingrich tells the story of how, "in August of last year, before Katrina, I went to see Cheney and Rice and Rumsfeld, and I said, look, you have an enormous systems crisis. . . . I said, 'You're going to have a catastrophe.'"

Or Iraq. "For reasons I don't understand," he says, "in June of 2003, [the Bush administration] decided to go for an American occupation. . . . I was screaming at Rice, Cheney, and Rumsfeld. . . . Now, had we appointed Khalilzad to be ambassador in June of 2003, I think we would have saved at least 1,000 American lives, and we would have ended the war much earlier."

When I finally ask Gingrich point-blank what would have happened had he not resigned as speaker, he gets a far-off look in his eyes. My question is specifically in the context of the House, but Gingrich doesn't take it that way. Rather, he heads straight for the bigger picture. "It's hard to go back and imagine," he says in a wistful tone. "It would have been a different world."

For the time being, Gingrich has had to settle for more modest satisfactions. He has the Center for Health Transformation, his for-profit health care consulting business, and Gingrich Communications, his political shop, which combine to give him a staff of about 25—more than some congressmen. When he's not in his Washington office or at his home in suburban Virginia, he's typically appearing on Fox News, where he's on contract as a commentator, or traveling the country delivering speeches—often for astronomical fees—in front of groups that range from Michigan's Ottawa County Republican Party to the National Plastics Expo. "I once asked Gingrich years ago how he'd like to be remembered," his political Svengali, Joe Gaylord, tells me. "His reply was that 'I'd like people to think of me as a patriot and a teacher.' I think he's in both roles right now."

For all the material and psychological comfort those roles may provide Gingrich, he clearly believes that they also entail making others uncomfortable. To the extent that he has a stump speech for his nascent presidential campaign, it involves explaining to his audiences that the United States is on the brink of calamity. In late June, on the same day that he later blitzes the Providence zoo, Gingrich offers his dark vision to a gathering of venture capitalists and private equity managers at a tony seaside resort in Newport, Rhode Island. His ostensible topic is health care, but, in order to put the crisis into context, he explains, he must offer a broader societal critique. And that critique begins, as it does in seemingly every speech Gingrich makes these days, with a particular historical analogy. "I believe that the scale of total challenge we face is more like April 1861 than any other period since then," Gingrich says. He goes on to explain that April 1861 was the month Fort Sumter was fired upon, setting off a chain of events—from the Civil War to the construction of the transcontinental railroad to the printing of paper currency—that no one at the time foresaw. "You go back through the cold war, the Second World War, the

Great Depression, the First World War—each of those were large, singular, focusable events. In some cases, they were excruciating, but they were containable," he says. "We're going to be hit over the next 15 or 20 years with so many different things simultaneously that the total number of solutions we have to come up with is going to stretch our capacity as a society to talk to itself well enough to actually reach agreement to get something done."

For Gingrich, the deeper problem, as he might put it, is not so much the size of the challenge, but that no one is prepared to face it—especially not President Bush. Gingrich's relationship with W has never been close. Part of that is because the two men have not had many occasions to interact: When Gingrich was leading the Republican Revolution in Washington, Bush was in Austin learning how to be a governor; by the time Bush was ready to move onto the national stage, Gingrich was in political Siberia. When Bush became president, Gingrich had good relationships with Dick Cheney (from their time together in the House), Donald Rumsfeld (from their work on defense issues), and Condoleezza Rice (whom he met at Stanford's Hoover Institution, where he's a visiting fellow), so he tended to communicate his ideas through them. But, more than the lack of personal connection, it seems clear that Gingrich's biggest problem with Bush is that he doesn't put much stock in Bush's intelligence. "There is a certain smartest-kid-in-the-class syndrome here," says one Gingrich friend, trying to explain the relationship—or lack thereof—between the two men.

To raise the topic of Bush with Gingrich, I read him a quote he gave to *The New Yorker* shortly after September 11, in which he said of the president, "You have to remember, this is a Texas governor learning to be leader of the world." Looking back over the last five years, I ask, does he think Bush has learned that role? "I think he's a lot better than he was in 2001," Gingrich replies. And that's as far as he'll go. Two days before, U.S. forces in Iraq had killed Abu Musab Al Zarqawi, and, while Gingrich is obviously pleased with the news, he's angry at Bush for the way he delivered it. "This was the moment to say, 'We got Zarqawi, but you need to remember . . . this is a worldwide campaign with worldwide complications, and it's going to go on a long time,' because every time the country looks up, they need to be reminded of that." He adds, "I think the administration is trapped in normalcy."

And that, in Gingrich's view, is a tragedy, because normal leaders are not what these times call for. "The genius of guys like Lincoln and Reagan and FDR—the great communicator leaders— is that they're actually educators, so they understand when they use a phrase that they have to explain it, because, by definition, you won't understand it or they wouldn't need to be using it," he says. "I think Bush is like a lot of managers who think, if they repeat it, it's your problem to figure it out. Now, no great teacher believes it's your problem to figure it out, because most of the students won't." He goes on, "I think Bush represents a Harvard Business School model of leadership, as opposed to an educator-communicator model." It's an odd insult coming from a man who once taught a business course at Kennesaw State University, but it's an insult nonetheless.

In June 2006, Gingrich told me he wouldn't make a final decision about whether to run for president until 2007. "Sometime late next year, we'll look," he explains, "and then, if at that point there's still a huge vacuum, and if at that point there's enough interest, we'll probably do something." In the meantime, he's making sure that, when that moment comes, he'll be ready to pull the trigger. He's a long shot to secure his party's nomination, but perhaps not as desperate a long shot as you might initially think:

While he may be anonymous to visitors at a zoo, he still has fantastic name recognition among the people who vote in GOP presidential primaries. And, in June 2006, Gingrich was the top vote-getter in a 2008 straw poll at the Minnesota Republican Party state convention.

"There'll be a moderate candidate like Giuliani or McCain," predicts conservative activist and longtime Gingrich friend Grover Norquist, "and, as soon as conservatives realize they don't want that, they'll grab the prominent conservative, who could be [Senator George] Allen or could be Newt." Gingrich, Norquist continues, "is by far the best speaker and presenter. . . . He's got star quality; people want to come and listen to him." Even if Gingrich doesn't win—as almost certainly will be the case—by running for president, he'll ensure that more people, not to mention more reporters, listen to what he has to say, a benefit he himself acknowledges. His presidential posturing will have gotten him, and his ideas, some of the attention he believes they deserve.

But is attention all that Gingrich thinks he's owed? He repeatedly emphasizes that he doesn't miss being in charge, that he doesn't need to be president. "Nixon had this remarkably effective, deeply intense will to power," he says. "Reagan and I have a will to ideas." He's constantly boasting about the influence he has behind the scenes—about the 53 hours of classified briefings on Iraq and the war on terrorism the administration gave him in one month alone; about his access to Cheney, Rice, Rumsfeld, and now Karen Hughes, who had him into her State Department office a few months ago to pick his brain on public diplomacy; about the reception he receives from congressional Republicans when he's on the Hill. "Almost everybody answers my calls," he says.

And yet, Gingrich's actions often seem to betray his frustration that, when people do answer his calls, he's the one giving the advice, rather than the one deciding whether or not to take it. A couple of years ago, for instance, Gingrich spoke to House Republicans about the Medicare bill. As Indiana Representative Mark Souder, who came to the House in 1994 as part of the Republican Revolution, recounts, "He gave the best defense of the bill I've ever heard—better than the president, better than anybody. Then he proceeded to say at the end, 'If you don't vote for this, I want you to come explain to me why.' And it was like, 'Newt, you're not even a congressman anymore. We're not going to your office.'" Souder adds, "There's an old country music gospel song by the Oak Ridge Boys that goes something like, 'Nobody wants to play rhythm guitar behind Jesus / everyone wants to be the leader of the band.' Newt Gingrich is no rhythm guitar person."

Indeed, Gingrich's self-regard is such that his current lack of power inclines him to cast a gimlet eye on the entire American political system. One morning in Washington, after he has finished a rooftop interview with Black Entertainment Television and before he goes to speak at the Brookings Institution, Gingrich sits in a borrowed office inside a TV production facility and talks to me about his political hero, Abraham Lincoln. Lately, Gingrich says, he's been spending a lot of time thinking about Lincoln's Cooper Union speech. "Here's a guy who's basically saying, 'I can take 7,300 words to center the North on an explanation of who we are, on which I'm prepared to stake my candidacy for the presidency,'" Gingrich says, becoming so immersed in this retelling that, as is often the case, he seems to forget that there's anybody else present. "And he spent three months personally writing it, and he then goes to the newspapers that night to make sure they get it technically right in their editing. He then gives the same speech in Rhode Island, Massachusetts, and New Hampshire, and goes home. And that's it. He doesn't say anything for the rest of the year."

Finished with his reverie, Gingrich comes back to earth and evidently notices the quizzical look on my face. What does Lincoln's Cooper Union speech have to do with his presidential ambitions? Before I can ask, Gingrich continues. "It is totally outside the Washington conversation," he says, a bit petulantly. "So you can imagine if we'd had the modern Washington, and everybody here would have gossiped about the fact that this defeated yokel from Springfield gave this speech. It would be a one-day story in ABC's The Note or something, and it would disappear. We wouldn't understand what Lincoln was doing." He goes on, "So all I'm saying is, you could have a moment in time where the country would be prepared for a serious conversation, and the question will be whether or not the political and the news-media class could actually present a serious conversation that the country is ready for."

Just minutes earlier, Gingrich's press aide, Rick Tyler, had interrupted to tell his boss that Fox News wanted to know whether he was available to do a segment that weekend. Gingrich said yes to the request, so I ask him, in light of his doubts about the news media's ability to present a serious conversation, if he thinks going on Fox—which is not exactly renowned for facilitating serious conversations—is really a useful exercise.

Gingrich is momentarily flustered, but he quickly sees a way to reconcile the contradiction. "If I'm on by myself, it is," he replies, explaining that he tries to avoid panels with more than one guest because they typically "degenerate to the dumbest idea." Warming to the subject, he continues, "It depends partly on the quality of the questions people are willing to ask you. Hannity and Colmes and O'Reilly are more focused on what's today's news story. But what I try to do is take today's story and try to link it to a larger lesson." Now Gingrich is smiling. "And I can do that on those shows," he says, a note of triumph creeping into his voice, "because they treat me with respect." At least someone, it seems, appreciates his genius.

Ron Paul

Full Name Ronald Ernest Paul

Current Residence Lake Jackson, Texas

Date and Place of Birth August 20, 1935; Green Tree, Pennsylvania

Education
  B.A., Gettysburg College, 1957
  M.D., Duke University School of Medicine, 1961

Military Service
  Flight surgeon, U.S. Air Force, 1963–1965
  Air National Guard, 1965–1968

Nonpolitical Positions Held
  Obstetrician and gynecologist, 1968–1978, 1985–1996
  Author of nine books about economics and foreign policy

Political Offices Held
U.S. Representative from Texas, 1976, 1978–1985, 1996–present

Family
  Married to Carol Wells; children: Ronnie, Lori, Rand, Robert,
    and Joy

The Surprising Relevance of Ron Paul:
The Crank   *Michael Crowley*

A star had just been born when, a day after the May Republican presidential debate in South Carolina, I met Texas Representative Ron Paul for lunch on Capitol Hill. The meeting had been scheduled for several days; but, as luck would have it, the previous night Paul had gone from an oddball obscurity to a major sensation in the political world when, answering a question about September 11, he seemed to suggest that the attacks were justified by an aggressive U.S. foreign policy in the Middle East. "They attack us because we've been over there. We've been bombing Iraq for ten years," Paul explained. The ever-macho Rudy Giuliani was quick to pounce. "That's an extraordinary statement," he marveled. "And I would ask the congressman to withdraw that comment and tell us that he didn't really mean that." The crowd roared its approval. A previously flagging Giuliani suddenly enjoyed his best moment of the race.

But it was also, oddly enough, Paul's best moment. The response to his comments was fast and furious: Angry Republicans, including the party chairman in Michigan, former Senate candidate Michael Steele, and unnamed South Carolina sources cited on Fox News, called for his exclusion from future debates. Sean Hannity couldn't wait to bully Paul in a post-debate interview. John McCain even added a line to his stump speech bashing him. But the outrage was instructive: Suddenly, Republicans were taking seriously a quirky 71-year-old Texas libertarian whose national support has hovered in the zero-percent range.

Nor was the attention all negative. Far from it. Paul won several instant polls on the debate, including one at the conservative Newsmax.com and a Fox News text-message poll. Incredibly, Paul's name began beating out "Paris Hilton" as the number-one query on the popular blog-searching website Technorati. (Granted, it's possible that Paul's fervent supporters are manipulating such online metrics.) The incident prompted a feisty exchange among the ladies of ABC's "The View," of all places. And, to top it off, within a day of the debate, Paul's campaign had raised $100,000—about one-sixth of his entire haul for the first three months of 2007. Paul's spokesman says the campaign headquarters has been "inundated with phone calls" ever since—80 percent of them supportive.

When Paul ambled through the door of a cheap Mexican joint on Capitol Hill last May, he hardly looked like a freshly minted celebrity. His slight frame, elfin face, and reserved persona suggest the doctor he used to be, not a politician. But Paul turned heads all the same. As he approached his table, a man seated nearby extended his hand with a broad smile and a hearty "congratulations." Paul explained that he had received a similar reception among his colleagues in the House. "I've had probably ten people come up to me and compliment me—including people I thought were war hawks," he said. "It was a tremendous boost to the campaign."

Who would have expected it? At its outset, Paul's campaign promised to be a curiosity. The nominee of the Libertarian Party in his previous run for the presidency (in 1988), Paul seemed likely to play a predictable gadfly role—using his stage time to press hoary libertarian bugaboos like the abolition of Social Security, the legalization of drugs and prostitution, and—Paul's special obsession—a return to the gold standard. Instead, thanks mainly to his adamant opposition to the Iraq war, he has assumed a far more serious role. In a Republican field that has marched in lock-step with George W. Bush on the war, Paul's libertarian isolation-ism has exposed an intraparty fissure over foreign policy that is far wider than has been acknowledged, encompassing not only dis-gruntled libertarians but some paleocons and social conservatives, as well as such GOP lions as William F. Buckley, George Will, and Bob Novak. As populist-isolationist Pat Buchanan wrote in an op-ed last spring, Paul was "speaking intolerable truths. Understand-ably, Republicans do not want him back, telling the country how the party blundered into this misbegotten war."

Paul, for his part, thinks his view is commonsensical. "This is a very Republican position," he told me. "I just think the Republi-cans can't win unless they change their policy on Iraq."

Before Paul became an antiwar hero, his support consisted largely of libertarian activists—people like Michael Badnarik, the Libertarian Party's 2004 presidential nominee. Badnarik refuses to get a driver's license (even though, he conceded to me, "I have my car operational") and warns against anyone who might try to force a smallpox or anthrax vaccination on him. ("You bring the syringe, I'll bring my .45, and we'll see who makes a bigger hole.") Badnarik recounts rallying support for Paul at a recent conference of the Free State Project, a group of libertarians who have relo-cated to New Hampshire in the hope of concentrating their power and more or less taking over the state government. "I asked how many people would drive without a license and not pay income taxes, and three-quarters raised their hands," Badnarik recalls. "I'm choking up. I've got my heart in my throat. And I said, 'We need to do something—and Ron Paul's campaign is the shining star. We need to contribute the full two thousand dollars now. Tell all your friends.'"

Pep talks like that helped Paul to raise more than $600,000 overall in the first quarter of 2007—a pittance compared with the top candidates, but more than several better-known competitors, including former GOP governors Tommy Thompson, Mike Huckabee, and Jim Gilmore. With the help of the Free State Project, Paul actually placed second in money raised in New Hampshire, ahead of Giuliani and McCain and trailing only Mitt Romney.

But libertarians are a fractious bunch, and some hardcore activists have mixed feelings about the man now carrying their banner. For instance, libertarian purists generally support a laissez-faire government attitude toward abortion and gay marriage, as well as "open border" immigration policies and unfettered free trade. Yet Paul opposes gay marriage, believes states should outlaw abortion, decries high immigration rates, and criticizes free trade agreements—though mainly on constitutional grounds. (These divergences may be explained by Paul's socially conservative East Texas district, which lies adjacent to Tom DeLay's former district and which President Bush last carried with 67 percent of the vote. Being pro-choice simply doesn't fly there.)

As a result, Paul's candidacy leaves some of his erstwhile libertarian fans cold—particularly the intellectuals who congregate in Washington outfits like the CATO Institute or *Reason* magazine. "He comes from a more right-wing populist approach," explains Brian Doherty, a California-based *Reason* editor and author of *Radicals for Capitalism*, a history of the libertarian movement. "Culturally, he strikes a lot of the more cosmopolitan libertarians as a yokel." (Doherty himself is a Paul admirer.)

And, while some libertarians criticize Paul from the left on social issues, others are swiping at him from the right over the war. "Will Libertarianism Survive Ron Paul?" asked one article on the America's Future Foundation website, before continuing, "Paul's prominence threatens to make his blame-America instincts the defining characteristic of libertarianism in the public imagination. If libertarianism becomes inextricably associated with radical pacifism, will young people with classically liberal instincts be discouraged from serious political engagement?"

Paul's provocations have roiled the waters back home as well. After the fateful debate, the largest paper in Paul's district ran a story headlined, "SOME SAY PAUL SHOULD RESIGN." More ominously, a former longtime aide, Eric Dondero, is now planning to knock his former boss out of Congress in 2008. A self-described Barry Goldwater–style "pro-military libertarian," Dondero first worked for Paul during his 1988 presidential campaign and finally left his office three years ago. He says it was bad enough begging Paul to support the 2001 congressional resolution authorizing military force in Afghanistan. But Paul's September 11 moment in the debate was the final straw. The next day, Dondero posted a blog item on RedState.com declaring his intention to unseat his one-time hero. "One of the really bad things about his piss-poor [debate] performance," Dondero told me, "is that now everyone in the country is going to think that all libertarians think the same way that he does."

Paul seems only to relish his newfound notoriety. "I enjoy dealing in the area of ideas," he told me over lunch. "And I want to make a difference." Paul also carries with him a certainty that he will be vindicated—and not just on Iraq. He is utterly convinced, for instance, that the United States is headed for an economic disaster that can only be averted by the adoption of the gold standard, a topic that has obsessed him for years. When I ask him why, at 71, he's putting himself through the ordeal of a national campaign, this—not Iraq—is the point to which he returns: "If there's an economic collapse," he says almost wistfully, "maybe I'll be in the right place at the right time." It's another slogan not suited for a bumper sticker, and another you would only hear from Ron Paul.

Chuck Hagel

Full Name Charles Timothy Hagel

Current Residence Omaha, Nebraska

Date and Place of Birth October 4, 1946; North Platte, Nebraska

Education

Brown Institute for Radio and Television, 1966

B.A., University of Nebraska at Omaha, 1971

Military Service

Sergeant, U.S. Army, 1967–1968

Awarded two Purple Hearts

Nonpolitical Positions Held

Newscaster and talk-show host in Omaha, Nebraska, 1969–1971

Administrative Assistant to Representative John Y. McCollister, 1971–1977

Manager of Government Affairs, Firestone Tire & Rubber Company, 1977–1980

Cofounder, VANGUARD Cellular Systems Inc., mid-1980s

Deputy Director and CEO of the Economic Summit of Industrialized Nations (G-7), 1990

President of McCarthy & Co., investment bank, early 1990s

Chairman of the Board of American Information Systems, 1992–1995

Political Offices Held

   U.S. Senator from Nebraska, 1996–present

Family

   Married to Lilibet Hagel; children: daughter Allyn and son
   Ziller

The Unmooring of Chuck Hagel: Look Back in Anger

John B. Judis

What distinguishes the politician from the political agitator is a lively concern for his own job security. Politicians sometimes say what they believe, but they don't usually say things that might jeopardize their political future. Until recently, Chuck Hagel was a consummate politician, and a successful one at that. He defeated a popular sitting governor in his first Senate race in 1996 and won reelection, in 2002, with 83 percent of the vote. While he occasionally strayed from the GOP fold on foreign policy—an ardent internationalist, he had criticized both the Iraq war and neoconservatism generally—his credentials as a loyal Republican were never in doubt. He has long been a predictable vote on issues of importance to the American Conservative Union, the U.S. Chamber of Commerce, and the Christian right. And he remains so. It's not well-known, but Kyoto foe Hagel is still skeptical that humans are triggering global warming. "We always had climate change," he told me during a recent interview. "The issue is what is causing this. We still do not know."

By 2004, Hagel was preparing to run for president in 2008. He assembled a kitchen cabinet of advisers and a wider group of friends who were committed to fund-raising for him. His PAC gave money to the Iowa Republican Party. He planned to run on his conservative credentials—he boasted that, in 2006, he had voted with the White House more frequently than any other senator—while remaining critical of the Iraq war. Hagel isn't a household name, and, in a field dominated by John McCain and Rudy Giuliani, the Nebraska senator certainly faced an uphill struggle. Still, there was reason to believe that Republican voters would at least give him a hearing.

Then, quite suddenly this year, Hagel began saying and doing things that no rational Republican who was running for president would say or do. In an *Esquire* article and later in a nationally televised interview with George Stephanopoulos, Hagel raised the specter of impeaching George W. Bush. The president is "not accountable anymore," Hagel told *Esquire,* adding, "You can impeach him, and before this is over, you might see calls for his impeachment." In March, he went a step further. Despite his misgivings about the war, Hagel had voted with the White House at key junctures, including the October 2002 resolution authorizing force and the committee vote to confirm John Bolton as U.N. ambassador. But, on March 27, he provided the swing vote to pass a Democratic measure on Iraq. The resolution, virtually the same as one that Hagel had opposed only twelve days before, set a March 2008 goal for the withdrawal of U.S. troops. On the Senate floor, Hagel ripped the administration for "escalating our military involvement in Iraq."

Republican voters might have put up with, even applauded, Hagel's criticism of how Bush was conducting the war; but they are unlikely to accept his decision to join Democrats on a crucial partisan vote and even less likely to accept his speculation about impeaching Bush. Indeed, in the wake of the Senate vote, Hagel's longtime patron and mentor, former Nebraska representative John McCollister, implicitly rebuked Hagel in a letter to the *Omaha World-Herald*, writing, "I believe that some people disregard the awful consequences of a premature withdrawal and want to end the war, period. Others have a consuming, burning hatred of George W. Bush as their dominant legislative priority. Those who carelessly throw out talk of 'impeachment' are of the same stripe." Meanwhile, Nebraska Attorney General Jon Bruning announced that he was considering challenging Hagel in the Republican primary if he seeks reelection to the Senate. "Senator Hagel has lost touch as a Republican," says Bruning, "and he has not behaved as one."

Having become an outcast in his own party, Hagel is now hinting that he may leave the GOP altogether and run for president as an independent—never mind the astronomically long odds that would accompany such a bid. "I think a credible third ticket, third party, would be good for the system," Hagel declared recently on "Face the Nation." Asked whether he might run on an independent presidential ticket with New York Mayor Michael Bloomberg, the usually poker-faced Hagel broke into a wide grin. "It's a great country to think about a New York boy and a Nebraska boy to be teamed up leading this nation," he said. One member of Hagel's kitchen cabinet says, "It is never going to happen." But the fact that Hagel even raised the possibility shows how far he has traveled politically.

In short, Hagel—having spent his career building a reputation for steady, loyal conservatism—has stopped acting like a politician and begun acting like an agitator or crusader, a man with a cause that overrides any political calculation; and, in doing so, he has probably ruined whatever shot he once had at becoming president. Why did he do it? Tightly wound and stocky, with steely blue-gray eyes, Hagel is known for what a former staffer calls his "huge temper." And there is no doubt that, today, Chuck Hagel is acting out of anger. Anger about Iraq, yes, but also anger fueled by things that happened many decades ago. Anger that he had suppressed for a long time.

According to his two younger brothers, Chuck Hagel takes after his grandfather, who managed a lumber mill in Ainsworth, Nebraska. Their grandfather, recalls Chuck's brother Tom, "was your stereotypical dominant Teutonic male—very, very German, very dominating, very hard-driving. He set the rules: his way or no way. And my father was kind of like that. But Chuck was more like that."

Their father at one point worked for the same mill, but he was an alcoholic and had difficulty holding a job. When Chuck was growing up, his family moved from one small town to another as his father got jobs working for lumber mills. His father's fondest memories were of his service in the Pacific in World War II. "We were a family that grew up with the Legionnaires' Cap and a sense of responsibility to the country," Hagel recalls. Much of his father's hope for the future rested on Chuck, who was a star football player in high school. But he died in 1962, when his eldest son was 16, and Chuck's football career ended when he injured his neck in December of his freshman year of college. With his athletic career over, Hagel floundered in school. In 1967, on the verge of being drafted, he enlisted in the Army.

Hagel was eager to go to war. Trained as a rifleman, he volunteered to go directly to Vietnam rather than spend six months in West Germany. In Vietnam, he was joined after three months by Tom, who, to his amazement, was sent to the same unit. They fought together in the jungle and Saigon during the Tet offensive. At different moments, each had to save the other's life. The last time came in the spring of 1968, when a mine went off under their armored personnel carrier outside Saigon. As Chuck later told a newspaper reporter, when he grabbed Tom, who had been knocked unconscious, he was "dead weight, blood pouring out of his ears." Before he could pull Tom out, the ammunition in the carrier blew up, severely burning Chuck and blowing out both his eardrums.

Soon afterward, the brothers were sent back to the States, but they arrived home with very different reactions to their war experiences. Tom was tortured by guilt over the people he had killed and seen killed. He believed that the war had been a waste and was immoral. "To the day I die, I will be ashamed I fought in this war," he wrote to their younger brother Mike, who couldn't serve because of a bad knee. When he came home, he drank heavily. After a year, he entered college and eventually became a law professor at the University of Dayton. Today, Tom—bearded, taller and thinner than his brother, his eyes betraying sadness rather than anger—considers himself a liberal Democrat.

Chuck, by contrast, remained convinced that he had done his patriotic duty by fighting. "Chuck believed it was right for us to be there, that we were defending freedom," Mike Hagel recalls. The future senator later told Myra MacPherson for her 1984 book about Vietnam vets, *Long Time Passing*, that he believed "If America was involved, then it's right." Unlike his brother, Chuck did not go on a bender when he came home; but he also didn't return to the life he had led before going to war. He went back to college at the University of Nebraska in Omaha. After living for six months with Tom near campus, he rented a house in the country. He went to classes but kept to himself for a year. "It was the strangest thing, so out of character for someone like me," he told MacPherson. "Then I woke up one morning and said, 'OK, enough of this. It's time to get back into society.'" In many ways, he simply put the war behind him— or so he believed. "I went about trying to get my life in order and not reaching back into what happened," he told MacPherson. "I don't have these same problems that Tom has about guilt and these emotional feelings."

But Tom told a different story about his older brother. "I've seen him break down," he explained to MacPherson. "I know we share some nightmares. He has just suppressed them so deeply. But he's going to have to walk through the valley sometime."

Chuck Hagel may not have dwelled on his own experiences in the war, but, like Colin Powell, his view of the world would come to bear the imprint of Vietnam. After graduating from college in 1971, Hagel went to Washington, where he got a job on McCollister's staff. When Reagan took office in 1981, Hagel was appointed deputy director of the Veterans Administration. He followed that job with a brief, but spectacularly successful, career as a cell phone promoter. Then, in 1986, Hagel took over the United Service Organization (USO) and revived it. When he was elected to the Senate in 1996, he surprised his colleagues by making the Foreign Relations Committee, which had become a backwater under North Carolina Senator Jesse Helms, his first choice.

Hagel's worldview was almost entirely self-taught—in speeches, he still mispronounces George Kennan's last name "Keenan"—but it was not the worldview of a typical Nebraskan. The state had been a center of isolationist sentiment before each world war. Its farmers were interested in foreign trade but not really in foreign policy. Yet Hagel was a committed internationalist who looked upon the United Nations, the World Bank, the International Monetary Fund, the World Trade Organization, and NATO as essential ingredients of U.S. foreign policy. "Borderless challenges will require borderless solutions," he declared in his first major foreign policy address in September 1998. But his internationalism was tempered by realism about what the United States could accomplish overseas. He was wary of attempts to use American power to create democracy. Like former National Security Advisor Brent Scowcroft, who would become a friend and adviser, Hagel thought the United States should seek stability, security, and prosperity. He later called his outlook "principled realism."

Like Powell, Hagel was hesitant to throw American soldiers into combat unless it was absolutely necessary, and he blanched at politicians who advocated going to war but had no personal experience of it. After a rancorous debate over foreign policy with a Republican primary opponent in 1996, Hagel said to an aide, "He has no idea what it is like to have his face down in the mud and having bullets flying over his head."

During his first term, Hagel applied his "principled realism" to U.S. policy toward Saddam Hussein. He voted for the Iraq Liberation Act of 1998, which committed the United States to removing Saddam and promoting a "democratic government" in Iraq, but he expressed reservations about its intent to fellow Nebraskan Bob Kerrey, a sponsor of the bill. "He was very skeptical about the desirability of democracy being established," Kerrey recalls.

Hagel was even more skeptical about using military force to oust Saddam. "With the current tensions in this region and the grim prospects for peace in the Middle East, this area of the world could erupt like a tinderbox," Hagel said in a floor speech that February. When McCain advocated air strikes against Iraq's Republican Guard, Hagel cautioned that "the military option alone will not work," and he warned against the "trap of doing something, anything, just because we said we would and the world expects us to."

Hagel first began to have misgivings about the Bush administration's foreign policy after the president's 2002 State of the Union address, in which Bush used the term "axis of evil" to describe Iraq, Iran, and North Korea. When Powell came before the Foreign Relations Committee the following month, Hagel chided him about the speech. "Actions and words have consequences that are very dangerous at a time in the history of man when there's little margin of error left," he said. That August, after Dick Cheney had made the case for invading Iraq in a speech before the Veterans of Foreign Wars in Nashville, Hagel recoiled. He warned against attempts "to scare the American public by saying this guy is a couple of months away from not only possessing nuclear weapons, but a ballistic missile to deliver those." A few days earlier, he had told *Newsweek*, "It's interesting to me that many of those who want to rush the country into war and think it would be so quick and easy don't know anything about war. They come at it from an intellectual perspective versus having sat in jungles or foxholes and watched their friends get their heads blown off. I try to speak for those ghosts of the past a little bit."

Hagel voted for the resolution authorizing the administration to use force against Iraq—but he did so, he said, on the basis of assurances from Powell and Bush that the United States would pursue a diplomatic strategy first. Hagel's speech in favor of the resolution could easily have been given by an opponent of the war.

"To succeed, our commitment must extend beyond the day after to the months and years after Saddam is gone," he said. "The American people must be told of this long-term commitment, risk, and costs of this undertaking. We should not be seduced by the expectations of 'dancing in the streets' after Saddam's regime has fallen." As it became clear to Hagel in the winter of 2003 that the administration was bent on going to war regardless of what U.N. inspectors found, his criticisms of the administration grew harsher. In December, Hagel co-authored a *Washington Post* op-ed with Joe Biden. They wrote, "Going it alone and imposing a U.S.-led military government instead of a multinational civilian administration could turn us from liberators into occupiers, fueling resentment throughout the Arab world." At the University of Notre Dame the following month, Hagel said he did not "see democracy taking quick root in Iraq and spreading throughout the Arab world."

Following the invasion, Hagel alternately criticized and expressed confidence in the administration's conduct of the war. He joined McCain, Biden, and Senator Jack Reed—a Democrat and former Army captain who is Hagel's closest friend in the Senate—in urging Bush to send more troops to pacify the country. In September 2004, he worried that "we're in deep trouble in Iraq," and, in November, he complained, "I don't think we have enough troops. We didn't have enough going in." But then, in December, he expressed optimism that the elections the Bush administration planned for Iraq would bring "peace and security in the Middle East." He was a critic, but not yet a heretic.

Sometime in 2006, Hagel's outlook darkened. Partly, that was because of what he saw happening on the ground in Iraq. But, partly, it was because he was once again thinking about a subject he had long repressed: Vietnam.

Hagel had begun revisiting his experience in Vietnam years earlier. In 1999, Nebraska public television aired a documentary, "Echoes of War," based on Chuck and Tom Hagel's visit to Vietnam to open the new U.S. consulate in Saigon. He also became a regular speaker at Vietnam memorial events. Hagel himself says that his interest in Vietnam was reignited sometime in 1999, when he listened to a tape of Lyndon Johnson's conversation with Senator Richard Russell about the war. On that tape, when Russell advises Johnson to pull out of Vietnam, Johnson agrees that U.S. intervention could end in disaster but expresses fear that, if he does withdraw, he will be impeached.

Hagel probably did begin reading about Vietnam in 1999, when he and his brother visited the country, but the opinions he expressed during that visit and over the next two years were no different from those he had expressed 20 years before. While critical of the way the war was prosecuted, Hagel claimed that it had ultimately proved beneficial. "If the United States had not made a stand in Vietnam, . . . the face of Southeast Asia would look very different from what it does today," he said during his 1999 visit. Two years later, speaking at the Vietnam Memorial, he made exactly the same point.

Tom Hagel says his brother's reevaluation of Vietnam began in earnest a few years later. "It was the run-up to the invasion of Iraq where you [began to] see all of this just flood out," he says. "Since that time, standing back, watching and talking to him, there were at least a few times a year, it was like watching someone growing increasingly obsessed and frustrated with what he sees going on around him and feels powerless to change it." According to Tom, during "the last year or two," as Chuck read more about the history of the war, his views on Vietnam changed dramatically. "I have never seen him change an opinion on anything in my life so quickly as he did after this information," Tom says. "It shocked me when he told me about it."

The first public inkling of Hagel's changed outlook would come in a profile of him in November 2004 by *Washington Post* reporter Robert Kaiser. Hagel described the learning process he was going through. "I read everything I could about Indochina, about the war, about the French, about Vietnam, about our policy, what got us there. . . . And the more I read, the more I understood. . . . I got a sense that there was just so much dishonesty in it. And it was chewing these kids up. . . . So I started connecting all the deaths and all the suffering and the chaos and wounds. I started to sense a dishonesty about it all." Hagel now saw the war in Vietnam, like the war in Iraq, as a war of choice—one that had been built on an edifice of lies.

Hagel began to believe that the United States had gone to war in Vietnam and had continued fighting partly for narrow political reasons—to avoid being impeached, in Johnson's case, or to avoid being "the first American president to lose a war," in Richard Nixon's words. He and his brother had been "used" for ignoble ends. That's what Tom Hagel had been saying all along. Says Mike Hagel, "Chuck totally agrees with Tom now."

Sometime in the last year, Hagel began to apply these conclusions to Iraq. Two things spurred him to do so. First, during several trips to the Middle East with Reed, he came to believe that the United States was throwing soldiers into the midst of another nation's civil war. "Chuck and I had the realization that this was a profoundly political and not a military problem," Reed says. "The Iraqis have to resolve this civil war and conflict."

Second, Bush's response last December to the Baker-Hamilton report greatly disturbed Hagel. He had enthusiastically backed the commission's recommendation to "engage directly with Iran and

Syria" and to move "combat forces out of Iraq responsibly." He expected that the administration would accept the report's recommendations; and, when Bush ignored them and opted instead to send more troops to Iraq, Hagel had a sense of déjà vu. When I asked him if Bush's surge had brought the comparison with Vietnam into focus, he said that was "exactly right." The arguments Bush is using to justify his "escalation," Hagel told me—he refuses to use the word "surge"—"are the same arguments we used in Vietnam."

Hagel was struck, he said, by "the dishonesty of both wars." And he sees the soldiers as victims of this dishonesty. Tom Hagel thinks it is this realization above all that is driving his brother's anger. "He knows what these people are getting into that we send over there," Tom says. "And he is so incredibly frustrated that he can't convince his colleagues that this is so important, this is so vital, this is so real that you've got to listen to me and follow my suggestions."

It was this frustration, Tom believes, that was "driving him to run for president." But the same frustration was also leading his brother to make statements and cast votes that undermined his chances of ever making it to the White House.

Hagel will not be pleased with this portrait of his political evolution on Iraq and Vietnam. As I learned when I interviewed him, he is not given to introspection and gets annoyed at questions that have a psychological dimension. But it is precisely Hagel's determined resistance to introspection that lends the story of his evolution poignancy and credibility. He is a man who decided, as he told his biographer Charlyne Berens, to take "the American Legion path" when he came home from Vietnam—and did so for many decades. It was only when faced with the onset of a new war—one that he saw "chewing" up a generation like his own—that he was forced to reconsider his past.

Hagel's fury over Iraq has unsettled his political life. He has been at odds with the White House for at least five years, but he has now alienated some of his Republican colleagues in the Senate. Even his friendship with McCain, who was once his mentor, appears to be on the rocks. In early February, Hagel called a McCain resolution on the Iraq war "intellectually dishonest." When a reporter from GQ asked Hagel this winter how serving in Vietnam had affected his decisions on Iraq, he drew a cruel contrast between his service and McCain's: "When I got to Vietnam, I was a rifleman. I was a private, about as low as you can get. So my frame of reference is very much geared toward the guy at the bottom who's doing the fighting and dying. . . . John McCain served his country differently—he spent five years as a prisoner of war. . . . I don't think my experience makes me any better, but it does make me very sober about committing our nation to war." In March, after Hagel had voted for the Democratic resolution on withdrawal from Iraq, McCain fired back. "My views are not framed by events that happened thirty years ago," he said. "I don't think it would be fair to my constituents, intellectually, to have my views formed only by that one experience of my life. That's maybe where Chuck and I have some differences." McCain's comments were as cruel as Hagel's. And they were also hypocritical, given that McCain invariably uses his own experience as a prisoner of war to attract support for his current stance.

In Washington, Hagel is reviled by neoconservatives. "I think the appeasers ought to have a candidate in the Republican primaries, and he's their ideal standard-bearer," wrote Michael Ledeen of the American Enterprise Institute. At the same time, he is cheered by conservative war critics like Grover Norquist and Robert Novak and by center-left foreign policy experts. Former National Security Advisor Zbigniew Brzezinski says of Hagel, "I like the guy, and I admire his views. We see eye-to-eye on the majority of issues. I won't say we see eye-to-eye on every issue, but if you ask what we don't agree on, I wouldn't be able to answer."

Last winter, I heard from people close to Hagel that he was preparing to announce an exploratory committee to run for president. That would have allowed him to raise money for a presidential campaign without yet committing himself to the race. And, when his office sent out "urgent" e-mails in large type announcing that he would give a press conference in Omaha on March 12, I expected, as did most other members of the media, that he was about to announce the committee's formation. But Hagel, with the Nebraska governor and McCollister seated in the front row, and with CNN and MSNBC carrying the event live, surprised the press by postponing any announcement. It was a bizarre performance by a politician who, in the past, had been very sure-footed and decisive. Pundits termed it Hagel's "March madness."

Hagel claimed that he wasn't ready because he still wanted to devote himself to Senate business; but, according to his advisers, he had become plagued by political uncertainty. He wanted to see if McCain's campaign continued to flounder, and he also wanted to see if he could raise enough money to run. At the time, he still insisted that he had a chance to win over Republican voters. "If I didn't think that, I wouldn't have interest in any of this business," he told me at the end of March.

By May, Hagel appears to have concluded that he has little chance as a Republican. When I asked him whether anything in particular had convinced him to consider running as an independent, he predictably said, "No," but he made clear that he had been stung by his party's revolt against him. "My loyalty is first to country, and I appreciate some in my party don't accept that," he said. Still, no one I talked to believes Hagel will actually run as an independent. Some people who know him think he is going to quit politics entirely, while others believe that he will be loath to turn his back on a challenge from an upstart like Bruning. One person who has worked with him questions whether Hagel has lost his moorings. "I just don't know what is going on in that guy's head," he says. "I can't tell if he is unusually smart or just lost it."

Yet what Hagel seems to have lost is not so much his sanity or his grasp of world politics—his recent floor speech opposing the Reid-Feingold bill, which would have entirely cut off war funding, was a model of sober intelligence—but rather the part of the political cerebellum that allows politicians to put career before conviction. In my final conversation with him, I asked whether he saw irony in the fact that, while his anger about the war was driving him to run for president, what he had said and done about the war was putting the Republican nomination out of reach. I told him that he seemed to be paying a price for honesty. Hagel laughed. "Of course there is a price for honesty in politics," he said. "Are you paying it?" I asked. He replied, "I'll let others make that judgment."

The Creeping Realignment: The Parties and the Presidency in 2008   *John B. Judis*

E very presidential election has its peculiarities, but the 2008 edition is shaping up to be more unusual than most. Two of the leading candidates in the race for the Democratic nomination are an African American and a woman. African Americans and women have run before but were never in a position to win a major party nomination. On the Republican side, three of the leading candidates for the nomination made their reputation as moderates in a party that, since 1980, has been thoroughly dominated by conservatives. The most reliable conservatives, such as Kansas Senator Sam Brownback and former Arkansas Governor Mike Huckabee, have no realistic chance of winning the nomination.

These anomalies might be explained away. Democrat Hillary Clinton benefits, after all, from being the wife of the former president, and Barack Obama made his name with a brilliant speech at the Democratic convention in 2004. John McCain ran second in 2000, and Rudolph Giuliani earned his reputation in the wake of the September 11 terrorist attacks. But there is nothing coincidental about the Democrats considering an African American and a woman while the Republicans are having a difficult time finding a genuine conservative. These seeming anomalies are the products of a creeping realignment that began almost two decades ago—a realignment that was interrupted by September 11 and then resumed in the 2006 elections.

Obama and Clinton represent important constituencies within a Democratic coalition that threatens to displace the older conservative Republican coalition of business and social conservatives. Obama and Clinton are following a path similar to Catholic politicians like Al Smith and John F. Kennedy, who also laid claim to the nomination partly on the basis of their constituency's growing strength within the Democratic Party. Mitt Romney, John McCain, and Rudolph Giuliani are leading Republican candidates by default in a party whose conservative standard-bearers have suffered defeat or discredit during George W. Bush's years in office. The two most prominent conservative candidates, Virginia Senator George Allen and Pennsylvania Senator Rick Santorum, were both defeated for reelection in 2006. The Republican quandary appears to have brought former Senator Fred Thompson out of retirement, but Thompson was a protégé of arch moderate Howard Baker and was known in the Senate as a close ally of McCain.

The Democrats are running in 2008 from an overall position of political strength; the Republicans from weakness. The Democrats are putting forward candidates that reflect their base. The Republicans are being forced to choose among candidates who are accusing each other of "flip-flopping" to pander to their party's conservative base. Because the center of American politics has shifted leftward, the Democrats will have an easier time retaining their base and appealing to the political center. The Republicans have to figure out how to retain their base. In addition, of course, the Democratic candidate will be able to run against the dismal record of the Bush administration, while the Republican will have to distance himself from his own party's record.

But the Democrats do not have a lock on the presidency. The current Democratic realignment is not like the New Deal realignment. It is not about to provide massive popular majorities. It is halting and jagged. It will likely result in narrow Democratic congressional majorities—on the average, but not necessarily in every election, over the next 12 to 16 years. Similarly, the shift in public opinion has moved from the right to the center—though it has not moved as far as the political left. The median voter is somewhere in the political space occupied by moderate Republicans and Democrats—say, the middle-ground occupied by California Governor Arnold Schwarzenegger and Florida Senator Bill Nelson. The average voter is neither a conservative Republican nor a liberal Democrat.

To win the presidential election, neither the Republican nor the Democratic candidate will be able to rely solely on his or her party's faithful. Instead, they will have to reach out to voters in this elusive center and in states that have not been in the habit of electing either doctrinaire conservatives or liberals. That puts a premium on political positioning and on the ability of the candidates to get voters to overlook the political positions on their platform where they disagree and focus instead on those issues on which they do agree. George W. Bush was pretty good at this in 2000. Al Gore was pretty bad at it in 2000, and John Kerry was even worse in 2004. Democrats, in other words, have good reason to hope for a presidential victory in 2008—the trajectory of U.S. politics is moving in their direction—but, based on their recent past performances, they also have good reason to fear another defeat.

I.

Political scientists V. O. Key and W. D. Burnham developed the theory of political realignment to explain the epochal rhythms of the American electoral history. The U.S. two-party system and the separation of power between the executive and congressional branches have tended to screen out political dissent until it becomes so loud that it disrupts the system itself and causes an upheaval in party alignments and a shift in governing coalitions. That happened, notably, in 1860, 1896, and 1932. These realignments, which Burnham called "America's surrogate for revolution," caused a sudden shift in coalitions, worldview, and political geography. After 1932, for instance, blue-collar Republicans became Democrats; much of the solidly Republican Midwest became Democratic, too; and Americans abandoned the laissez-faire individualism of the 1920s for the interest-group liberalism of the New Deal.

But, since 1932, there has not been a similar sudden realignment. Instead, realignments have taken place gradually, with stops and starts. The conservative Republican realignment began in 1968, lapsed during Watergate, revived in 1980, and reached its culmination in 1994 at the same time as a centrist Democratic realignment was already under way. Realignments occurred more gradually partly because of the growing decentralization of party structures that made it possible for conservative Southern Democrats to co-exist with the Northern liberals. But realignments also attenuated due to the smoothing out of the business cycle after World War II. The 1896 and 1932 realignments had both been precipitated by depressions. Without that kind of severe economic jolt, political change became more jagged, subject to lesser shocks, such as a recession or a scandal.

The newest creeping realignment began in the late '80s and was first clearly manifested in the 1992 elections, when third-party candidate H. Ross Perot split the Republican vote in the same way that George Wallace's third-party candidacy in 1968 had fractured the Democratic Party majority. After suffering a congressional setback in 1994, the Democrats began to gain ground again from 1996 through 2000, with Gore winning the popular vote and Democrats winning enough seats to bring about a tie in the Senate.

Three groups entered the Democratic Party over the last decades to make up for the blue-collar and ethnic whites that had been previously lost to issues of race, religion, and national security. First, and most surprising, were college-educated professionals—part of the Ralph Nader generation—who embraced the post-'60s regulatory state, feminism, the civil rights revolution, and cultural libertarianism. According to the extensive American National Election Survey (ANES), the vote for a Democratic presidential candidate among professionals went from 31 percent in 1952 to 57 percent in 1992 and remained at 56 percent in 2004.

The second group comprised women voters. Women once voted disproportionately Republican, but, in response to the Republican embrace of the religious right and the widespread entry of women into the workforce, they turned disproportionately Democratic, especially single, young, and professional women. Democrats received more male than female votes from 1952 through 1960; from 1964 to 1976, allegiances wavered; but, from 1980 to the present, Democrats have received a much higher percentage of votes from women and, from 1992 through 2004, an absolute majority. Thirdly, the Democrats benefited from the support of minorities. Blacks shifted decisively to the Democrats during the '60s. Hispanics (except for Cubans) had backed Democrats even earlier than that; still, even more shifted Democratic during the '90s.

The worldview of this new Democratic coalition in part reflected changes in the U.S. economy and society. The onset of a new highly competitive global capitalism undercut the older industrial unions and accelerated the movement from an industrial to a post-industrial capitalism of well-paid professionals and low-wage service workers. Democratic presidential candidates, and many new arrivals in Congress, took their cue from the professionals who had become Democrats and from the public-interest organizations those professionals founded, staffed, and funded. The labor movement has remained important, but the professional and service-worker unions have eclipsed the older industrial and construction unions. And labor, along with the older public-interest groups like Common Cause or NARAL, increasingly compete for attention and influence with Internet-based organizations.

Professionals and their organizations now back campaign-finance reform, lobbying reform, environmental regulation, and consumer regulation, but they don't back deficit-busting spending programs or most tax increases, even when they are targeted to the wealthy. For the most part, these Democrats don't think government has a responsibility to create jobs, but to prepare workers to get jobs and keep them. They are often sympathetic to unions, but don't think they are all-important. They favor women's rights and civil rights; they oppose the intrusion of the religious right into government social policy and science. They are internationalists in foreign policy—and oppose the Iraq war. They have a relaxed attitude toward immigration and free trade. In U.S. politics, their outlook is center-left, but not left-wing.

There was plenty of reason for conflict within this new Democratic coalition—over trade, immigration, welfare reform, abortion, and government spending—but opposition to a conservative Republican Party, which was increasingly identified with the business-backers of Washington's K Street and with the religious right, united the different segments of the Democratic coalition behind the professionals' center-left views. This coalition is strongest in what had once been the Republican Northeast, the upper Midwest, and the far West; and the Democrats are now competitive in the lower Midwest, the Hispanic Southwest, and the Southern border states, including Florida. The party is weakest in the Southern Bible Belt, the upper Rockies, and the Prairie states.

Much of the Democratic coalition's strength lies in the new post-industrial metropolitan areas that can be found in traditionally Republican as well as Democratic states. In these "ideopolises"—typified by greater Boston, Raleigh-Durham, Austin, Denver, Chicago, and Los Angeles—both city and suburb have become part of a social-economic whole whose politics are defined by the Democratic professionals and also by minorities, including immigrants, who work in the service industries of these metro areas. Democrats used to win the central cities and lose the suburbs; now they sweep the entire area.

II.

In the electorate of the 1990s, there were two key swing groups—one social and the other ideological—that determined elections. In many states in the South and Midwest, the white working class, which used to be solidly Democratic, still makes up a majority of voters. (These voters can be roughly defined as white wage-workers without four-year college degrees. According to the Census, 69 percent of whites over 25 don't have college degrees.) After 1992, it became a rule of thumb in elections that, if Democrats could get about 44 percent or more of the white working-class vote nationally—which means at least breaking even outside the Deep South—they could win a presidential election.

In the South, the first wave of white working-class voters left the Democrats over civil rights, followed by evangelical Protestants offended by the Democrats' identification with feminism and counter-culture. Many white working-class voters in the North-east, Midwest, and far West also shared these concerns, par-ticularly about race, but many of these voters were still tied ten-uously to the Democrats—through labor-union membership, religion (if they were Catholic), concern about the economy, and the residual identification of the Democrats as the party of the common man and the Republicans as the party of business. In the 1992 and 1996 elections, Bill Clinton was able to win those voters over. In 2000, Gore was not.

The other swing group is independent voters. Independents used to be transitional voters—young people who had not yet made up their minds about which party they wanted to join. They were of no political consequence. But, in the '70s, indepen-dents acquired a political identity. At that time, many of them were conservative Southerners who had begun to vote Republican but were reluctant to label themselves as such. According to politi-cal scientist Alan Abramowitz, "In the ten presidential elections between 1952 and 1988, Democratic candidates received an average of just 40 percent of the major party vote among independent identifiers."

In the last two decades, a new group of independents has emerged who represent a politics of their own and now make up about one-third of the electorate. They often lean toward one party over another, but they like to see themselves as being above partisan conflict. They disdain Washington and the parties them-selves as the preserve of special interests. They favor campaign and lobbying reform. They tend to be more secular-minded than other voters and leery of the religious right. They worry about deficit-spending.

In the Northeast, these independents have tended to be liberal in their outlook. But, in the West—and particularly in the non-Pacific West, such as Montana, Colorado, and Arizona—they have tended to be more libertarian. These Western independents are opposed to any interference in private life—from guns to abortion—and opposed to many government programs that liberals would traditionally favor. Some independents are white working class; others are professionals. Many of them voted for Perot in 1992. In 1996, they backed Clinton over Robert Dole; but, in 2000, they narrowly favored Bush over Gore.

III.

By 2000, the Republican Party had begun to recognize the shift toward the center. In that year, both Republican candidates, John McCain and George W. Bush, cultivated the center: McCain in his primary campaign and Bush in the general election. After the election, when James Jeffords' defection gave Democrats control of the Senate, the movement toward the center and toward the Democrats intensified. But the September 11 terrorist attacks arrested this realignment and provided an opportunity for Bush and the Republicans to restore their older, conservative Republican majority.

President Bush's aggressive response to the September 11 terrorist attacks and his initial success in Afghanistan revived the Republican advantage on national security—an advantage that had helped both Ronald Reagan and George H. W. Bush win presidential elections. George W. Bush's administration and the

Republican Party were able to use national security issues to their advantage in the 2002 congressional elections and in the 2004 presidential election.

Some Republican strategists attributed the party's success in 2002 and 2004 primarily to its mobilization of its own voter base rather than to its success in winning over swing voters. But this is a misreading of these elections. The Bush administration did increase turnout in some Republican districts, but it won because it brought back voters who had deserted the party in the '90s. The Republicans brought back suburban professionals in 2002 and white women in 2004 (think, "security moms"). In 2002, for instance, Republican Jim Talent defeated Missouri Senator Jean Carnahan by reducing the Democratic margin in the county outside of St. Louis. In 2004, according to exit polls, Bush won white women by 55 to 44 percent—a 10 percent increase from 2000.

Republicans in these elections did seek to capture the center on economic issues. Republicans touted, for instance, their support for a prescription-drug benefit for senior citizens. But the 2002 and 2004 elections didn't fit the usual pattern. Bush and the Republicans made those elections into referenda on the Republican performance in fighting the so-called "war on terror." The 2002 and 2004 elections became wartime elections, similar to the elections of 1942 and 1944. Voters who thought that the threat from terrorists abroad (among whom Bush succeeded in lumping Saddam Hussein) was the most important issue overwhelmingly backed the Bush administration in both elections. That was what drew white women—particularly white working-class women—and some suburban professionals back into the Republican camp.

Voters in these elections were either sufficiently distracted by the threat of terrorism that they ignored those issues on which they had previously favored the Democrats, or, faced with the threat of foreign terrorism, they embraced or moved toward the Republican stance on a whole range of issues. In 2002, for instance, the Republicans' reputation on fighting terrorism carried over to voters' view of their performance on the economy. In a poll conducted on the eve of the election, more voters blamed the Clinton administration rather than the Bush administration for the recession. And, in exit polls, voters said they trusted the Republicans more than the Democrats to manage the economy—an unheard-of result for a party in power during a recession. Even voters' opposition to abortion rose sharply during this period.

In these elections, Bush and the Republicans sensed what political psychologists who studied the impact of September 11 have confirmed: Voters, facing what they saw as an existential threat, tend to turn toward strong leaders cast as political saviors and to fall back on the older verities of family, nation, and religion. Bush and the Republicans reinforced these tendencies through evoking the threat of terrorist attacks during the 2002 and 2004 elections and in casting themselves as the guardians of U.S. security and morals.

Bush's failure in Iraq finally began to impress itself upon some voters during the 2004 election. He lost the most serious ground in that election among college-educated suburban professionals. Voters with post-graduate degrees had backed Republicans 51 to 45 percent in 2002; in 2004, they backed Democrats by 52 to 46 percent. These voters began to make a distinction between the war in Iraq and the war on terrorism and to discount the Republican attempts to exploit the fear of foreign attack. But enough voters still linked the war in Iraq to the war on terrorism to enable Bush to defeat Kerry.

After the 2004 election, many more voters gave up on the war and on Bush. The failure in Iraq—along with the administration's response to Hurricane Katrina and the scandals among congressional Republicans—created an impression of reckless incompetence and corruption. That gave the Democrats issues on which to campaign in 2006, but, more important, it removed the ideological advantage that Republicans had enjoyed in 2002 and 2004 and returned U.S. politics to where it had been in 2000. The trends that began in the '90s re-emerged with a vengeance in the 2006 congressional elections, leading to a Democratic takeover of both the House and the Senate.

The same groups that had helped Clinton to win in 1996 and had contributed to Gore's popular-vote victory in 2000 voted Democratic in 2006. Democrats' margin among women voters went from 51 to 48 percent in 2004 to 55 to 43 percent in 2006; single white women went from 51 to 49 percent in 2004 to 58 to 42 percent in 2006; the overall margin among minorities went from 71 to 29 percent in 2004 to 76 to 24 percent in 2006; and college-educated voters went from 49 to 48 percent in 2004 to 53 to 46 percent in 2006. Democratic strength in post-industrial metro areas continued to grow, with Democrats displacing Republicans in suburban Denver, southern high-tech New Hampshire, Ft. Lauderdale, and Philadelphia.

The Democrats also made gains among the swing voters who had gravitated back to Bush. White working-class voters who earn between $30,000 and $50,000 had backed Republican congressional candidates by 60 to 38 percent in 2004. In 2006, the two parties each received 49 percent of these voters. That translated into healthy majorities in states like Ohio, Indiana, and Pennsylvania. Independent voters also swung toward the Democrats. They had backed Republican congressional candidates by 48 to 45 percent in 2002. In 2006, they backed Democrats by 57 to 39 percent. And this included the libertarian independents from states like Colorado, Montana, and Arizona as well as the more Democratic-leaning independents of the Northeast. In Montana, for instance, Democratic Senate candidate Jon Tester carried independents by 59 to 35 percent.

Regionally, Democrats completely dominated the 2006 election in the Northeast by 63 to 36 percent, and Democrats went from a 51 to 48 percent deficit in the Midwest in 2004 to a 52 to 47 percent advantage. Democrats also made surprising inroads in places that the Republicans had claimed as their own, including Colorado, Kansas, Montana, Arizona, Missouri, Ohio, Virginia, North Carolina, and Florida. The only region in which the Republicans held their own was the Deep South: Alabama, Georgia, South Carolina, and Mississippi. While Democrats won't necessarily be able to reproduce these successes in a presidential contest, the results in 2006 showed the Democrats with a base in the Northeast, upper Midwest, and far West roughly equal to, if not greater than, the Republican base in the deep South and the prairies. The remaining states are up for grabs, with many of them, like Colorado and Ohio, even more receptive to Democrats than before.

Some of the Democratic victories were directly attributable to Republican scandals, to overreaching by the religious right, or to Bush's mishandling of the Iraq war. But, in most cases, discontent over the war or scandal acted as a catalyst that led to the re-emergence of late '90s trends away from the conservative Republican worldview of Ronald Reagan, Pat Robertson, Trent Lott, and George W. Bush. Voters, including the crucial 18-to-29-year-olds, began to embrace or re-embrace a much more centrist worldview, one that is more congenial to the Democrats than to conservative Republicans.

In April 2007, the Pew Research Center conducted an extensive poll, "Trends in Political Values and Core Attitudes: 1987–2007," that demonstrated this shift in political worldview. The Americans of the early '80s blamed government regulation for inflation and unemployment and cheered Reagan's assertion that government is the problem, not the solution. Echoes of that attitude can still be found, but there is now widespread support among most Americans for different kinds of government intervention in the economy. These include raising the minimum wage (84 percent), strengthening environmental protection (83 percent), encouraging affirmative action for women and minorities (70 percent), and creating a national health-insurance program (66 percent).

The Pew poll also reveals an erosion of support for social conservatism. In 1987, for instance, only 42 percent of Americans disagreed that "school boards ought to have the right to fire teachers who are known homosexuals." In April 2007, 66 percent disagreed. In May 1985, 47 percent favored "making it more difficult for a woman to get an abortion." In April 2007, only 35 percent wanted to make abortion more difficult to get. The Pew poll also finds "a reversal of the increased religiosity observed in the mid-1990s." For instance, in 1999, 55 percent of Americans polled said "prayer is an important part of my life." Now only 45 percent do. One of the fastest growing voting groups is "seculars"—people who either profess no belief in God or refuse to state a religious preference—who have gone from 8 percent in 1987 to 12 percent today (17 percent of independents are "seculars").

But, while the Pew and other polls record a decisive shift away from Republican conservatism, these results don't mirror the worldview of the Democratic left. Americans are very skeptical that the government can run a national program. By 62 to 34 percent, Americans agree that, "when something is run by the government, it is usually inefficient and wasteful." That's an attitude born of Hurricane Katrina and the Iraq war, but it would still pose an impediment to an ambitious liberal agenda, including national health insurance. Americans' social attitudes have veered away from the religious right and from Jesse Helms–era views on race. But 55 percent still oppose gay marriage, and 62 percent oppose "preferential treatment" for blacks and minorities. About one-third or more Americans still want abortion to be illegal. In other words, the shift has not been from the right to the left, but from the right to the center or center-left.

IV.

This shift in regional balance and worldview favors Democrats over Republicans, and it should help the Democrats retain Congress in 2008 and beyond. Democratic presidential candidates should also enjoy a contextual advantage: not having to answer as many embarrassing questions about their party's record or to overcome as many damaging presumptions about what they stand for and would do in office. This advantage was reflected in the large lead—12 percent in the spring of 2007—Democrats held in polls that pitted an unspecified Democratic against an unspecified Republican presidential candidate. And, during the next 12 to 16 years, one would expect that a shift in the political center and Democratic congressional majorities will be reflected in Democratic presidential victories. But, while circumstances favor a Democratic presidential victory in 2008, that by no means rules out a Republican one.

Structural reasons alone impede an easy Democratic victory. The United States does not have a parliamentary system where the party that wins Congress automatically wins the presidency.

Instead, the presidential election is separate and operates under a different political dynamic. Take, for instance, the idea of a presidential candidate winning the center. The political center is an average of divergent attitudes, not a single attitude that dominates every state and region. In congressional elections, a party can field diverse candidates whose views, while generally congruent to the party's on some important economic or foreign policy issues, may differ on other matters or on social issues. What exactly congressional candidates espouse will depend upon the "center" of the district or state they are running in.

In 2006, Democrats ran candidates in the Northeast and far West who were consistently liberal on social, economic, and foreign policy issues. But, in the lower Midwest, Pennsylvania, the upper rim of the South, Florida, the Rocky Mountains, and Prairie states, the party's candidates diverged from a traditionally liberal stance on abortion, guns, or on particular economic or foreign policy issues. That was a key, for instance, to easy Democratic gubernatorial victories in Pennsylvania, Ohio, Kansas, and Colorado; this flexibility was also key to congressional victories in Indiana, Kentucky, and North Carolina. Presidential candidates, by contrast, don't have the luxury of holding contradictory positions on social or economic issues. They can't back a ban on partial-birth abortion and oppose gay marriage in Missouri while supporting full abortion rights and gay unions in California. Presidential candidates have to run a single, unified campaign.

Politically, the presidential electorate is divided into base states and swing states. Swing states possess a large proportion of white working-class voters—60 percent of the electorate in Pennsylvania, 70 percent in Iowa, and 80 percent in West Virginia—and a large proportion of libertarian independent voters. These voters espouse heterogeneous views that don't exactly fit those of either Republican conservatives or Democratic liberals. Which way they vote depends on which issues or concerns are paramount in a given election. If West Virginia voters worry most about losing their gun rights, they are likely to back a Republican, as they did in 2000 and 2004. If they worry about special interests controlling Washington or about jobs, they are most likely to back Democrats. For the last 16 years, presidential elections have come down to which party can maintain its political base while winning over these swing voters, who live along the southern tier of the Midwest, the Southwest, and in Southern border states, including Florida and Louisiana.

Republicans have sought to win white working-class voters through appeals to their social conservatism, patriotism, and fear of foreign threats. Democrats have wooed them by stressing economics, but they have only succeeded when they were able to neutralize the Republicans' social appeal. In 1976, Jimmy Carter trumpeted his "born-again" Christianity. In 1992, the Clinton campaign promised to "end welfare as we know it." Gore and Kerry failed to adopt any positions that could win over these socially conservative voters. If anything, both Gore and Kerry were prevented from doing so in order to win the Democratic primary electorate. In 2000, for instance, Gore got into a bidding match with Bill Bradley in the primary over who could have the toughest gun-control program. In 2004, Kerry thought he had to flip-flop on war funding and fudge his position on gay marriage in order to challenge Howard Dean.

Republicans have wooed libertarian independents through appeals to frontier individualism and attacks on "big government." Democrats have had to resort to identifying Republicans with Washington corruption and with the most authoritarian side of the religious right. Republicans won this argument in the last three presidential elections. With the war in Iraq assisting, the Democrats were able to get these voters on their side in the 2006 congressional elections.

Of course, presidential elections are not simply decided on issues. A candidate's stand on the issues is only part of the image that he or she projects; and it is on the basis of that image that many voters finally make their choice. Generally, voters want a presidential candidate who they think cares about them and understands them—better still, someone who is "one of us." Presidential candidates can communicate the latter either positively or negatively through the programs they favor or oppose, but equally important is how a candidate seems to voters. Among recent candidates, Bill Clinton and George W. Bush succeeded admirably in convincing voters in swing states like Louisiana and Missouri that they were "one of them." George H. W. Bush, Al Gore, and John Kerry failed. In 2004, for instance, many voters who agreed with Kerry's economic views still voted for Bush because they saw Kerry as a Northeastern liberal elitist who didn't care about them.

When foreign threats loom, voters sometimes also look for presidential candidates who are heroes. In the nation's founding years, voters elected military heroes like George Washington, Andrew Jackson, and William Henry Harrison into office. (In the early nineteenth century, the main "foreign" threat was from Indians.) In the twentieth century, voters elected Theodore Roosevelt, the leader of the Rough Riders, and former General Dwight D. Eisenhower. Heroes like these attract less attention in peacetime, as former Senator and Congressional Medal of Honor winner Bob Kerrey found out when he ran for president in 1992. In 2008, however, voters may be looking for a wartime hero.

V.

In the 2008 election, the Republicans are running candidates who could appeal to swing voters in the general election. Three of the leading Republicans come out of the moderate wing of the party. As mayor of New York City, Rudolph Giuliani made his reputation being tough on crime, but he was also pro-choice, in favor of gun control, and a supporter of gay rights. In 1994, Giuliani endorsed Democrat Mario Cuomo for governor against Republican George Pataki. Meanwhile, Mitt Romney championed a universal health-insurance program as governor of Massachusetts and was once the darling of the pro-gay Log Cabin Republicans. John McCain backed campaign-finance reform and opposed the Bush admin-istration's tax cuts. He fought waste in the military budget. During Bush's first term, he even contemplated leaving the Republican Party. And Fred Thompson was pro-choice prior to his first Senate campaign and was a supporter of McCain's campaign-finance reform bill.

Some of these Republicans might also appeal to swing voters. Thompson, a well-heeled lobbyist who won office in 1994 by driv-ing around Tennessee in a red pickup truck, has shown a re-markable ability to project himself to voters as "one of us." And Giuliani and McCain are seen as heroes: Giuliani for his leader-ship after September 11, and McCain for his wartime imprison-ment and bravery.

But, to win the nomination, these Republicans have attempted to woo the party's most conservative voters. Romney has repudi-ated his past positions on abortion, gay rights, and gun control. Giuliani has tried to soft-pedal his support for gun control and gay rights. And McCain has sought the favor of religious leaders whose influence in the Republican Party he had once deplored. All three have backed the Bush administration's foreign policy to the hilt: McCain perhaps out of conviction and the others primarily, it seems, out of ignorance or expediency. That has made all three candidates less capable of moving to the center should they win the nomination.

Whether the Republicans are viable in November will depend on how much use they can still make of the "war on terror." Giuliani and McCain seem particularly determined to sound the tocsin of terrorism. Can they do that without associating themselves with the current administration's failures in Iraq? Plus, whoever wins the Republican primary will have to find a way to distance himself from the sentiments he may have expressed to secure the nomination. A Republican candidate who ran on Bush's record and whose positions simply reflected those of the party's conservative base could potentially lose every state except for those in the Deep South and the Rocky Mountains.

The three leading Democrats, Hillary Clinton, Barack Obama, and John Edwards, are clearly identified with the party's liberal wing. Their possibilities of success in the swing states will depend on their ability to convince white working-class voters in Missouri or West Virginia to ignore the Democratic stands on abortion and gun control, and to focus instead on Bush's failures in Iraq as well as on the Democrats' promise of prosperity. Equally, a Democratic nominee's fate in Colorado or Montana will depend on getting voters to ignore his or her support for gun control and "big government" and to focus instead on Republican corruption and ties to the religious right. A candidate's ability to do this will depend on positioning and on how he or she appears to voters.

None of the Democrats enjoy the heroic stature of McCain or even Giuliani. Edwards is a former trial lawyer and undistinguished one-term senator. Clinton and Obama possess celebrity, but not the allure of the hero. Edwards, the son of a textile worker, may be able to convince voters that he is "one of them." But Clinton and Obama have formidable built-in disadvantages when it comes to the ineffable "one of us" quality. Besides being a Northeastern liberal, Clinton is also a woman. While her gender may serve her well in the Democratic primaries, it could prove a bar to support in the general election. As Thomas Edsall observed after the 2006 election, of the 42 "red-to-blue" races that the Democratic Congressional Campaign Committee chose to fund, 20 of 25 male candidates won, and only 3 of the 17 women won. One reason may be Americans' personal cultural barriers to entrusting a woman with the nation's security.

Obama has a similar, if not greater, hurdle. As Harold Ford's defeat in Tennessee's Senate race in 2006 showed, the race card still carries considerable weight in U.S. politics, particularly in the South and in border states, including Ohio, Kentucky, and Missouri. A military figure and hero like Colin Powell might have overcome voters' prejudices against a black candidate. But Obama, with only one term in the Senate and two best-sellers, will have a more difficult time. He has too many blank pages in his resume on which voters can inscribe their fears. In the 2008 election, the question will be whether a Clinton or an Obama candidacy suffers the fate of Al Smith's candidacy in 1928—path-breaking but destined for defeat—or achieves the path-making precedent of John F. Kennedy in 1960.

VI.

If a Democrat does win the presidency in 2008, he or she will very likely have a Democratic Congress with whom to work. That could lead to Democrats achieving things that they have advocated for decades, but it could also lead to gridlock and disappointment. A Democratic president in 2009 with a Democratic Congress will be in a very similar position to Bill Clinton after the 1992 election. The new president will be under pressure from party organizations and activists to undertake dramatic change—most likely, a single-payer national health insurance system, a quick exit from Iraq, and a renewal of the global-warming treaty with caps on carbon emissions. But these kinds of changes will not come easy.

Major economic initiatives will run into the imperatives of the global economy to reduce the federal deficit. These initiatives will also encounter public skepticism about large government programs, which is almost as pronounced now as it was in 1993 and 1994 when Bill Clinton tried to get Congress to pass a national health-insurance bill. Republicans are also likely to retain the 41 seats in the Senate necessary to block Democratic initiatives—and a few Democrats can always be counted on to join them on crucial votes. In addition, a Democratic president may find it difficult to pull out of Iraq: America's investment there and in the Middle East is extraordinarily large. Indeed, the next president might have to expend his or her political capital in digging the United States out of the mess that Bush has created overseas. In doing so, a new Democratic president could be pinioned between disillusioned supporters and a hostile Republican opposition.

If a Republican president is elected, along with a Democratic Congress, the constraints could be even more severe. As Stephen Skowroneck recounted in *The Politics Presidents Make*, presidents from one party who have tried to impose their will on a Congress dominated by the rival party have had "wrenching political impacts." Congress voted for impeachment against Andrew Johnson and Bill Clinton; it would have impeached Richard Nixon had he not resigned; John Tyler barely escaped impeachment;

Ronald Reagan saw his presidency almost destroyed by scandal; and Woodrow Wilson suffered the repudiation of his foreign policy. The only president to escape unscathed was Dwight D. Eisenhower, a testimony to his immense political skill and wisdom but also to his relative passivity toward Congress. There is a temptation to attribute these wrenching presidential episodes to character flaws in individual presidents, but, collectively, as Skowroneck notes, they demonstrate the perils to the presidency and to the nation of a politically divided government.

A Republican president in 2009 would likely be caught between a deeply divided Republican Party and a hostile Democrat-controlled Congress. Would he continue the Bush administration's disastrous foreign policy? With his domestic initiatives blocked, a McCain or Giuliani might even be tempted to undertake rally-around-the-flag foreign adventures in the name of the "war on terrorism." If so, the Democratic opposition would not be constrained by the responsibility of carrying out its own foreign policy. It would be Nixon in Vietnam revisited. It's not a pleasant prospect for a Republican president or for the country to contemplate.

From the standpoint of party history, the Republicans of 2008, like the Democrats of 1980, need time to regroup. Here, after all, is a conservative party whose most prominent and successful representatives have been three moderates: California Governor Arnold Schwarzenegger, Florida Governor Charlie Crist, and New York Mayor Michael Bloomberg. Indeed, Bloomberg, who is contemplating an independent campaign for the presidency, finally left the Republican Party. Yet the party's leaders in Washington and the presidential candidates insist that Bush failed because he was not conservative enough. That's the kind of contradiction between performance and ideology that led the Democrats in the

'80s to reassess their politics; and it should lead to a similar reassessment among Republicans.

The Democrats, for their part, need to discover whether they can finally enact the economic, social, and environmental programs that have been around since the Bill Clinton years but which were blocked by a Republican Congress and president. The 2008 election—which promises to be the biggest political free-for-all in decades—could provide the Democrats with an opportunity to get things done. That will require a major political effort as well as good fortune overseas. If the Democrats succeed, they could establish the kind of majority that New Deal Democrats enjoyed. The New Deal majority endured not just because of the memory of Herbert Hoover, but also because of legislation like Social Security. But, if Democrats fail to achieve lasting reforms to anchor their majority, the party will be left with a continuation of the creeping realignments and unstable equilibria that have characterized—and plagued—American politics since the '60s.

Coda: Warner and the Agony of Running for President

Ryan Lizza

Mark Warner and I had each had a couple of cocktails. They say up in the air one drink feels like two, and so things were, as Warner would later remind me the day he announced he wasn't running for president, "a little foggy." We were aboard a campaign donor's jet, flying back to Virginia after two intense days of New Hampshire politics. Democrats who show up to listen to presidential hopefuls stump in the dead of August two years before the election are a tough crowd. And Warner's pitch, earnest and wonky—"We've fallen to sixteenth in the world in terms of broadband deployment!"—did not always electrify. Yet he seemed to impress the right people. After an event in North Conway with a state representative named Tom Buco, Warner's political aide Mame Reiley shrieked, "Governor, Buco is having multiple orgasms!"

So were the donors. Warner raised almost $10 million, partially by tapping a network of new political money based in the Northern Virginia tech community. He was like a one-man Friendster, adding new buddies to his network everywhere he campaigned. He is the only politician I've seen who carried business cards. Nobody escaped a conversation without a little body contact and a card. (His aides called it "getting the full Warner.") Everyone was a potential friend. "Here, take this," he told a young woman at the Buco event, pressing a card into her hand. She was 17.

In Washington, Warner also had lots of new friends, especially among the class of Democratic operatives thirsty for a winner in 2008. Newcomers seemed truly enamored of him and spoke glowingly of what it was like to work for a politician who hadn't been ruined by years inside the Beltway. "His staff loves him," one recent hire told me, noting the contrast with Al Gore in 2000 and John Kerry in 2004. The press also had a crush, setting Warner up as the electable Hillary slayer and the only fresh face in the Democratic presidential field.

But, no matter how well things seemed to be going for Warner, privately he was filled with self-doubt. He had built a machine that was hurling him forward toward a presidential race that he actually didn't want to enter. "I told him," says his friend and longtime media adviser Jim Margolis, "if you don't want to do this, you have to stop it all now. Because the easy thing is to just say yes. The momentum is only going to get more intense, so this is the time to stop it."

In July, Warner took his family to Spain and Italy, where he hoped to put to rest the nagging reservations about running. His indecision consumed so much of his family's time in Europe that his wife, Lisa Collis, banned the conversation. "There came some times when Lisa said, 'Mark, you know—no more. We're on vacation,'" Warner told me shortly after he returned from Europe. Last week he told me, "I had come back from that vacation assuming this decision would have been put behind me. But it really wasn't."

Most, though not all, of his staff also assumed the decision was already made. "People like you and me don't take seriously when guys like that say they might not run," says Jim Jordan, a Warner adviser. In August, his political team started scheduling him at a presidential pace to get Warner adjusted to the rigors of the coming contest.

Up in the air flying home from his successful but draining trip to New Hampshire, Warner turned around in his seat to chat with me. It was his daughter's birthday, and, instead of being with her, he had been buying garlic bread at a farmer's market in Keene and answering hostile questions from TV reporters about why he refused to denounce the Nevada caucuses as "reprehensible." Even worse, he was now trapped on a seven-seater airplane with a reporter who had been shadowing him for an exhausting 48 hours. I pressed him on whether he was really going to run. His response shocked me at the time. He bent in close, looked me in the eye and asked, "Would you want to do this?"

Looking back, I don't think Warner meant that the indignities of the campaign trail were too much of a bother. He had a cheerful approach to the absurdities of life on the road. He didn't seem to mind when a poodle dressed in a pink bow relieved itself as he courted its owner in New Hampshire. After being trapped in conversation with a September 11 conspiracy theorist at a Hardees in Virginia, he was more philosophical than disdainful, marveling at how many seemingly rational people spin similar tales.

Warner also had a way of making the campaign trail more tolerable by encouraging a jovial, almost carnival-like mood. He kissed babies but also joked about having to kiss babies. When someone suggested he buy his daughter a birthday present at a store called the Hemporium, Warner deadpanned, "I'm pro-organic hemp." In most campaigns, at the end of the day the candidate retires to his suite to read briefing books while the staff and traveling press hit the bars. Not Warner. He personally organized the entire caravan for drinks and dinner.

He invited a rotating band of old friends out on the trail to keep him company. They were all rich and seemed to have names like Rex D. VanMiddlesworth, a guy who tagged along on the trip to New Hampshire. "One thing you'll have to get used to when hanging out with Warner," said a journalist who had spent lots of time with the governor and his traveling party, "is the fact that his fabulously wealthy friends are always trying to pay for things." They served as a life raft for Warner when he was feeling adrift on the road. "They help me keep it real," he told me. "Because most of my friends are not political. Sometimes, at the end of the day, the person you want to have the beer with—[to them] you're not a candidate. You're not anything else. You're just hanging out with a buddy. And you need honest feedback . . . if you've got something you don't feel comfortable sharing with a staff person." But, in hindsight, Warner's effort to create a bubble of normality around him was also a sign that he craved a normal life more than he craved being president.

Of course, nobody believed Warner when he said a yearning for a real life was the reason he decided to skip the race. Immediately, the entire presidential-industrial complex, including many of Warner's own staffers, began pinging each other with queries about the "real reason" he was folding one of the sturdiest tents in the '08 field. Was there a skeleton? My own experience with Warner suggests that he was, at the very least, wary of the modern-day vetting process for presidential candidates. When I first interviewed him in a hotel suite in Las Vegas back in June, he turned serious at the end of our chat and made a point of reminding me about the enormous responsibility that a journalist has when writing about a public figure. That same day, he summoned another national reporter to his suite to complain about a profile this person had written months earlier.

One night in New Hampshire, after a few drinks at a pool hall in a college town, the conversation turned to the political troubles of another potential '08 contender. I told a story that had been making the rounds about how this politician once spit on his wife. Warner's huge jaw dropped and his face blanched. The table fell silent. "I guess that's not that funny to you, is it?" I muttered. He shook his head.

After his announcement, I asked Warner if he had been worried about the vetting process. "Not really," he insisted. "You know, politics is a body contact sport. I've run for elective office twice. . . . I sat with my family and said, 'If we go through with this, there will be people—who knows what kind of attacks people will make.' But, you know, I think my family and I were ready to take that on."

Margolis says he spent the day Warner dropped out on the phone with reporters explaining that there was no scandal that sidelined Warner. "There was nothing that anyone was concerned about," he told me. "In fact, I sent an e-mail on Thursday afternoon to Mark and others saying I've now told like 20 reporters that there is absolutely no truth that he is gay, that he has a health problem, that he is about to have a sex-change operation, or that the oppo research was really bad."

Another staffer offered the more interesting theory that part of Warner's decision may have been about whether he actually wants to be president at this moment. "Who really wants this job?" the adviser asked. "Do you want to be the one to extricate America out of Iraq, decide whether to strike Iran? It's big-boy time. I believe Mark Warner is up to it, but I wouldn't be surprised if this was one of the ingredients in the soup. This isn't going to be fun." Warner once hinted at this same idea in an interview. We were talking about his foreign policy experience, and I noted that, compared with some other Democrats in the field, he wasn't really that inexperienced. He said that wasn't the important question. "If you do this," he told me, "having the notion that you might be able to do it better than Person X doesn't get you through the night. You've gotta feel it in your own gut."

This week, when I listened to that same August interview with Warner again, I realized Warner was already hinting at the decision he would make. In between campaign stops in New Hampshire, he brooded over what being president would do to his three daughters, ages 16, 15, and 12. "At some point, being the governor's daughter, that fades," he told me, sounding in hindsight like a guy who had already made up his mind. "You can move out of the state, you can move somewhere else and redefine who you are. If you are ever a child of a president, that's who you are for the rest of your life."

Every governor or senator thinks about running for president. Most do so because they are ambitious and see the presidency as the next rung on America's political ladder. The big question they often ask is strategic. How can I make it through the process and get elected? In the end, that's not the question Warner asked. His advisers swear that the nuances of the primaries and the details of how to topple Hillary Clinton never came up in his final deliberations. Warner asked not whether he could be president, but whether he should be president. The irony of Warner's answer is that the kind of person who dwells on that question is the kind of person you want to be president.

Appendix:
Where They Stand

Iraq

	Position in 2002	Position in 2007	Defining Sentiment
DEMOCRATS			
Clinton	Voted for war.	Withdrawal in 2008, but leave a significant force in place.	"If I had been president, . . . I certainly would never have started this war."
Obama	Opposed the war.	Remove all combat brigades by March 2008.	"I am not opposed to all wars, I am opposed to dumb wars."
Edwards	Co-sponsored a war resolution.	Apologized for vote; leave Iraq in the next 12–15 months.	"I was wrong."
Richardson	Pro-war, but wanted more diplomacy.	Establish a 2007 departure date.	Pull out *all* troops, but leave some Marines to protect the embassy.
Kucinich	Opposed the war.	De-fund the war.	"It is simply not credible to maintain that one opposes the war and yet continues to fund it."
REPUBLICANS			
McCain	Voted for war.	In favor of surge; maintain troop levels indefinitely.	"If we walk away from Iraq, we will be back."

	Position in 2002	Position in 2007	Defining Sentiment
Romney	Generally supportive.	Maintain troop levels.	Favors a surge "so long as there is a reasonable prospect of success."
Giuliani	Generally supportive.	Maintain troop levels.	"I think that it would be a terrible mistake to cut and run."
Thompson	Voted for war.	Leaving would be irresponsible.	"We are left with nothing but bad choices."
Brownback	Voted for war.	Opposed surge; wants to withdraw gradually.	"While we cannot make a precipitous withdrawal, we can transfer more security responsibility to the Iraqis."
Gingrich	Extremely supportive of war.	Keep pushing forward.	"Has developed an 18-point plan of tweaks to the current strategy, such as reorganizing war bureaucracy."
Paul	Opposed the war.	Leave as soon as possible.	"We just marched in. We can just march out."
Hagel	Voted for war.	U.S. should begin "phased withdrawal."	Iraq is "the most dangerous foreign policy blunder in this country since Vietnam."

	Iran	Defense Budget	Signature Move
DEMOCRATS			
Clinton	Thinks U.S. should engage with Iran directly, but it may be necessary to take military action to prevent Iran from getting nuclear weapons.	Has called for an expansion of Army and Marine end-strength.	Would appoint Bill Clinton as an international envoy to rebuild goodwill around the world.
Obama	Says he would negotiate directly with Iran and Syria, but has said that he would consider missile strikes to prevent Iran from getting nuclear weapons.	Would expand end-strength of Army and Marines by 92,000 troops.	Places a very high importance on securing loose nuclear weapons from Soviet Union and stopping the spread of AIDS.
Edwards	The U.S. should negotiate directly, but "under no circumstances can Iran be allowed to have nuclear weapons."	Money saved by withdrawing from Iraq will go to repairing the military and expanding some of the Army.	Places a very high importance on ending global poverty.
Richardson	Wants to negotiate with Iran directly and "lead a global diplomatic initiative" to prevent them from building nuclear weapons.	Would cut defense budget and use funds to reduce the deficit, ensure universal health care, and improve education.	Would push for a U.N. force in Darfur; focus on global terrorism and nuclear arms trade.

	Iran	Defense Budget	Signature Move
Kucinich	Open up relations with Iran and Syria.	Would cut defense budget and use funds to reduce the deficit, ensure universal health care, and improve education.	Establish a Department of Peace to oversee reductions in the military budget and advocate non-military solutions for foreign policy problems.
REPUBLICANS			
McCain	Has called Iran the most serious foreign policy crisis since end of the cold war; would consider military strikes.	Wants to increase the size of the Army and Marines and boost spending for missile defense.	Wants a "League of Democracies" to be at the core of a new international order.
Romney	Is opposed to engagement with Iran.	Would peg defense spending at 4 percent of GDP and add 100,000 more troops to the Army and Marines.	Would call for a "summit of nations" to help moderate Muslims develop the infrastructure they need to modernize.
Giuliani	Says Iran is "more dangerous than Iraq."	Has called for increasing the Army by 70,000 troops.	Backs "intense" interrogation of terrorist suspects.

	Iran	Defense Budget	Signature Move
Thompson	Favors helping Iranian dissidents overthrow the regime in Tehran.	Generally favors higher military spending.	"I think that our relationship with China over the next few decades is probably the single most important issue facing our country."
Brownback	Supports efforts to strengthen opposition forces in Iran; says U.S. must act "very aggressively" to stop Iran from going nuclear.	Would increase defense budget; says Pentagon should "step up" missile defense.	Says U.S. "must take pro-active steps to promote democracy and human rights abroad."
Gingrich	Says U.S. should make regime change a goal.	Consistently favored increasing the defense budget, especially missile defense.	Says the U.S. is fighting "World War III" against those—Iran, Syria, Hezbollah—that want to destroy Israel.
Paul	Flatly opposed to a military strike on Iran.	Reduce military spending significantly.	"It is shameful that Congress ceded so much of its proper authority over foreign policy to successive presidents during the twentieth century."

	Iran	Defense Budget	Signature Move
Hagel	Flatly opposed to a military strike on Iran.	Generally favors higher military spending.	A committed internationalist who calls his outlook "principled realism."

Energy

	Energy Policy	Defining Characteristic
DEMOCRATS		
Clinton	Wants to cut oil consumption in half by 2025 and tax current oil profits to pay for alternative energy research.	"We're not spending far more on military security in the Persian Gulf than it would cost to jumpstart a clean energy future."
Obama	Has co-sponsored a bill aiming for a two-thirds reduction in emissions by 2050.	Supporter of replacing gasoline with liquefied coal, which could lead to increased emissions.
Edwards	Has called for an 80 percent reduction in greenhouse-gas emissions by 2050 through a cap-and-trade system.	Has suggested banning all new coal-fired power plants unless they recapture the CO_2 they create.
Richardson	Would use tax credits and regulations to "bring along" the private sector, improve energy efficiency, and invest in alternative technology.	As governor, signed a bill requiring New Mexico to get 20 percent of its energy from clean sources by 2020.
Kucinich	Subsidize new energy technologies through NASA, sign Kyoto treaty, require that 20 percent of energy be from renewable sources by 2010.	"Sustainability is a principle that must infuse our whole approach to life; . . . the economic practices must always yield to protect the environment."
REPUBLICANS		
McCain	Sponsored legislation to reduce emissions two-thirds by 2050 through a cap-and-trade system.	One of the most environmentally minded Republicans, McCain has criticized Bush for inaction on global warming.

	Energy Policy	Defining Characteristic
Romney	Create incentives for alternative fuels and energy conservation to lessen dependence on foreign oil.	"Republicans should never abandon pro-growth conservative principles in an effort to embrace the ideas of Al Gore."
Giuliani	Has promised nuclear power, expansion of offshore drilling, and investment in new oil refineries; no policies to cut CO_2 emissions.	Has said, "I do believe in global warming," but criticizes Al Gore's movie and offers no policy solutions.
Thompson	Favors oil-drilling in Alaska, terminating CAFÉ standards, and de-funding renewable and solar energy.	Mocks "fevered" theories of global warming.
Brownback	Advocates subsidies for ethanol, bio-diesel, and nuclear power; supports emissions standards if they don't cripple auto industry.	Has expressed concern about global warming but hasn't spoken seriously about how to reduce CO_2 emissions.
Gingrich	Offer tax credits to companies promoting new energy technologies; opposes cap-and-trade systems; calls Kyoto a "bad treaty."	On global warming: "The evidence is sufficient that we should move toward the most effective possible steps to remove carbon from the atmosphere."
Paul	Has opposed all bills that provide funding for alternative fuel research; supports drilling in ANWR.	"The last thing we need is centralized government planning when it comes to our precious energy supplies."
Hagel	Offer tax credits to companies promoting new energy technologies; opposes cap-and-trade systems.	"We've known we've had an impact, absolutely, but exactly what impact human society has had on climate we're not quite sure."

Capitalism

	Taxes	Trade	Social Security
DEMOCRATS			
Clinton	Voted against most GOP tax cuts, is "not sure" if Bush tax cuts should be repealed entirely.	Mostly a free-trader, although she voted against CAFTA.	Against privatization.
Obama	Against extending Bush tax cuts. Supports eliminating marriage penalty while extending child tax credit. Supports scaling back capital gains and dividend tax cuts and re-examining tax benefits for the top 1 percent of earners.	Mostly a free-trader, although he voted against CAFTA.	Looks for fixes that don't involve privatization.
Edwards	Would repeal tax cuts for oil companies and for individuals making over $200,000.	Favors environmental and labor standards in all trade deals.	Against privatization.
Richardson	Cut income taxes substantially as governor, but opposed Bush tax cuts.	Says "fair trade must also be free trade."	Against privatization.

	Taxes	Trade	Social Security
Kucinich	Repeal tax cuts for top brackets, and restore brackets to Bill Clinton–era levels.	Would repeal NAFTA and secede from the WTO upon taking office.	No crisis, leave program as is, make up possible shortfalls with tax revenue.
REPUBLICANS			
McCain	Opposed tax cuts in 2001 and 2003 because they didn't come with spending cuts; now favors keeping them.	Strongly in favor of all "free trade" treaties.	Partially privatize.
Romney	Proposed a tax hike as governor, and refused to endorse Bush tax cuts in 2003, but now supports keeping them.	Strongly in favor of all "free trade" treaties.	Find some way to "reform" the system.
Giuliani	Says he would extend the Bush tax cuts; curbed spending as mayor.	Says he "supports free trade but also wants to make sure countries such as China are playing fair."	Partially privatize.
Thompson	Supports Bush tax cuts.	Strongly in favor of all "free trade" treaties.	Partially privatize.

Capitalism (*continued*)

	Taxes	Trade	Social Security
Brownback	Supports Bush tax cuts; would like to replace income tax with a national sales tax and repeal estate tax.	Strongly in favor of all "free trade" treaties.	Partially privatize.
Gingrich	Supports Bush tax cuts; wants to eliminate estate tax and simplify tax code.	Strongly in favor of all "free trade" treaties.	Partially privatize.
Paul	Supports all of Bush's tax cuts.	Favors free trade but has criticized free-trade treaties on constitutional grounds.	Abolish Social Security.
Hagel	Supports all of Bush's tax cuts.	Strongly in favor of all "free trade" treaties.	Partially privatize.

Immigration

	Favored Policy	Key Quote

DEMOCRATS

Clinton	Supported Bush plan: Strengthen borders, implement new enforcement laws, provide a path to citizenship for undocumented workers in the United States.	Republican efforts to criminalize undocumented workers "would literally criminalize . . . even Jesus himself."
Obama	Supported Bush plan: Strengthen borders, implement new enforcement laws, provide a path to citizenship for undocumented workers in the United States.	Has said he will "not support any bill that does not provide [an] earned path to citizenship for the undocumented population."
Edwards	Increase border security, offer a path to citizenship for undocumented workers, work with Mexico to better control the border.	"Immigration reform is central to alleviating poverty in the United States."
Richardson	Tougher law enforcement, more border guards, better detection of those that overstay their visas, and earned legalization program; opposes border fence.	As governor, signed legislation to allow illegal immigrants to get a driver's license and qualify for in-state tuition.
Kucinich	Would grant legal permanent residence to immigrants living in the U.S. for five or more years, with work authorization for those here less than five years.	Supports restoring benefits to legal immigrants withdrawn by the 1996 welfare reform legislation.

Immigration *(continued)*

	Favored Policy	Key Quote

	Favored Policy	Key Quote
McCain	Supported Bush plan: Strengthen borders, implement new enforcement laws, provide a path to citizenship for undocumented workers in the United States.	Has twice co-sponsored an immigration bill with Ted Kennedy that has gained wide support in the Senate.
Romney	Opposes Bush-backed guest-worker plan. Wants a system for employers to verify legal status of workers. Opposes allowing illegal immigrants to gain legal status apart from existing procedures.	As governor, gave state troopers power to arrest immigrants who were in the state illegally and opposed tuition breaks for illegal immigrants.
Giuliani	Provide a path to citizenship for some illegal immigrants (if they learn English), but not ahead of those in the system legally; create a tamper-resistant ID system to verify legal status; supports a fence along border.	As mayor, barred New York City employees from reporting illegal immigrants seeking government assistance.
Thompson	Vague policies.	Would tell Mexico to abandon "left-of-center" economic policies that he says spur immigration.
Brownback	Supported Bush plan: Strengthen borders, implement new enforcement laws, provide a path to citizenship for undocumented workers in the United States.	With McCain, generally considered the least popular candidate among conservative immigration groups.

	Favored Policy	Key Quote
Gingrich	Opposes McCain-Kennedy; would deploy technology to enforce employment laws and increase border security.	Favors a guest-worker program that keeps tabs on immigrants with biometric data.
Paul	Strongly opposes Bush plan: Wants a heavy focus on border security.	Supports ending "birthright citizenship."
Hagel	Supported Bush plan: Strengthen borders, implement new enforcement laws, provide a path to citizenship for undocumented workers in the United States.	During immigration debate: "We have to keep trying to find ways to make this a workable, realistic and responsible comprehensive immigration bill."

Health Care

	Supports Universal Health Care?	Favored Method	Defining Characteristic
DEMOCRATS			
Clinton	Gradually, by end of her second term as president.	Focus on containing costs by spending more on prevention, ending discrimination by insurers, and placing more scrutiny on the effectiveness of treatments.	Has worked with Gingrich on incremental reforms, such as computerizing records.
Obama	Yes, in first term as president.	Create a pool of regulated private insurance plans, and offer subsidies for those who can't afford care.	Has been vague on details of his plan.
Edwards	Yes, in first term as president.	Employer mandates, insurance regulation, state-created health-care markets.	Would raise taxes to pay for the program.
Richardson	Yes, in first *year* as president.	Lower Medicare eligibility age, and allow Americans to buy into the congressional health care plan.	Claims that his plan could be paid for without an increase in taxes.
Kucinich	Yes.	Medicare for all.	Only candidate to support a single-payer system.

	Supports Universal Health Care?	Favored Method	Defining Characteristic
REPUBLICANS			
McCain	No.	Says we need to restrain health care spending.	Would "bring all parties to the table and hammer out a principled solution."
Romney	Possibly.	In favor of individual mandates and "market reforms."	Has backed away from the universal health care plan that Massachusetts passed in 2006.
Giuliani	No.	Leave health care to the market.	"I don't like mandating health care."
Thompson	No.	Hasn't said.	Doesn't like Cuba's health care plan.
Brownback	Possibly.	Would rely on "market-based solutions."	Has said "we need high-quality, affordable health care for everyone."
Gingrich	Ambiguous.	"Market-based" solutions, such as health savings accounts and tax breaks.	Runs a think tank focusing on bringing new technology to the health care industry.
Paul	No.	Tax credits for health premiums.	Has said, "When government and other third parties get involved, health care costs spiral."

Health Care *(continued)*

	Supports Universal Health Care?	Favored Method	Defining Characteristic
Hagel	Possibly.	Hasn't said.	Convened a committee of experts in 2006 to make recommendations on improving care and cutting costs.

Social Issues

	Abortion	Death Penalty	Gun Rights
DEMOCRATS			
Clinton	Pro-choice, but supports prevention and education to reduce number of abortions.	Supports death penalty.	Supports modest gun control; F rating from the National Rifle Association (NRA).
Obama	Strongly pro-choice, against "partial-birth abortion ban."	Supports death penalty only in narrow instances.	Supports gun control; F rating from the NRA.
Edwards	Strongly pro-choice, against "partial-birth abortion ban."	Supports death penalty but wants to reform the system.	Supports gun control for criminals and kids.
Richardson	Strongly pro-choice, against "partial-birth abortion ban."	Supports death penalty.	Opposes gun control.
Kucinich	Once pro-life; now receives 100 percent positive ratings from pro-choice group NARAL.	Opposes death penalty.	Strongly in favor of gun control.
REPUBLICANS			
McCain	Strongly pro-life, consistently receives 0% ratings from NARAL.	Supports death penalty for federal crimes.	Says he believes in "no gun control."

Social Issues *(continued)*

	Abortion	Death Penalty	Gun Rights
Romney	Once pro-choice, now against abortion except for rape, incest, or to save the life of mother.	Supports death penalty for terrorism, killing sprees, and killing of law enforcement.	Previously favored assault-weapons ban, but joined the NRA in 2006.
Giuliani	Favors abortion rights, but with greater restrictions; would not fight hard to keep *Roe v. Wade*.	Supports death penalty.	Strongly in favor of gun control as mayor of New York City.
Thompson	In 1992, said abortion shouldn't be criminalized, but now is against abortion rights.	Supports death penalty.	Opponent of gun control.
Brownback	Strongly anti-abortion, and against funding for preventive-pregnancy services.	Has questioned whether death penalty fits with a "culture of life."	Staunch opponent of gun control.
Gingrich	Thinks abortion should be illegal, but not sure how to implement a ban.	Has pushed to increase use of death penalty.	Staunch opponent of gun control.
Paul	Strongly pro-life; consistently receives 0% ratings from NARAL.	Opposes death penalty.	Staunch opponent of gun control.
Hagel	Strongly pro-life; consistently receives 0% ratings from NARAL.	Supports death penalty.	Staunch opponent of gun control.